NON-VOCAL COMMUNICATION

TECHNIQUES AND AIDS

FOR THE SEVERELY PHYSICALLY HANDICAPPED

EUGENE T. MCDONALD
Research Professor, Speech Pathology
Pennsylvania State University

SHIRLEY MCNAUGHTON
Director, Symbol Communication
Research Project
Ontario Crippled Children's Centre

DEBERAH HARRIS-VANDERHEIDEN
Director, Communication Research
And Evaluation
Trace Center

GREGG C. VANDERHEIDEN
Director, Trace Center
University of Wisconsin, Madison

Edited By
GREGG C. VANDERHEIDEN
KATE GRILLEY

Art Editor
JANA FOTHERGILL

University Park Press
Baltimore • London • Tokyo

NON-VOCAL COMMUNICATION TECHNIQUES AND AIDS FOR THE SEVERELY PHYSICALLY HANDICAPPED

Based Upon Transcriptions Of The 1975 Trace Center National Workshop Series On Non-Vocal Communication Techniques And Aids

COPYRIGHT STATEMENT

In order to maximize dissemination of the information contained, no copyright or other restrictions on dissemination have been made. Most of the photographs and drawings contained herein, however, are covered by other copyrights and, therefore, should not be duplicated in any way without obtaining permission from the author or source of the photograph or figure. (See Figure Listing) It is requested that any excerpting of information from this document be done carefully to retain its accuracy and that use of this document be appropriately acknowledged.

Thank you.

Library of Congress Cataloging in Publication Data

Main entry under title:

Non-vocal communication techniques and aids for the
  severely physically handicapped.

  Bibliography: p.
  1. Communicative disorders in children—Congresses.
  2. Physically handicapped children—Language—Congresses.
  3. Communication devices for the disabled—Congresses.
  4. Pasigraphy—Congresses. I. McDonald, Eugene T.
II. Vanderheiden, Gregg C. III. Grilley, Kate.
IV. Trace Research and Development Center for the
Severely Communicatively Handicapped.
RJ496.C67N66   616.8'55'06   76-21835
ISBN 0-8391-0952-0

CONTENTS

---

* This section has been significantly expanded from the original workshop transcriptions in order to provide a comprehensive reference for the many different approaches and techniques which have been developed.

LIST OF FIGURES

ACKNOWLEDGEMENTS

The authors would like to express their appreciation to Mr. Warren P. Brown, Ms. Mary Jo Luster and Ms. Barbara Caddock who organized and co-ordinated the workshops upon which this document is based; to Mr. Richard Foulds, Director, Biomedical Engineering Center of the New England Medical Center, and Drs. Donald Olson and Harriet Gillette of the Rehabilitation Institute of Chicago for hosting the workshops; to Ms. Jana Fothergill and Ms. Janet Laier for their tireless efforts in assembling this document; and to the many researchers and clinicians without whose co-operation this assemblage of information would not be possible.

The authors would also like to express a special note of appreciation to the Division of Personnel Preparation of the Bureau for the Education of the Handicapped (OE) for their support of the national workshop series which formed the basis for this document. The workshop series was conducted under grant OEG-0-74-3321. The opinions expressed herein, however, are those of the authors and do not necessarily reflect the opinions or position of the Bureau or the Office of Education.

Eugene T. McDonald, Ed.D.

Dr. McDonald is a registered psychologist and research professor of speech pathology in the Department of Special Education of the Pennsylvania State University. He is a fellow of the American Psychological Association, the American Speech and Hearing Association and the American Academy for Cerebral Palsy. He is author of <u>Understanding Those Feelings: A guide to Parents of Handicapped Children, and Articulation Testing and Treatment</u>, and is co-author of <u>Cerebral Palsy</u>. Dr. McDonald is also the author of the <u>Deep Test of Articulation</u>.

Dr. McDonald has worked extensively with non-vocal physically handicapped children through his consultantships at two residential programs for cerebral palsied children - the Matheny School in Peapack, New Jersey, and the Home of the Merciful Saviour for Crippled Children in Philadelphia, as well as many day care centers for handicapped children. His article, "Communication Board for Cerebral Palsied Children" which appeared in the JSHD XXXVIII, 1, was based upon his work at the Home of the Merciful Saviour. Dr. McDonald has also recently completed a lecture tour of handicapped children's centers in Australia as a guest of the Australian government.

Shirley McNaughton Ms.Ed.

Ms. McNaughton is the Director of the Symbol Communication Research Project at the Ontario Crippled Children's Centre, Toronto, Ontario. She was part of the team which first discovered the symbols developed by Charles Bliss and adopted them for use with non-vocal children. In addition to her position at the Cripped Children's Centre, Ms. McNaughton is also the Program Director for the Blissymbolics Communication Foundation, the organization which has been given exclusive license for the Blissymbols.

Ms. McNaughton presents a very practical approach to communication development in non-vocal physically handicapped children, an approach which is based upon her many years as a teacher of these children both before and after the initiation of the Blissymbol program.

Deberah Harris-Vanderheiden, Ms. Ed.

Ms. Harris-Vanderheiden, who has two degrees in Special Education, is a generically certified Special Education teacher and is currently completing work toward a Ph.D. in Exceptional Child Development at the University of Wisconsin. Ms. Harris-Vanderheiden is a member of ASHA, CEC, and AAMD.

Ms. Harris-Vanderheiden is the Area Co-ordinator for both the Language and Communication Research, and the Training and Clinical Services Programs at the Trace Center. Her research efforts have included: director of a Blissymbol research program for mentally retarded children, field evaluation of independent communication aids, and research into vocabulary development and acquisition of language in non-vocal physically handicapped children. Ms. Harris-Vanderheiden's current efforts at the Trace Center include: development of inservice training workshops, a study of language acquisition in non-vocal physically handicapped children, and co-ordination of a service delivery program for non-vocal physically handicapped children and adults.

Gregg C. Vanderheiden, M.S.

As Co-founder and Director of the Trace Center, Mr. Vanderheiden has been an active participant in the field of non-vocal communication techniques and aids. Mr. Vanderheiden's efforts have been directed toward information dissemination, training of professionals, conducting a state-of-the-art survey of the needs in this area, and directing the interdisciplinary research efforts of the Trace Center. Mr. Vanderdeiden has served as principal investigator on numerous grants from the National Science Foundation and BEH/OE, which dealt with the exploration, development and evaluation of communication aids and techniques.

Mr. Vanderheiden has given papers and presentations at conferences of many professional societies (ASHA, CEC, AAMD, NCC, AAESPH, ACEMB, AAAS) and has published articles and chapters relating to his research in the area of communication. Mr. Vanderheiden holds two degrees in Engineering (Electrical and Biomedical) and is currently pursuing a Ph.D. in Language and Cognitive Development in the Exceptional Child.

To the educators, clinicians and researchers, both in America and abroad, on whose work this document is based.

INTRODUCTORY REMARKS - (Gregg C. Vanderheiden)

Good Morning. The problem we will be addressing in this workshop will be that faced by teachers, clinicians and parents in trying to develop an effective means of communication in their non-vocal physically handicapped children. When we talk about the non-vocal child we are referring to the child for whom speech is not now a functional means of meeting his communication needs. This does not necessarily mean that the child has no speech or vocalization at all, nor does it mean that the child may not develop fully functional speech in the future - as some of the children will do. In this workshop we will simply be referring to the children who are presently severely communicatively (and therefore developmentally) handicapped because they are unable to fulfill their communication needs with their limited or non-existent speech abilities.

Now you'll notice that we have put the "completely non-vocal," the "non-vocal with potential for later development of speech," and the "partially vocal" all together and will be addressing them together during the course of the workshop. We have done this for the following reasons: 1) they all have the same problem - an insufficient communication system; 2) they all need to augment their present communication in order to compensate for partial or complete inadequacies in their oral communication system; 3) non-vocal communication systems haven't decreased speech development for those who may have the potential for speech - in fact evidence indicates that communication aids tend to promote speech; and 4) children who are partially vocal tend to use whatever vocal capabilities they have and fall back on their non-vocal technique only when their vocal skills or the unfamiliarity of those with whom they are communicating prevent effective communication via speech.

We will be discussing these topics more later, but as we go along remember that these approaches have been applied to children with all of these degrees of vocal ability and that each child can utilize the techniques in combination with his own speech capabilities to develop an effective communication system.

We've talked a bit about the fact that the children may vary in their speech abilities. But there are many other ways the children may differ as well. As you will see later, these variations make it necessary to develop or become familiar with a wide range of different possible solutions or approaches, in order to be able to develop effective communication systems for these widely varying and very individual children. Some of the variables, if you will, that become important here are: age, cognitive abilities, specific physical abilities, visual acuity, mobility, environment, and communication needs. (Although this

1

workshop was directed toward the needs of the non-vocal child, the materials were presented so that much of it could also be used in developing communication in adults as well.)

To provide an idea of the different types of individuals that will be addressed by this workshop consider the following examples:

A 3-year-old cerebral palsied, athetoid quadraplegic, no speech, no activities of daily living, non-ambulatory, estimated normal intelligence,

A 10-year-old, cerebral palsied, spastic quadraplegic, non-ambulatory, no activities of daily living, no head control, good control of eyes only, average mental abilities.

A 20-year-old, head/neck injury, quadraplegic, no speech, has language,

A 5-year-old, cerebral palsied, athetoid quadraplegic, mentally retarded, no speech, no controlled movements,

A 56-year-old, Parkinsons disease, severely dysarthric, confined to bed,

An 11-year-old, cerebral palsied, spastic quadraplegic, estimated trainable-educable mentally retarded, cannot focus closer than 20 feet, non-ambulatory.

A 6-year-old, cerebral palsied spastic quadraplegic, severe-profound mentally retarded, no speech, no communication, non-ambulatory,

A 12-year-old, cerebral palsied, athetoid quadraplegic, educable mentally retarded, 8-10 words recognizable only to a few people, ambulatory.

From these few examples it is evident that no single approach will be applicable to all cases. This workshop will therefore present a wide range of different approaches along with some guidelines that may be helpful in selecting appropriate approaches or techniques for the individuals you are working with.

ORGANIZATION OF THE WORKSHOP

The objective of this workshop is to bring together information on the various aspects involved in developing communication in the non-vocal, physically handicapped child (or adult), and to present it in such a way that it will facilitate the maximum dissemination and use of this information. The workshop was organized in this manner because there is a great need for summary information in this area and because no such information is currently available. The participants were chosen to represent all of the disciplines involved in developing a communication system for the non-vocal physically handicapped child including speech and language clinicians, teachers, occupational therapists, physical therapists, parents, biomedical rehabilitation engineers, rehabilitation equipment distributors, program directors and school administrators. Participants were also chosen because of their ability to further disseminate the information presented, either through formal training programs or by establishing communication development programs that could act as models for others in their area. The material has been chosen to provide the participants with an overall profile of the problem, and the various approaches to solving it which have been developed around the world. Because of limited program time, emphasis has been placed on those topics for which little information is available elsewhere.

ORGANIZATION OF THE PRESENTATIONS

The material to be presented has been organized into three areas: Definition of the Problem, Description of the Tools, and Description of Programs Demonstrating the Application (of some of the tools described). In the Definition of the Problem section the importance of communication to development will be discussed along with the impact that lack of functional communication has on the non-vocal physically handicapped child. The need for early intervention and for providing a supplementary means of communication will be discussed in addition to indications for early identification of children at risk.

The presentation then shifts to a discussion of the tools that can be employed to develop an effective supplementary channel of communication for a non-vocal physically handicapped child. First various techniques will be discussed for providing the physically handicapped child with a reliable means to indicate or respond. Then various symbol systems ranging from objects to pictures to words to Bliss Symbols will be presented along with considerations in selecting an appropriate symbol system for a child.

Descriptions of several programs which have applied these tools will then be presented. In these programs the various physical techniques for indication are applied with different symbol systems to demonstrate the application of both to meet the needs of different children. Results of the programs, including impact on the children, will be discussed.

Finally, there will be a short discussion on assessment of the non-vocal physically handicapped child. Although it was not part of the original workshop program, we have added this brief discussion at the suggestion of the participants of the first workshop in Chicago. The discussion will center around the aspects that should be included in assessment, the applicability of formal assessment materials and the development of informal techniques.

THE PROBLEM

LANGUAGE FOUNDATIONS - (Eugene T. McDonald)

DEFINITION OF COMMUNICATION AND ITS SIGNIFICANCE

As we begin to consider different means of providing communication for the non-vocal child, it is important to discuss what we mean by "communication." A very important point for us to keep in mind is that communication cannot take place within just one person. There must be a listener or reactor. When developing communication aids for children we must also do something about the environment in which the child lives if communication is to take place. Communication is a function that takes place among persons who group themselves together to form a community. I want to emphasize the relationship of "communicate" to the concept of community. We suspect that many of the communication problems of severely involved children stem from the fact that their community does not interact with them. Because they can't talk, non-vocal children often find themselves living in environments where people don't talk to them. Moreover, people tend to not interact with them socially in other ways as well. As a result non-vocal children, who are often non-ambulatory and unable to manipulate objects, have little opportunity to gain experience through interaction with others, thus seriously jeopardizing their development.

It would be impossible to exaggerate the significance of communication. It has been the cohesive force in human cultures. It is a vehicle for social interaction and it is essential for personal development. We have all seen older, physically involved children who appear to have very restricted personality development. They are often unmotivated, we say. They are children who seem to be content to remain dependent upon others. They are children who don't seem to do as much as they are physically capable of doing. Perhaps they give us these impressions because they have not developed personally. One of the reasons for their restricted personal development is that they have not had the stimulation which comes from interaction in a communicative way with those persons around them. They have come to be, and are content in being, dependents in the community. Perhaps this is because they are not, and don't know what it means to be, a member of their community.

FOUNDATIONS OF LANGUAGE DEVELOPMENT

I plan to represent some models on which we can hang some very elementary ideas about the development of language. We need this background in order to follow the arguments I will present for early identification of children at risk for failure to develop communication skills and for early intervention. We will be talking about the process which involves transferring information from one person to another person or persons. The first model depicts the 'foundations of language develop-

6

ment.' (Figure 1) We are suggesting that language, a component of communication, develops as a result of a child's interacting with its environment. For language to develop from these interactions, the child must have a sensorium which provides his nervous system with information about what is going on in the environment. The motor system, however, does not have to be intact for language to develop. We have seen many children who are severely handicapped motorically, but who give evidence of well developed receptive language and good manipulation of language in another modality. For language to develop the environment must provide appropriate stimulation for the child; and it must reinforce certain of the child's reactions so that these reactions will be likely to occur again. In other words the environment must provide language stimulation and must reinforce language behaviors if language for communication is to develop.

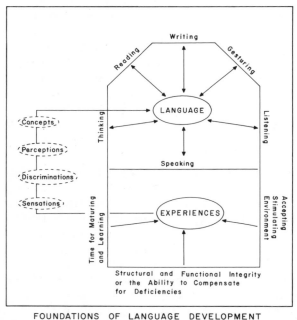

FOUNDATIONS OF LANGUAGE DEVELOPMENT

Figure 1.
Foundations of Language Development

Unfortunately, many severely involved children don't find this kind of environment. The mother does not get positive feedback from her efforts to communicate with the child. When she plays with him she does not get smiles or cooing. She does not hear the beginnings of vocal play, and consequently she does not get the kind of reinforcement she needs to continue this kind of stimulation. Also it may be that when the child attempts to respond, his behaviors are so bizarre or so abnormal that the mother gets negative feedback. She is pained and hurt by what she sees in her child when she attempts to communicate with him. Her natural reaction is to talk and play less with the child, and as a consequence the child has fewer opportunities to interact with his environment.

The interactions which take place during the time of maturation and learning give rise to experiences, the first of which are very simple. The child merely senses that something is occurring. It may be that he hears something or doesn't hear anything. He feels something, he doesn't feel anything. A little later he begins to notice that there are differences in these sensations and at that point he is discriminating between stimuli. He later begins to develop perception by adding to these discriminative sensations some interpretation: mother's voice, father's voice, the dog barking. A little later he will generalize his perceptions into concepts - the building block of language.

Some Language Models

Language is employed in several ways which we will refer to as modalities for language use. Some ways of using language are receptive, some are expressive, and one is central. Perceptive uses of language would be listening and reading, with reading, of course, coming at a much later age. Expressive modalities would be speaking and gesturing, and the central modality would be thinking. It is possible to develop language without developing expressive skills. We have seen children who don't speak, and who are so severely physically handicapped they are capable of only the most elementary type of gesturing (eye movements or head nod) but who give evidence of a very rich receptive language development.

Speech is the most commonly employed modality for using language. Our model of speech production barely suggests the complexities of the speaking process. (Figure 2) In speech production three major proces-

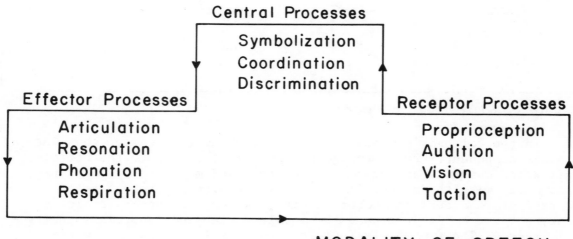

Figure 2. Modality of Speech

ses must be coordinated: receptor, central and effector. As receptors we have the auditory, proprioceptive and tactile senses. Vision may be helpful but is not nearly as important as these other senses for the development of speech. The central process could be organized in a number of different ways but basic to the relationship between speech and language is symbolizing function. It is in the central area that the input from the receptors is organized in such a way that it can be given some symbolic features and an appropriate motor command issued to the muscles of the speech producing mechanism.

Several effector processes are involved in speech production: respiration, phonation, articulation and resonation. In some cerebral palsy children breakdowns in these processes which probably indicate that the child is at risk can be detected at an early age.

In the widely used model of the source-filter theory of speech production (Figure 3) are counterparts of the effector portion of our model of speech production. The lungs represent respiration, the larynx represents phonation, and the supralaryngeal tract.represents resonation and articulation. This model also corresponds to the effector component in Fairbanks control theory model of speech production. (Figure 4).

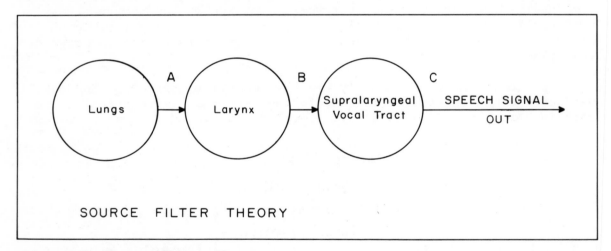

Figure 3. Source Filter Theory

In the Fairbank's model the input from the environment goes into a storage component. From storage a signal is directed to the effector unit which consists of a motor, generator, and modulator. To compare this model with the source-filter model envision a circle labeled 'lungs' drawn around the motor, a circle around the generator labled 'larynx," and a circle around the modulator labeled 'supralaryngeal vocal tract.' The two models indicate that air is directed from the lungs into the larynx and from the larynx into the supralaryngeal tract from which sounds are emitted. The acoustic output is sensed, heard and fed back into the comparator which, if there is an error signal,

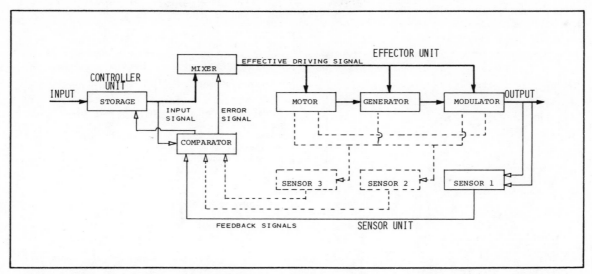

Figure 4. Control Theory Model

would report that some change is necessary. There is also sensory input into the comparator from the tactile and proprioceptive end organs, which come from the structures of the effector unit. This theory envisions a closed loop system; however, in the initial stage of speech learning it has to be an open loop. Only after the child has developed a program which gives him satisfactory match of output with what he has stored about input, does the system operate as a closed loop servosystem.

The storage component of the model might be expanded by adding a model of the memory system. (Figure 5) Envision these components of the memory system as included in the storage unit. An environmental input enters the sensory registers or sensory buffers on an ongoing basis as we are constantly being bombarded by visual, auditory, tactile and proprioceptive stimuli. Information doesn't remain in the sensory register very long unless we attend to it, thus removing it from the sensory buffer and transferring the information into a short term store. I want to stress this process because many cerebral palsied children are not good attenders; they have not developed attending skills. They may have sensory systems which work very well, but unless they can attend to sensations present in the sensory buffer they can not transfer information into short term store or long term store. Therefore, to teach this child to communicate you must be sure that he is attending to the stimuli you are presenting.

By attending, we get information into our short term store which is sometimes called the temporary working memory. Material doesn't stay in the store very long and there is a limit to how much the short term store can hold. It has been suggested that we can hold 7 plus or minus

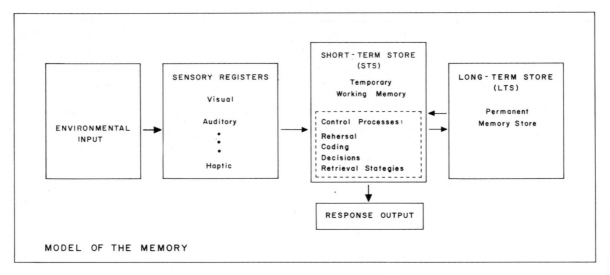

Figure 5. Memory Model

2 bits in this unit. Since material disappears from the short term
store very quickly it is necessary to transfer it to long term storage
if it is to be retained. To effect this transfer there are many procedures we can use. We can categorize, classify, encode, make decisions
and develop retrieval strategies. It has been demonstrated that many
children with learning problems have difficulties in this area because
they haven't developed strategies for getting information from the
short term store into the long term store; hence, the information disappears. When evaluating children, we should consider their memory
function and, if they have difficulty here, find some ways to help
them learn how to get material into their long term store. Once information is in long term memory it seems to be stored permanently. Scanning and other retrieval strategies however must be developed if the
child is to make ready use of material in the long term memory.

   Directing our attention again to the servosystem model (Figure 4)
which we have elaborated by incorporating the memory system model, we
can now take a look at the total speech process as defined by the
model. First, there is an idea or message to be expressed which
activates the central nervous system causing motor commands to be
issued. These motor commands bring about patterns of contraction of
respiratory, laryngeal, and articulatory muscles. The result of this
muscle action is an acoustic signal. The acoustic signal will consist of a time series of formant patterns, transients, noise and so on.
The output signal will consist of phonic symbols organized into words
and sentences. The model includes a self-monitoring system. At the
point where we have acoustic symbols as an output we can get auditory
feedback. At the point in the model where there is muscle contraction
and movement of structures there can be tactile and kinesthetic feedback. This kind of feedback loop has to be developed early. If it is
not developed early, the child will experience difficulty in developing

self-monitoring skills. We see some children speak intelligibly when talking to their therapist but outside the situation where their helpers are, their speech becomes difficult to understand. One suspects that these youngsters are having difficulty monitoring their own speech and that their speech problem may stem from lack of an effective feedback system.

From these models it is apparent that there are many places where things might go wrong during the development of speech. For this reason it is important to identify, at a very early age, children who are having problems in order to help them to develop the specific skills necessary to develop communication and, if possible, fully functional speech.

IDENTIFICATION OF CHILDREN AT RISK - (Eugene T. McDonald)

Consideration of the developmental sequences of speech production is an important step in trying to identify at an early age those children who are at risk for failure to develop normal communication skills. It is especially informative to relate expressive developmental milestones to the physiology of speech production.

During the first two weeks an infant normally produces undifferentiated vocalizations. He cries and produces other reflexive sounds. Parents sometimes report that their baby is a quiet baby; it doesn't cry, it doesn't make any noises. It is abnormal for a child to be too quiet. If an infant is not producing undifferentiated vocalizations during this early period one would be alerted to the possibility that the child might have some problem and that he should be watched.

By the end of the first month these vocalizations become differentiated. Differentiation in sound production requires a little higher level of neuromuscular function. A listener can hear differences. For example, the mother will say that she can tell if the baby is hungry or wet by his cry. A little better control of the speech producing system is required to produce these differentiated cries. If at the end of the first month the child has not developed the ability to produce differentiated vocalizations that child ought to be followed carefully for a while.

At two months of age the child "plays" with the vocalization of a single vowel varying the pitch and loudness. He now is exerting more control over his speech mechanism in changing the tension in his larynx.

At four months a very interesting thing happens. The child begins to employ more supralaryngeal activity which results in production of consonants. Instead of just making vowels he begins to produce and play with consonant-vowel combinations. It is important to note that at this time he is able to produce only one consonant-vowel syllable per exhalation. Many older cerebral palsied children have not progressed beyond this stage and they continue to produce one syllable on an exhalation. They don't have the control of their exhalation necessary to combine syllables into a string of syllables. If at four months a child is not producing a consonant-vowel syllable on an exhalation this observation should be regarded as a sign of potential difficulty in developing speech.

To understand the significance of producing single syllables on an exhalation rather than a string of syllables we must consider how the rest breathing pattern is modified for speech production. In rest breathing, inspiration and expiration are about equal in duration, that is, we spend just about as much time inhaling as we do exhaling. The ratio of inhalation to exhalation is about one. The ratio changes markedly to support speech production. Inspiration is performed very rapidly and exhalation is prolonged. In speech breathing, inspiration occupies only about one-sixth of the breathing cycle. Speech is produced during the remaining five-sixths of the cycle.

Many cerebral palsied children particularly are unable to make this modification. They can't produce the quick inhalation or if they do, they are unable to coordinate exhalation and vocalization. They may lose a lot of air before they begin to talk or, in some cases, they have a laryngeal block and are unable to initiate phonation at all. Children who can't modify the rest breathing pattern try to talk on their short exhalation. This will allow them to produce a single syllable but is insufficient to sustain continuous speech.

At five months the child begins to vocalize to attract attention. This is a different type of landmark but an important one. Recall that the child has been vocalizing - first producing undifferentiated and later differentiated vocalizations. At five months the normally developing child begins to realize that his vocalizations are important, that he can use vocalization to get some kind of reward. This is an important stage in the child's development. If the parents do not reward his vocalizations with attention, if his environment does not respond in a way that his vocalizing behavior is reinforced, he is less likely to continue vocalizing. I've already alluded to the fact that if the handicapped child's vocalizations are in any sense bizarre his parents may not be emotionally able to provide positive reinforcement for his attempts to vocalize. We must help them understand why the child is not vocalizing as other children, and help them learn how to react to his efforts in a positive way. This parental reaction is essential if the child is to develop an awareness of the social utility of speech.

At 6 months the child has enough respiratory control to produce several consonant-vowel syllables on an exhalation. He can shift from his rest breathing pattern to a speech breathing pattern and isn't restricted to producing only one syllable per exhalation. He can inhale quickly and prolong exhalation sufficiently to support productions of chains of syllables. Chaining is essential for learning to produce the consonants. At the boundaries between syllables, phonetic events occur which do not occur intra-syllabically. As we combine sounds across symbol boundaries more complex articulatory maneuvers take place. A child can learn to produce these maneuvers only if he has opportunities to produce several syllables on an exhalation.

At 7 to 9 months the child practices inflections. He produced inflections earlier, but on a single vowel. At this age inflections occur on the strings of syllables uttered on an exhalation.

At 9 months the child imitates vocalizations. If you cough, the infant will cough; you clear your throat, the infant will clear his throat. It's always exciting to hear that response for the first time. Imitation indicates the child has enough neuromuscular control that he can command his system to do something he wants it to do - produce a sound he has heard in his environment.

At 12 months the average child has a vocabulary of about 3 words, which is an indication that the child is learning to form and use symbols. At this stage the child can not only make noises, but he can make noises which conform to communicative noises of his community. He can produce sounds which represent things. By 18 months he has about 20 words and is proceeding very rapidly in developing meaningful utterances. At 18-24 months he makes 2 word sentences and at 24 months his expressive vocabulary includes about 200 words.

The foregoing discussions illustrated that speech production is a very complex process. There are many places where this process can break down or functions which are part of the process fail to develop. By comparing a child's speech producing activities with the developmental milestones described we can identify early those children who are likely to have difficulty in developing intelligible speech.

A second method for identifying children at risk is through their histories. Our medical colleagues can provide information about problems associated with the pregnancy, the delivery, the early condition of the child, and so on. If there are signs suggestive of brain damage we should be aware that the child may have difficulty developing speech and follow him with the milestones of speech development in mind.

A third source of information to be considered is our own examination findings. Evaluation of the child's oral motor function, laryngeal functioning, and his respiratory functioning can provide some indications that the child might encounter difficulty in developing the control necessary for speech production. Also to be considered is the child's breathing rate and breathing pattern. Look for rapid breathing. Children with rates over 30 cycles per minute have difficulty producing vocalizations. Does the child shift the rest breathing to the speech breathing pattern? Check for tension associated with attempts to vocalize in the child who gives signs of trying to respond vocally or trying to initiate vocalization but who remains speechless. Look for tension in his extremities, and tension in his respiratory musculature. Such generalized tension is often associated with heightened tone in the laryngeal musculature and is incompatible with the production of vocalization.

When assessing oral motor functions look for persistent strong suckle or grossly defective chewing, sucking and swallowing patterns. The neuromuscular integration required for non-speech movements is different from that required for speech movements; however, unless suckle is inhibited and the low level vegetative patterns of chewing, sucking, and swallowing are developed, the child can not develop the higher level motor acts necessary for speech. This is not to say that a child who has oral motor problems will not be able to overcome them and later develop normal chewing, sucking and swallowing patterns nor that work on chewing, sucking or swallowing will result in better speech. If the child retains very defective vegetative patterns however, it will be very difficult, if not impossible for him to develop intelligible speech. These signs, therefore should be taken as an early indication of trouble and work on these basic oral motor patterns should be initiated at a very early age.

The speech pathologist, parents and others must face the fact that many severely involved children will not be able to develop intelligible speech regardless of how much speech training they are given. For other children speech may become a functional mode of communication for them but only after years of work. They will be without communication for many or all of their developmental years. In one of our programs a very bright little eight year old boy uses a communication board. Recently I asked him what he liked about his communication board. He said it enabled him to talk about sports. As this was during baseball season, he and I talked about the baseball teams and his favorite players and team. If this boy had to rely on oral expression-speech to communicate, he never could have enjoyed that kind of an exchange with anyone.

Putting on my hair shirt for a minute, let me suggest for emphasis that it borders on malpractice for speech pathologists to insist that a child like this bright eight year old express himself vocally. It is wrong for us to allow administrators, parents and others to force us to put that child into a situation where he fails time after time as we try to get him to say 'yes' or 'no' or when we try day after day to get him to talk. It would be more sound to develop a supplementary means of communication and open up his life for him while we work on speech.

Information is available making it possible to identify at an early age children who are at risk for failure to develop oral communication skills. Techniques are also at hand which we can employ early to help at-risk children become expressive. The use of supplementary methods of communicating doesn't have to be regarded as failure, although it might be if we do not take steps to prevent such an assessment. The parents can be helped to understand that the early use of a communication board is much better than denying their child the opportunity to communicate while we are trying to see if he can learn to speak. They should be assured that these supplementary systems do not impair the child's chances of developing speech. In many cases early use of communication boards has facilitated speech development. Speech pathologists are trained to help people learn to talk so we have an unconscious feeling of failure if we can't help people learn to talk and have to use a non-speaking method of communicating. We must recognize that our job is broader than just teaching the child to talk; our job is to help the child learn to communicate.

THE TOOLS

INTRODUCTION AND FRAMEWORK - (Gregg C. Vanderheiden)

We have discussed some of the elements of the problem of providing the non-vocal physically handicapped child with a means of communication as well as the need for early intervention. We have mentioned that, for the child who currently is unable to communicate through speech, other supplementary means of communication could be employed to provide him with an effective means of communication. In this section, we will be describing some of the tools that can be used to develop such a supplementary system.

To provide a framework around which to present these tools, it is helpful to look at the basic components of an expressive communication system. To do this I would like to use the simple three-part model depicted in Figure 6. Here we can see the expressive system broken down into three basic parts:

1. A <u>physical mechanism</u> or means of indicating or transmitting the elements of a message to a receiver,

2. A <u>symbol system</u> and vocabulary to provide the child with a set of symbols which he can use to represent things and ideas for communication to a receiver,

3. <u>Rules and procedures</u> for combining and presenting the ideo-symbols so that they will be most easily interpretable by a receiver.

To get a better understanding of these components, let's take a brief look at what they might look like for a normal child and for a non-vocal physically handicapped child.

The <u>physical mechanism</u> which the normal vocal child uses to present or transmit the elements of his message is his oral speech mechanism. With this mechanism he is able to transmit specific sound patterns which represent different ideas or concepts. These sound patterns, or spoken words, form the child's <u>symbol system</u>. The child uses these symbols (spoken words) to transmit his ideas to a receiver. In presenting these words to a receiver, however, the child must follow certain <u>guidelines</u> concerning their combination and order of presentation if his message is to be easily and correctly interpreted by the receiver.

Fortunately, for the vocal child, the potential to develop these three components is present in infancy. Given normal stimulation, it develops early in the child's life and provides him with an effective means of communication and interaction with others during most of his growth and development.

A Simple Model of Expressive Communication Components

for Normal and Non-Vocal Motor Impaired Children

COMPONENT	FUNCTION	Component as represented in the normal speaking child	Component as represented in a child using a communication board
Physical Mechanism	To provide the child with a means of specifying or transmitting the elements of his message to a receiver	Oral speech mechanism	Pointing board
Symbol System and Vocabulary	To provide the child with a set of symbols which he can use to represent things or ideas for communication	Spoken words	Pictures Printed words Other symbols
Rules for Combining and Presenting Symbols	To provide the rules and procedures for presenting the ideo-symbols so that the message will be most easily understood by the receiver	Syntax Grammar, etc.	Syntax Grammar, etc.

Figure 6.

For the non-vocal severely physically handicapped child, however, physical and sometimes cognitive impairments often prevent the development of one or more of the components of his communication system. In the case of the physically handicapped child who is unable to communicate through his oral speech mechanism, at least two and often three of the components are missing or unavailable (the oral speech <u>mechanism</u> and consequently the use of vocal <u>symbols</u> and often basic communication skills as well). To supply an augmentative communication channel for the non-vocal child, alternative mechanisms of providing these basic components must be developed.

Column 4 in Figure 6 shows an example of how these components might be realized for a non-vocal physically handicapped individual using a communication board. The <u>physical mechanism</u> for such a child would be his pointing board. Using this board, the child would be able to indicate the various <u>symbols</u> (displayed on it) which make up his message. These symbols may be in the form of pictures, printed words or other symbols such as Bliss Symbols. Again, as with the vocal child, there are certain <u>rules</u> for combining and presenting the symbols so that they can be easily understood by the receiver.

Steps in developing a communication system

The basic procedure for developing a non-vocal communication system for a severely handicapped child would consist of:

1. Selecting/developing a technique aid to provide the child with an effective means of <u>indicating</u> the elements of his message.

2. Selecting/developing a symbol set and vocabulary system which are compatible with the child's <u>current</u> abilities and fulfill the child's communicative needs.

3. Developing the necessary communication skills in the child which will permit him to use his symbol set in such a way that he can be clearly understood by the message receiver.

In keeping with this model we will first present various techniques and aids which can be used to provide children having different physical handicaps and abilities with an effective means of <u>indication</u>. This section will then be followed by a discussion of different symbol systems which could be used with the various techniques and aids to provide the children with a means of conveying their messages to a second person. Some discussion of procedures for developing communication skills in these children will also be covered, along with the discussion of the symbol systems. Additional information on developing communication skills will be presented during the description of programs in the Results section of the workshop.

PROVIDING THE CHILD WITH A MEANS TO INDICATE -
(Gregg C. Vanderheiden)

The first problem we will be considering, then, is that of providing a child with a means of *indication*. Since these children cannot communicate through voice, they will have to communicate by selecting elements out of some vocabulary set (pictures, words, symbols, etc,) which will make up their message. To communicate in this fashion, however, they will need some way of indicating the words (pictures, etc.) from their wordlist which make up their message. The child on a regular communication board does this by simply pointing to the various pictures, symbols, letters or words on his board. This type of communication is probably the most common approach used today, and it is the one that will be used throughout most of the workshop to demonstrate the application of communication aids with the severely handicapped children. There are, however, a great many children, perhaps a majority of the children, who cannot point effectively. These children are so severely physically handicapped that they either have no pointing capability at all, or they are able to point to so few items that a functional vocabulary cannot be provided for them. For this reason, we, as clinicians, must be familiar with other types of techniques which can be used to provide even the most severely physically handicapped child or adult with a means of indicating the words, pictures, etc., that make up his message.

Importance of selecting the right technique

The problem, however, is not simply trying to provide the child with a means of indication that he is capable of using. At the same time that the technique must be <u>within</u> the child's capabilities, it must also <u>take best advantage</u> of these capabilities so that he can communicate in the most efficient manner. As we shall see later, the speed of a child's communication (or the lack of speed) has a tremendous effect on his opportunities to communicate as well as his educational progress. It is therefore very important to select the technique which will allow the child the greatest speed and ease of communication given his particular physical abilities. Since different techniques will be faster with individuals having different types of handicaps, there are no "best" approaches. It is therefore necessary to look at and become familiar with the various different approaches as well as their advantages and disadvantages when applied with children having different types or degrees of handicap.

Points to keep in mind when reviewing existing techniques

There are a couple of things which should be kept in the front of our minds as we look at the various techniques which have been developed.

20

First, for many of the children you are working with, none of the techniques will be applicable in the exact forms in which they will be
presented. There will probably be some one aspect of them which will
not fit with your child's capabilities or environment. In these cases
it will be necessary to adapt the techniques or to combine aspects of
several techniques to meet the needs of your child. A little later
we'll try to show you how that can be done and provide examples. As
the various techniques are presented, try to think of ways that a
technique might be adapted to work with your specific children or
adults.

The second thing I would like to mention is related to this same
basic idea. Many of the aids that will be presented during this session
will use words or the letters of the alphabet. Others will be connected
to typewriters or printers and will print out the children's messages as
letters are indicated. These aids may seem far beyond the capabilities
of pre-spelling or pre-reading children. If you remove the typewriters,
however, and replace the letters of the alphabet with pictures, or symbols, you will see that the same techniques for indication used in these
advanced aids could be used with children on a picture or symbol level.
It is important to remember that the same techniques for indication
which are used in the more expensive aids can almost always be implemented either in simpler and less expensive aids or manually by the teacher
in the classroom. Once again, we'll try to give examples as we go along.

THREE BASIC APPROACHES FOR PROVIDING A MEANS OF INDICATION

Although a great many techniques have been developed for the non-
vocal physically handicapped (NVPH) child, they are essentially variations on three basic approaches. These approaches are Scanning, Encoding, and Direct Selection.

Scanning communication aids - a brief introduction

The formal definition of Scanning which has been formulated by the
Trace Center is:

Any technique (or aid) in which the selections are offered to
the user by a person or display, and where the user selects
the characters by responding to the person or display. Depending upon the aid, the user may respond by simply signaling when he sees the correct choice presented, or by actively
directing an indicator (e.g., light or arrow), toward the desired choice. (Vanderheiden, Harris-Vanderheiden, 1976)

In less formal terminology, a technique is considered to be a scanning technique if the items in the child's vocabulary are presented to
him one at a time so that he can let you know when the item he wants is
presented. The simplest example of a scanning technique would be the
familiar "yes/no" guessing technique (see Fig. 7a). With this technique,

a second person would simply present choices to the child such as "You're thirsty?" "You're hungry?" "Does something hurt?" "Do you have to go to the bathroom?" etc. When (and if) the second person reaches the desired message, the child will signal in some manner, such as smiling, looking up, or by using some other pre-arranged signal.

Another example of a simple scanning technique (see Fig. 7b) would be the use of a communication board with a second person pointing to the pictures, words, or letters one at a time while watching for a response from the child. Figure 7c shows this same technique, automated somewhat, so that a rotating arrow does the pointing for the second person. With this aid the child signals the aid directly when he wants to stop the arrow. To signal the aid he could use some kind of switch which is specially fitted to take advantage of some movement over which he has good control. For the child who can spell, this technique could be automated even further so that as he selects the letters, the aid would automatically print them out on a typewriter or other device. (Fig. 7d) If the child is completely non-vocal, it would be highly desirable to have a communication aid which could move around with him and function as his "voice," if you will, as he moves around in his environment, in school and at home. For this purpose a portable aid such as the one featured in Figure 7e could be used.

The most significant thing to notice about the scanning technique is that it is extremely powerful. By powerful I mean it can be used with individuals who have only minimal control. If you can recognize a child's "yes" (or an affirmative signal of any form), you can use any of the non-mechanical techniques, no matter how severe the child's handicap. By the same token, if the child has a reliable and recognizable signal, it can almost always be tapped, using a special switch of some sort, and used to control the mechanical or electronic types of scanning aids. Anything from a gross motor movement to a muscle twitch can be detected and used as a control signal. The price that is paid for this power, however, is speed. Because a lot of time is spent presenting unwanted choices before the correct choice is arrived at, communication with this technique can be quite slow. There are ways to speed up the selection process using the scanning technique and these will be described a little later.

Encoding techniques and aids - a brief introduction

Because speed is so important when communicating, various techniques have been developed which use an encoding approach. The formal definition for encoding which has been formulated is:

> Any technique or aid in which the desired choice is indicated by a pattern or code of input signals, where the pattern or code must be memorized or referred to on a chart.

Figure 7. *Examples of techniques using the scanning approach: a) Yes/ No guessing; b) manual scanning of communication board; c) Rotating Pointer Communication; and d) Printing communica- tion board using Row column scanning; e) Portable, printing communication aid.*

When an aid is used, any number of switches may be used
(e.g., one, two, seven, etc.). The code may involve
activating the switch(es), sequentially or simultaneously.
(Vanderheiden, Harris-Vanderheiden, 1976)

The best way to clarify this definition is to look at some examples
of encoding techniques. One very simple technique would be to arrange
the letters of the alphabet in a matrix (see Fig. 8a). The child could
indicate which letter he wanted, such as the "L," by pointing to the
number 3 and then pointing to the number 2 to show that he wanted a letter in the third row, second letter across. An example of a simple
encoding technique which could be used with a child who can only control
his eyes is shown in Figure 8b. With this technique, the child would indicate which picture, word or letter he wanted on a vocabulary chart by
using his eye gaze to indicate the numbers which are printed next to
that picture, word or letter.

Once again, many of these encoding techniques could be automated.
Let's say we have a spinal cord injured person who has fairly good control of his upper neck muscles. These muscles could very easily be mon-
itored so that by simply tensing them he could send out Morse or some
other code. This code could then be decoded by an aid and displayed so
that the average person could see what letter he was trying to indicate.
Figure 8c shows an aid which is controlled by shoulder shrugs. The message receiver would only have to watch the display to see which letters
appeared, to determine what message the individual was trying to communicate. These techniques could also, of course, be fully automated so
that the letters would print out directly onto a typewriter or other
display. (Fig. 8d).

The encoding technique is generally faster if the individual has
some form of quick motion, or if the individual is able to point directly to a moderate number (eight or so) of different squares or switches.
For the individual who can operate only a few switches and whose movements are slow and erratic, (as may be found in some severely athetoid
or spastic cerebral palsied children) the encoding approach may be very
slow, even slower than scanning. The specific abilities of the child
must be taken into account before a comparison of the approaches can
be made.

Two other aspects should be noted about techniques that use the
encoding approach. First, this approach often requires more responses
and thus more work from the child. This may be good or bad, depending
upon how quickly the child fatigues and upon his physical abilities.
Secondly, the encoding technique is more abstract than the scanning
approach (where the choices are more directly presented to the child)
and for very young children or children with cognitive handicaps this
may present a problem. However, people who have implemented various
encoding techniques have found that children pick them up much faster

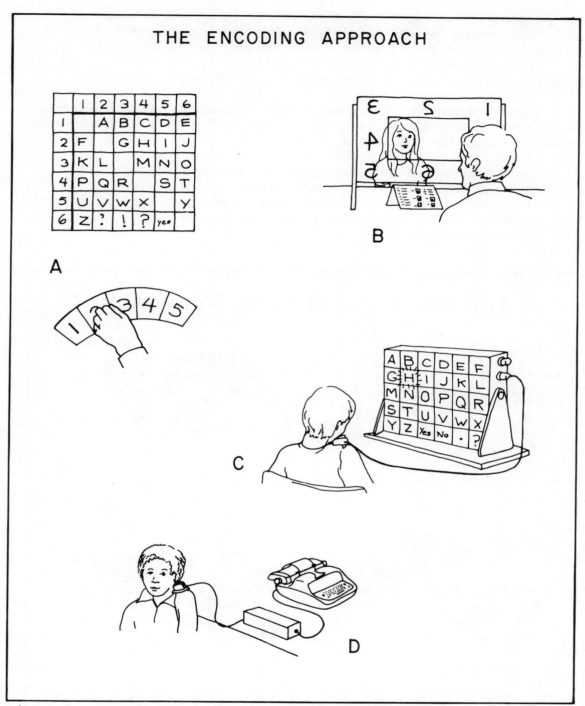

Figure 8. Examples of techniques using the encoding approach. a) Two movement encoding with number line; b) two movement encoding using eye gaze; c) Morse code decoder/display being controlled with shoulder (shrug); d) Morse code decoder controlling typewriter.

26

than originally anticipated. Later we will be discussing ways that can make the encoding technique fairly straightforward and easy to handle even for the child with limited cognitive ability.

Direct selection techniques and aids - a brief introduction

The third approach is called direct selection. This approach, which is the most straightforward and common of the three, has been formally defined as follows:

> Any technique (or aid) in which the desired choice is directly indicated by the user. In direct selection aids there is a key or sensor for each possible choice or vocabulary element. (Vanderheiden, Harris-Vanderheiden, 1976)

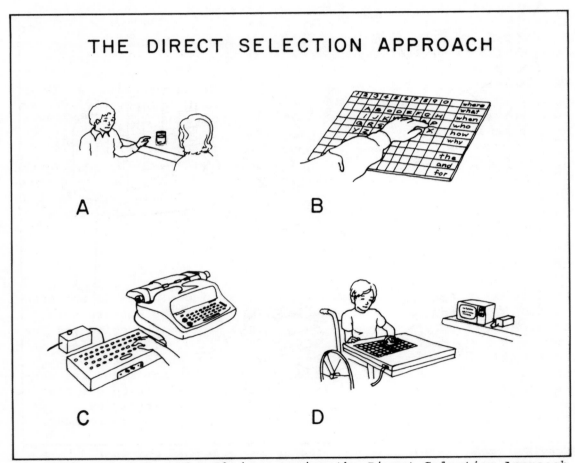

THE DIRECT SELECTION APPROACH

A   B

C   D

Figure 9.   *Examples of techniques using the Direct Selection Approach.
a) direct indication; b) pointing communication board;
c) expanded, recessed keyboard; d) portable printing communication board.*

The simplest example of direct selection is direct gesture, where a child simply looks at the door when he wants to go out, points to the bathroom when he wants to go to the toilet, points to a glass of water for a drink, etc. (Fig. 9a) Another very familiar example of the direct selection approach would be the letterboard or communication board. (Fig. 9b) Here again the child directly indicates with his hand or headstick the letters, words, pictures, etc., which he wants to use to make up his message.

Any kind of keyboard, including those that are expanded, guarded, or otherwise modified (Fig. 9c) would be examples of direct selection aids. Direct selection techniques can, of course, be used in portable, printing communication aids as well. (See Fig. 9d)

LEVELS OF IMPLEMENTATION

In introducing the three approaches, we have seen that the techniques within each approach can vary from fundamental techniques to more sophisticated aids. Figure 10 shows the various techniques we have been talking about, characterizing them by their degree of sophistication. Each of these levels has different advantages and disadvantages for children with differing abilities or in different situations. It is therefore important to understand the significance of these different levels, both when we are comparing one aid against another and when selecting an aid for a particular individual.

In general, each successive category represents an increase in the complexity of the aid. It also generally represents an increase in the independence of communication for the handicapped individual, as well as a decrease in the amount of effort needed by the message receiver to interpret the handicapped person's message.

Unaided techniques

Unaided techniques are communication techniques which do not actually involve any physical communication aid. These systems are very limiting in that they are usually only viable between the child and one or two people who know him well. The guessing game, or "intuition" is often thought to be effective between a mother and child for basic needs. It does not, however, provide the child with any means for asking questions or learning about his environment. This technique also does not provide the child with any viable means for expressing opinion or emotion or for interacting with others in his environment.

Fundamental aids

Aids in this category represent basic methods of implementing scanning, encoding, or direct selection techniques. Any of the approaches, no matter how complex they may be, could be implemented on the fundamen-

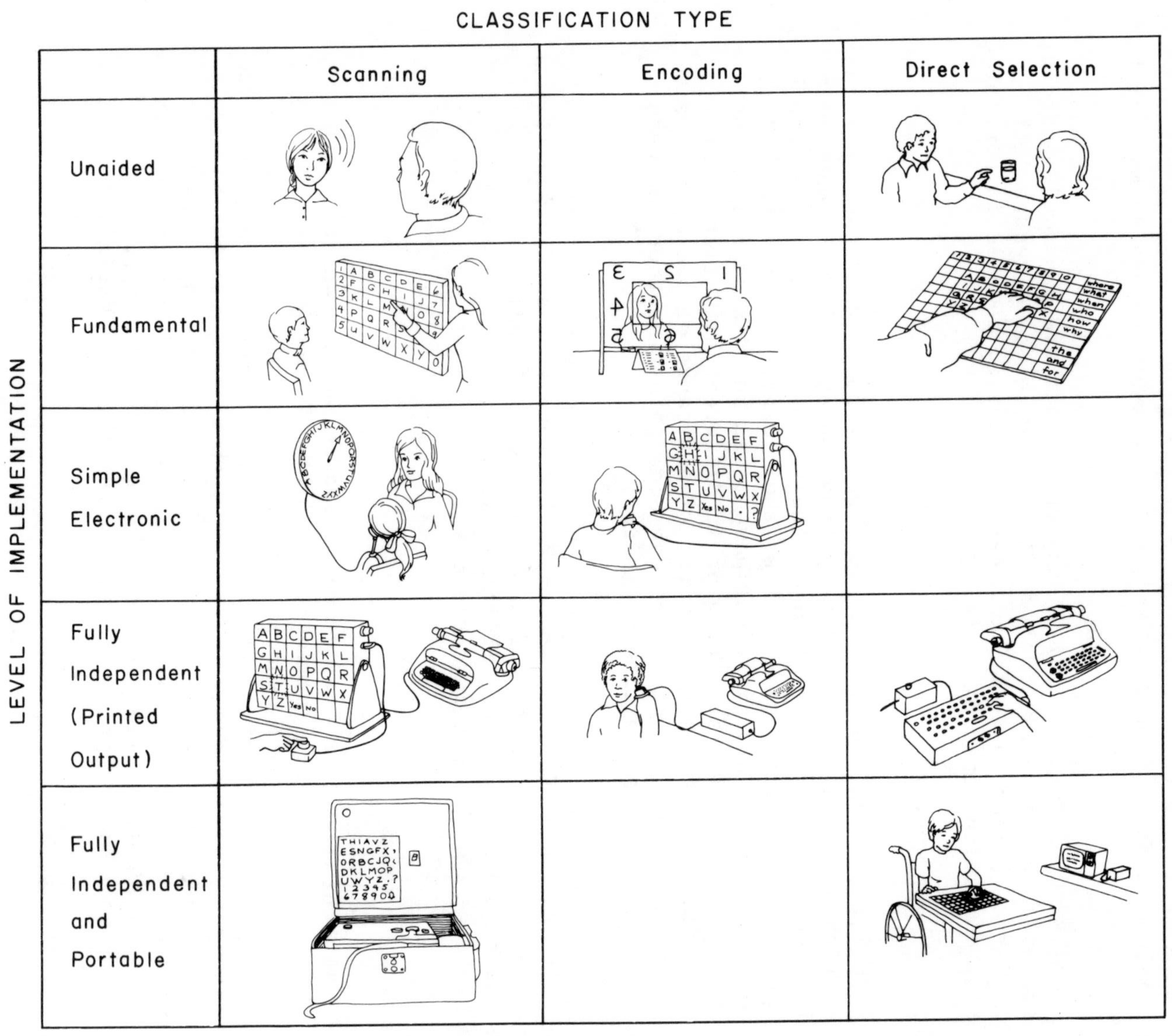

28

CLASSIFICATION TYPE

Direct Selection	Encoding	Scanning	
			Unaided
			Fundamental
			Simple Electronic
			Fully Independent (Printed Output)
			Fully Independent and Portable

LEVEL OF IMPLEMENTATION

Figure 10.

tal level with the work being done by the person working with the child. For example, the fully independent, portable encoding communication aid with printer could be implemented on this level by an individual who would watch the child, interpret his movements, decode them to determine which letters the child was trying to indicate and then write down the letters to assemble the child's message. As you can see, using the techniques in this manner can require a fair amount of effort on the part of the second person. Even when using a communication board, a second person is needed to interpret the child's movements, figure out which letters he's pointing to, and then assemble them to determine his message.

These techniques, however, do have a great advantage in that they are readily available to the teacher in the classroom. Most of the aids can be very easily fabricated by a teacher or by a local handyman. Their construction doesn't require any special kind of expertise as they generally don't incorporate any moving parts or electronics. It is only the amount of time and effort on the part of the second person to use these aids for communication that keeps these aids from being used on a more widespread basis and from fully meeting the communication needs of many of the children.

Simple electronic and mechanical aids

Aids in this category use some electronic or mechanical technique to interpret the child's motion and to indicate directly to the message receiver the letters, words, pictures, etc., which the child is trying to indicate. With these aids, the message receiver, therefore, does not have to interpret the child's movement, but still does have to write down or remember the characters and assemble the message for the child.

Because the child can (with the aid) directly indicate the letters, pictures, etc. which make up his message, very little knowledge of the system is required on the part of the second person. For this reason, the handicapped individual can generally communicate with a much greater number of people using this aid than he could using the simplier aids. Although the amount of work that has to be done by the message receiver is greatly reduced by using these methods, the undivided attention of this person is still required. This continues to be a problem if the child's message is more than a few words long or if he wants to partake in group conversation or do independent work.

Fully independent aids

The last two categories concern fully independent aids. An aid is considered fully independent if it has some kind of printout or display (like a calculator's display). With these aids the child has a fully independent means of assembling his message. He is able to select letters which are then assembled by the aid and printed out (or displayed) for the message receiver. The child needs no help in assembling his message and only needs the attention of the other person for the brief instant needed to read the completed message. With these aids the child is able to participate in group conversations or classroom discussions and only interrupt the class for the brief amount of time it takes to read a completed message (rather than the entire time it takes to assemble it).

Many of these aids have some sort of printer, typewriter, or television display. With these aids, the child is given not only a means of communication, but also a means of writing. This becomes very important if the child is placed in any kind of educational program. If the child is going to be held responsible for practicing his lessons, doing homework, independent work, and taking tests, it is necessary for him to have some means of writing without requiring the constant attention of a second person. This becomes even more evident when it is understood that a simple three-page book report can take between seven and twelve hours for someone to assemble, even if the child is using a letterboard (a relatively fast communication technique).

Fully independent and portable aids

Like the independent communication aids just discussed, these aids allow the child to assemble his message completely independently. They also, however, have the advantage of being fully portable. As such they can move around with the child and function as his "voice," rather than simply as a writing instrument.

In order to be portable, aids in this category incorporate some form of printout or readout other than a typewriter. For some of the aids, however, the typewriter is available as an accessory which can be controlled by the aid. This provides the child with the ability to write out longer messages in page form which is very valuable in educational or vocational settings. Another form of page output is the television display. These displays, which resemble the TV displays in an airport (listing the flight schedules) have the advantage of being both highly visible and completely correctable. Because of these features they are especially popular in educational settings. Their correctability is thought to be very important both for allowing the child to correct his mistakes and for allowing the teacher to separate inadvertent mistakes from mistakes made because the child truly does not understand something. The television display is also often less expensive than the specially adapted electrically controllable typewriters.

IMPLICATIONS AND ADVANTAGES OF THE VARIOUS LEVELS OF IMPLEMENTATION

Looking at the various levels, it may appear as though the further down the chart you go the more function you get. While it is true that the further you go down the chart the less work needs to be done by the message receiver, it is not necessarily true that the portable independent aids are the best aids for everyone. There are a lot of constraints which cause one aid to be much more applicable to an individual than another. For instance, most of the independent portable aids cannot be used with pictures or other symbols outside of the letters of the alphabet. For this reason these aids cannot be applied with children who are still on a picture level, children who cannot read, or children who will be communicating in only one or two symbol utterances. For these children, and for other children just starting out, the fundamental and simple aids are much more powerful since they can be used with letters, pictures, words, or special symbols. For developmental reasons or for children who may not be able to read or spell, therefore, simpler aids may be the more applicable aids.

Another restriction, which hopefully is a temporary one, is that children are often not able to acquire the aid which is most appropriate for them due to financial restrictions. As you move down the chart the cost of the aids goes up rapidly. Aids in the fundamental category generally run from between $5 and $50 if you make them yourself, or from between $10 and $150 if you were to buy them as commercially available aids. The next level, simple electronic and mechanical aids, would generally run in cost from $50 - $100 up to about $1,000. Fully independent aids run anywhere from $1,000 - $7,000, depending upon how many accessories and different printouts you want with them. Fully independent portable aids cost about the same as the stationary aids. It generally costs more to make something portable, but then you don't have to cover the cost of adapting a typewriter. For those aids which are portable and can also be hooked to a typewriter the cost usually runs around $1,500 extra for a typewriter or TV display as an additional accessory.

Part of the reason for the high costs at the present time is the large amount of demonstration and information dissemination that must be done in connection with selling the aids. As these aids become more and more widely known and used, these "missionary" costs will decrease along with production costs. You can, therefore, eventually expect to see a decrease in the cost of the aids. Unfortunately, the number of aids that will be sold will never reach the scale of the pocket calculator and so you shouldn't expect the price drop you've seen in the calculator industry. Instead I think that we should be looking for a solution to the cost problem through either legislation or awareness activities at the school administration level. Although the cost of the aids seems high when looked at in isolation, what is not seen is that it would cost from $4,000 to $8,000 a year to provide a child with a dedicated "second person" to interpret his messages and allow him to do independent work so that he could participate in an interactive classroom situation. When compared to the $400 cost of even the more advanced aids ($3,000 divided by 10 years = $300 plus $100 maintenance = $400/year) the cost of the aids does not seem nearly so high. The cost of the aid can also be compared to the $1,500 to $2,500 per year (or even $25,000 per year in hospital school settings) that is already being spent to place many of these children in educational programs in which they cannot really effectively participate. Independent aids, therefore, seem to be not only necessary and appropriate for many of these children, but also cost effective. I'd like to restate here, though, that we should remember that the advanced aids are not going to be appropriate for all children and that it is often better to start the child out on simpler aids until his need for the more expensive and more advanced aids has been established.

THE SCANNING APPROACH - (A more detailed look at specific scanning techniques)

Now that we have introduced and briefly discussed each of the basic approaches and the various levels of implementation, let's go back and look at each approach in more detail. As we do this we will be looking at the different ways in which the approaches introduced earlier can be used to meet the specific abilities of these children. In addition we can look at some of the restrictions of each of the approaches as well as examples of various aids which have been developed around the world using these techniques.

The first approach we discussed was scanning. As stated earlier, when thinking about the scanning technique the thing that should first come to your mind is that it is the most powerful of the three approaches. By powerful we mean that it can be used by even the most severely physically handicapped individual. If there is even one movement or signal that the individual can make consistently, the individual has the physical capability of controlling a scanning aid. All that needs to be done is to develop or select a switch which can be used to recognize that movement or signal. To understand this point better, let's go over some examples of different kinds of switches that could be used.

There are sight switches which attach to the frame of your glasses and will activate if you look at them. There are breath switches, both those that have paddles that you blow at and those which have a pipe stem which you sip and puff on. This method, by the way, does not require that you use your lungs; you sip and puff using your mouth in much the same way you would drink through a straw. There are pillow-like switches which can be activated either by heavy pounding or light pressure. Switches have been developed which can be used with almost any part of the body including the knee, thigh, elbow, head, tongue, and foot. In addition, switches have been developed which can operate off the electrical potential generated when you try to flex a muscle. As a result an individual does not necessarily have to even move. Simply by tensing a muscle slightly he can activate a switch. (For more information, see Masterchart in Appendix).

Although it has not been demonstrated in a practical manner at the present time, there is also research being done in the development of switches which run off brain waves. One experimenter developed a communication aid that could be operated using alpha wave output. The technique however, was extremely slow and took tremendous amounts of concentration. A more encouraging line of research has been conducted by specialists trying to develop a computer which can be controlled by thoughts. The aim is to have the operator "think" a word and have the computer be able to recognize his thought waves. If a small portable unit could be developed which could recognize even a small five word vocabulary (up, down, left, right, yes) a child would be able to direct a light to the word on a panel that he wanted to print out and then think "yes" to have it printed out. Theoretically this could be an extremely fast technique which would even approach the speed of normal speech. The feasibility of this type of approach, however, has not been explored in terms of these children. What the brainwave pattern of the athetoid cerebral palsied non-vocal child with limited language abilities is, I don't know. But if the brainwave patterns are regular enough to be used as a signal, they may be quick enough so that they could provide even the most physically handicapped child with a fairly efficient means of communication.

Overview of scanning techniques

There are many different types of scanning techniques. I will be going over a few of them here to show you different ways in which the technique can be implemented and to demonstrate that there are ways of making the scanning technique faster.

The first technique is the simplest and is called a "linear scan."* In the linear scan various message elements are presented one at a time and the child simply responds when the aid gets to the one he wants. (Example in Fig. 11) This is the most straightforward and simplest type

Figure 11.
Example of linear scanning technique.

---

*If the "line" is bent into a circle this same approach is sometimes also referred to as "circular scanning." The elements are still in a line however, and are covered under 'linear scanning.'

34

of scan and is probably the best one to use when starting out with a
very young child or a child with limited cognitive ability. This approach, however, is the slowest approach and while it works well if you
have ten pictures, it can become impractically slow if the child has a
50 or 100 word vocabulary. With a vocabulary of fifty words, for instance, it would take half a minute, on the average, just to get to a
single correct letter or word (with a one second response time).

To help overcome this speed problem, some people have utilized a
two-speed linear scan. With the two-speed approach, the individual has
two switches. One causes the scan to go quite fast until it gets close
to the desired letter. The child then releases this switch and lets
the aid scan slowly up to the letter he wants. When it reaches the
correct letter the child activates the second switch and the letter is
printed out. This approach, you will notice, requires more ability on
the part of the child. Not only does it require extra movements, but
it also requires that the child be able to hold down the "fast" switch
until the scanner has reached the vicinity of the desired letter. For
some children, particularly athetoid children, this may not be within
their capabilities and another approach may be more desirable.

Another technique which has been used to increase the speed of the
scanning approach is the "row-column" scanning technique. With this
technique the letters, words or pictures are arranged in a matrix or
checkerboard fashion. Figure 12 shows an example of a 7 by 7 matrix
which has 49 squares. To use the row column technique the aid (or per-

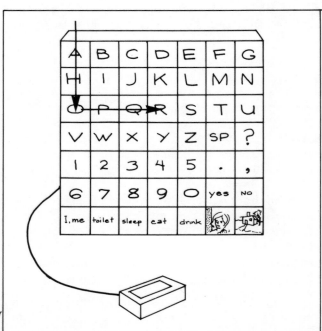

Figure 12.
Example of Row Column Scanning
Aid.

son working with the child) first lights up (or points to) the rows to let the child select the proper row. Then the aid lights each square (or points to each square) in that row until the child signals again, indicating that that is the letter he wants. Now, with a 10 by 10 matrix, the maximum number of steps it could take would be 14, whereas with the linear scanning the maximum would be 49. The average time would be 7 versus 24. From these numbers you can see the savings in time that results from using the row-column technique; we have gone from an average of almost half a minute to less than ten seconds to get any one letter or word from the display. Once again you will note that in order to achieve the increased speed, the child must do more work in that he must signal twice as often.

With either of the two techniques just discussed, one can increase the speed even further if the most frequently used letters, words, etc. are placed in the upper left hand corner where the scan begins. For instance, in the English language e, t, a, o, i, s, r, h, and l are the letters used most frequently. By putting these up in the corner where the scan starts each time, it is possible to reduce the average time needed to select the proper letter to about 2/3 the time it would have taken had the letters been arranged in alphabetical order.

If the child has enough control to use a joy stick (see Fig. 13), then another, more efficient scanning technique may be appropriate. This technique, called the directed scan, allows the child to control the direction that the indicator is scanning as well as to stop in on the correct choice. For the child who can use his eyes well, this technique can also be implemented on a manual basis where the child looks up, down, left, or right to direct the pointing of the second person. (See Fig. 14).

A pseudo-scanning technique is the "step-scan." With this technique the child hits a switch to move the light from each position to the next. Two or three switches are usually used for this technique; one to step downward, one to step across, and one to print the characters if a printing aid is used. (This is not a true scanning technique since the child actually moves the light himself - the aid does not actively present choices to the child and wait for his response to signal a correct presentation).

These are some of the different scanning techniques which have been developed. Each of them can be implemented in any of the levels, including: as a fundamental aid with a teacher doing the scanning, as a simple electronic aid, or as a fully independent or portable and independent aid. There is one final technique I would like to describe which would probably only be found in an independent communication aid. It was originally described by Rick Foulds, et. al., at the Biomedical Engineering Center of the Tufts-New England Medical Center. This technique, introduced as the "anticipatory scanning" technique, has also been called "predictive scanning" and the "computer-aided scanning"

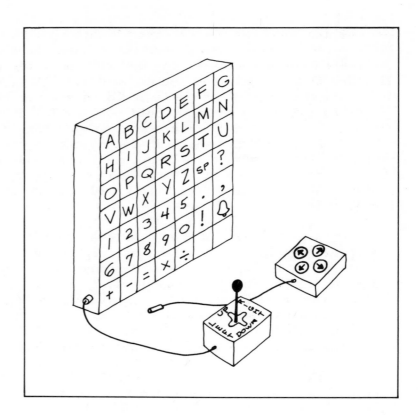

Figure 13.
Example of a directed
scanning aid with joy
stick or push button
control.

Figure 14.
Example of directed
scanning using eye gaze.

technique. The technique looks at the last letters that have been printed, and, based upon probability, tries to determine which letter the child will want next. For instance, if the last two letters were "t" and "h," the aid would know, (from probability tables), that the next most likely letters would be "e," "space," "a," "i," etc. The aid would then change the letters appearing in the scanning matrix so that the letters "e," "space," "a," "i," would appear in the upper left-hand corner of the display.* (See Fig. 15) These letters would then be the first letters presented to the child. Using this system the probability is 81.3% that the letter the child wants will be one of the first 6 letters presented by the aid. If the letters were presented in a fixed pattern (space, e, t, a, o, n, i, s, k, h) the aid would have to scan

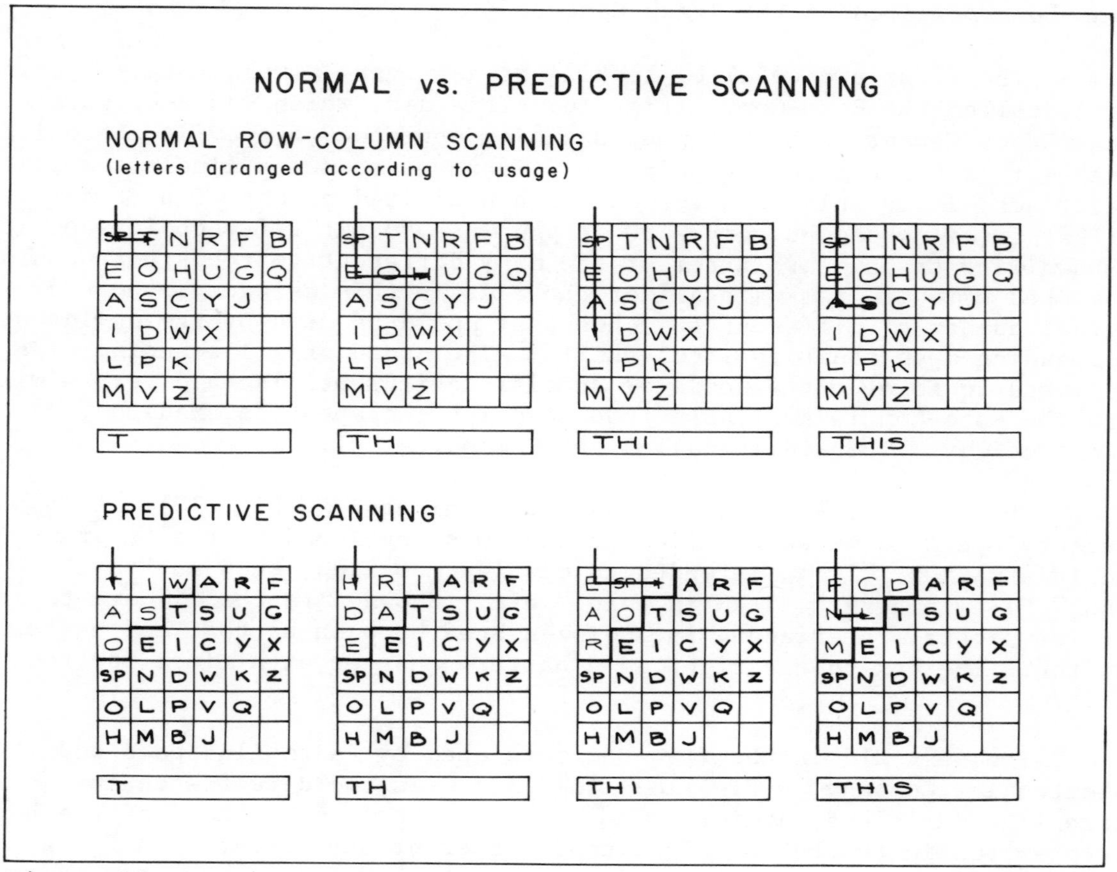

Figure 15.

---

*Instead of actually changing the first letters in the display as in Figure 15b - an alternate approach to anticipatory scanning uses a static display as in 15a except that the aid would jump the light to the six predicted letters first and then go to a traditional row column scan. A dim light might precede the bright light to prepare the child when this jump scanning approach is used.

over 10 letters in order to achieve the same 81% probability of presenting the letter the child wanted. Studies are now being conducted to see whether or not the increase in speed which is achievable through the anticipatory scanning approach is sufficient to offset the increased cost of implementing this advanced technique.

A partial survey of scanning aids

In this survey we will be moving from the simpler aids toward more complex aids. I will be giving only a few examples of different aids which have been developed or are under development. There are many others and I encourage you to check both the Master-Chart at the end of the book and also the Annotated Bibliography of Communication Aids which has been prepared at the Trace Center.

The first aid we'll be looking at is a very simple rotating pointer aid, called the Roto-Com. (Fig. 16) This aid, which was developed at the Trace Center, uses a linear scanning approach to provide the children with a basic means of pointing. Because it uses a linear scanning approach, it is only good for use with a limited number of pictures. (That is, it would be very slow if you were to put fifty choices on it). Shown with the aid are three of the many different switches that could be used with it. As with all of the aids in this category, there are a great number of different switches that could be used by the children, depending upon their physical skills. The speed of all scanning aids is adjustable to meet the needs of specific children. (An aid very similar to the Roto-Com is available from Adaptive Therapeutics, Madison, Connecticut. The aid is called the Communicator).

The next aid shown is the VAPC Communicator. (Fig. 17) It is a battery operated message indicator that was developed by the Veterans' Administration. It is intended to display messages, such as "yes," "no," "I am hungry," "I am in pain," etc. Shown with the aid are three of its several interfaces, including a breath, push-button, and magnetic switch. The box to the right is a battery charger with timer for the aid.

The next aid is the View-Com developed by Fairchild Space and Electronics Company. (Fig. 18) This aid uses the direct scanning technique described earlier. The aid is controlled by means of the hand-held switch in the bottom right-hand corner of the picture. Although this switch requires fairly fine motor control of the thumb, the aid could also be used with other types of switches. All the little squares containing messages can be removed or rearranged. In addition, blank squares are provided to allow individualization of the aid. There are two features which I'd like to bring to your attention concerning this particular aid. One is found on the bottom of the third column, the word "damn." Many parents and teachers feel that swear words such as this are necessary, but are reluctant to put them on indication boards for fear of endorsing them. Such words as "phooey," or simply an assortment of punctuation marks have been used with great success and provide children with a means of expressing frustration when they feel they need to. What is important is that some means of expressing frustration be provided. The other feature that I'd like to point out is in the bottom of the left-hand column. It is a square which controls a buzzer (which is built into the aid). Since many of these children do not have an effective means of calling the attention of those around them without going into complicated gyrations, this is an important feature. It is also important for calling the attention of people who may not be in the room.

The next aid is the SCRP "100 + 100" display. (Fig. 19) This aid,

Figure 16.
Roto Com shown with three interface switches; a pillow switch, a feather touch switch and a slam switch.

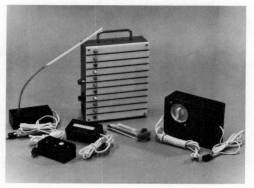

Figure 17.
VAPC Communicator shown with breath, push button and magnetic switches. Battery charger at right has built-in shutoff timer.

Figure 18.
The View-Com, a directed scanning aid.

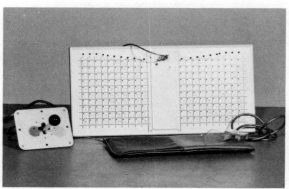

Figure 19.
The SCRP 100 + 100 display (a directed scanning aid for use with Blissymbols), shown with three types of input switches; joystick, dual pillow and paddle switches.

developed by the Ontario Crippled Children's Centre, Ontario, Canada, was designed specifically to be used with Bliss Symbols, although it could be used with words, letters, or pictures as well. Each of the squares on the aid has a small red light (LED) in the upper left-hand corner. The child indicates which symbol he wants by lighting the light in the appropriate square. This aid also uses a directed-scanning technique by which the child can control the direction of the jumping light and direct it to the square he desires. Using either the pillow switches (center), or the paddle switches (to the right), the child moves the dot up and down using one pillow (or one direction of the paddle switch), and moves the light dot to the left and right using the other pillow (or direction of the paddle switch). Alternately, the aid can be controlled with a joy stick (left) where the scanning direction is directly selected by the direction in which the joystick is pushed.

All of the aids shown thus far have been examples of simple electronic communication aids. The Alphabet Message Scanner (Fig. 20) by Prentke-Romich Company is also a portable simple electronic communication aid. It, however, offers the option of having a typewriter controller plugged into it, thus becoming a stationary independent communication aid. The scanner uses the row-column scanning technique where the aid first scans across the top row until signalled by the switch, and then scans down the column until signalled again. Note that this aid also has a "buzzer" square (botton right-hand corner).

Centre Industries in Australia developed a linear scanning typewriter controller shown in Figure 21. This aid, called the Clock-Face Selector, would be an example of the linear scanning stationary independent communication aid.

Figure 20.
The Alphabet Message Scanner,
a row column scanning aid which
can be used alone or in
combination with a printer.

Figure 21.
The Clockface Selector -
a linear scanning independent
communication aid.

Another linear scanning aid was developed by Palmstiernas Mekaniska Verkstad AB in Stockholm, Sweden. (Fig. 22) The aid, called the PMV

Printer, helps to alleviate the slower speed of the linear scanning process by introducing a two-speed scan. Two switches are then used by the individual, one which is held down to cause the aid to scan at the fast speed, and one which is hit when the correct letter is indicated.

One of the very early row-column independent communication aids was developed by Bush Electronics in California. Called the VISTA (Fig. 23), this aid was the only commercially available scanning aid in America for some time. The aid used an IBM typewriter which slid in from the back and could be removed for separate use.

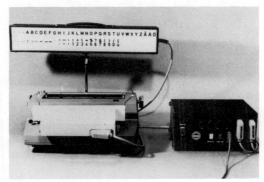

Figure 22:
The PMV Printer, a two-speed,
linear scanning, independent
communication aid.

Figure 23.
The VISTA, an early row-column
independent communication aid.

A more recent row-column scanning aid is the Whispertype™(Cyber Corp., Washington, D.C.) The Whispertype™has the capability of being controlled by a sound made into a microphone. It can also be controlled by a large variety of other interface switches which can be selected to best meet the needs of the handicapped individual. This Whispertype™is part of a larger family of communication aids collectively known as Cybercoms® All of the aids in the Cybercom®family use a standard display format or code to facilitate movement from one aid to another as the child's physical skill development permits. In addition to their normal typewriter output, these aids have also been interfaced with a variety of other outputs including a voice synthesizer.

Another row-column scanning aid, the "System 8," was developed by Zambette Electronics, Ltd., in England. (Fig. 24) The unique feature of the Zambette aid is the capacitance operated switch which requires only that the operator come near it to operate it. It thus requires no fine motor control.

The final stationary communication aid in this survey is the Tufts Interactive Communicator (TIC) developed at Tufts University, Medford, Mass. (Fig. 25) This aid is available in several versions, one of which incorporates the "anticipatory scanning" technique described earlier. The

---

®™ Cyber Corp., Washington, D.C.

anticipatory scanning model, which is in final development, will use a limited set of rules to look at the last three letters which have been printed when determining the next letters to be presented. A smaller, portable version of the TIC is also under development.

Figure 24.
The System 8, a row column scanning, independent aid featuring a capacitance operated proximity switch.

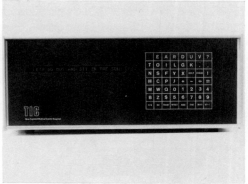

Figure 25.
The TIC, a row-column scanning independent aid with electronic display and strip printer. Available with Anticipatory Scanning Option.

The first fully portable scanning aid to become available was the Portaprinter by Portacom, Incorporated, New York. (Fig. 26) This aid uses a row-column scanning technique which is different from any of the others which have been developed. Instead of returning to the upper right-hand corner after each selection, the aid continues its scanning pattern. The letters are arranged so that they form very commonly used patterns, and frequently used letters are repeated on the face of the display. The aid is normally battery-operated but can control two 110 volt outlets for environmental control when it is plugged into the wall. The output of the aid is on a 1/4"-wide thermal strip printer tape which is displayed at the very front edge of the aid. (A similar aid, using the conventional row-column scanning approach, has also been developed by Prentke-Romich, Shreve, Ohio).

Figure 26.
The Portaprinter, a portable independent aid which operates in a modified row-column scanning pattern, with strip-printer output.

A third portable scanning aid is the Versicom, developed by the Trace Center, University of Wisconsin-Madison. (Fig. 27) This aid is capable of operating in many different modes to best accommodate the specific abilities of different children. With its optional LED display (comparable to a calculator display), this aid represents the first portable scanning aid which is correctable. The aid is able to print out entire words, phrases, or messages with a single indication by the user. Thus, the aid can be used with children who are still learning to spell or, by coupling it with pictures or symbols, could be used by non-spelling and non-reading children.

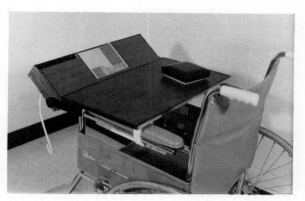

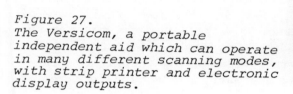

Figure 27.
The Versicom, a portable
independent aid which can operate
in many different scanning modes,
with strip printer and electronic
display outputs.

SCANNING AIDS - SUMMARY REMARKS

In closing the discussion of scanning aids, the thing to remember is that aids in this category could be controlled by almost anyone, no matter how severe their physical handicaps. If you can tell that the child is trying to signal you, then there should be some type of switch that can be found or developed which the child would be able to operate. Once he has a switch which he can operate, he has the physical means to use any of the scanning approaches or aids which have been described. The disadvantage of the scanning approach is that it can be quite slow for some types of handicaps. For this reason, other approaches have been developed which may be faster. These approaches, however, require increased physical skills. It is not always true that the scanning approach is the slowest technique for a given individual. If an individual has very restricted motion but is fairly quick with it, the scanning approach may indeed be faster, least fatiguing, and therefore the best technique for him.

ENCODING APPROACH

Encoding techniques are techniques which require some kind of multiple signal that must be either memorized or looked up on a chart. One of the advantages of this approach is that, for some people, it is faster than the scanning technique. Because this approach does not require a large back-lit display, these aids have the potential for being made smaller. Some of the encoding approaches also require pointing to a moderate number of switches (four to eight). These encoding approaches have the additional advantage of helping to develop motor control and pointing skills. Often, children who start out with encoding approaches can develop the skills necessary to point to larger numbers of squares or switches and can move on to the direct selection approach which will be described later. Finally, the encoding approach allows a child to access a larger number of vocabulary items than can be easily used with either the scanning or direct selection techniques. For this reason, children who are able to use the direct selection technique may use it in combination with an encoding technique to allow them to access an expanded vocabulary (see combination techniques).

The disadvantages usually cited are that encoding approaches generally require finer control and more motions than the scanning technique. They also require the user to utilize some code or at least a two-step process in specifying his output. For very young children, or mentally retarded individuals, this may pose a problem. As we shall see, however, the encoding approach can be made fairly simple. Further, it is possible to develop some approaches so that neither the child nor the message receiver would even realize that a code was being used. Since there is often no visual display (as there is with the scanning technique), feedback can be a problem with the encoding approach unless care is taken to provide feedback information to the child while he is selecting the letter. Of course, feedback should also be provided to the child after he has selected the letter, both in the form of presenting the letter to the child and presenting him with his message to that point.

Response requirements for the encoding approach may be more or less demanding than the scanning approach, depending upon the specific techniques used. In general, the encoding approach requires more refined or more numerous responses than the scanning approach. The encoding approach, however, does not require that responses be given at a specific instant in time, as is required with scanning techniques. The encoding approach may therefore be easier for individuals who have difficulty in making very rapid responses. (It should be noted, however, that with the scanning approach the child is able to anticipate the instant at which he must respond, and it would be unfair to compare his reaction time under this kind of a task with his reaction time to a stimulus which was suddenly presented to him).

The number and complexity of the individual's responses are all dependent upon the number of switches required for a specific approach and the type of switches that are used. As we discussed under the scanning approach, there are a great many different types of aids that can be used with these children. Although specific aids usually come with one or another type of interface switch, it should be remembered that if the child is not able to operate a specific type of switch, any one of the many other types of switches described could be hooked up to control the aid.

The number and complexity of responses required by the user changes, depending upon the various approaches used. In general, the greater the number of switches or movements used in an encoding scheme, the simpler the code will be. However, an increased number of movements requires greater dexterity on the part of the operator. Thus, a compromise between the two factors, simplicity of code and number of movements or switches, must be worked out. Different researchers and clinicians have chosen different balances between these two factors in the design of their techniques. The specific needs of the individual determine which approach is best suited for him.

Overview of encoding techniques

In the above discussion, much reference has been made to "aids" and "switches." As we get into discussing various specific techniques, however, it will become evident that many of the techniques do not utilize any electric or electronic aids at all. In addition, all of the techniques which have been implemented using electronic aids could also be implemented by a clinician using magic markers and paper to make displays, and performing functions herself that are normally automated by the devices. Thus, all of the techniques which will be described could be implemented immediately by the teacher, clinician, or aide in the classroom. In general, one can simply substitute the word "movements" or "squares" for the word "switches," and the word "teacher" for the word "aid" to translate the function of any electronic aid into a "fundamental" way of implementing the same basic techniques without an aid.

The most common encoding techniques are all based upon a simple pairing of two items (two numbers, two letters, a letter and a number, a number and a color, etc.) with the various items in the selection chart or vocabulary. We saw an example of this earlier (see Fig. 28a) where a number-pair was used to specify the letters of the alphabet. In that instance, the alphabet was arranged in a matrix and the numbers were arranged along the top and sides. This same technique could have been realized in a slightly different manner by simply arranging the number-pairs along the letters in a list fashion (see Fig. 28b). This listing provides the same information as the first listing, but makes it easier for the user to pick out the two-number code which should be used with the specific letters. Both techniques, however, are equivalent, and both techniques could be used with pictures, words, or symbols instead of the alphabet as shown in Figure 28c. Since all these techniques require that the child make two pointing motions to indicate the letter, word, picture, symbol, etc. he wants, they have been termed "Two Movement Encoding Techniques." By using a larger number of encoding numerals, you are able to expand the system to account for larger numbers of vocabulary items. In very large vocabularies, three numerals may be used instead of the two numeral pair.

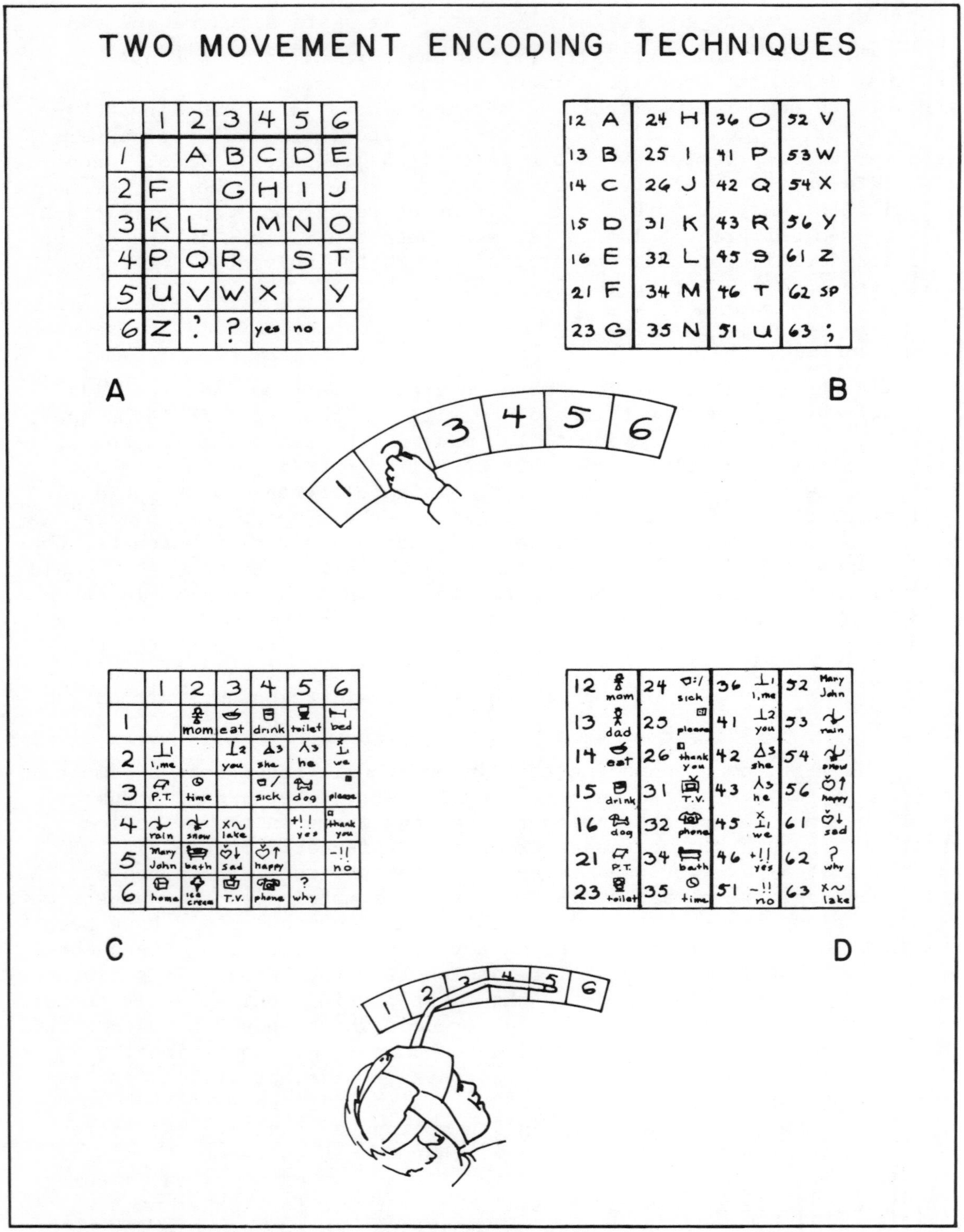

46

TWO MOVEMENT ENCODING TECHNIQUES

A

	1	2	3	4	5	6
1		A	B	C	D	E
2	F		G	H	I	J
3	K	L		M	N	O
4	P	Q	R		S	T
5	U	V	W	X		Y
6	Z	?	?	yes	no	

B

12	A	24	H	36	O	52	V
13	B	25	I	41	P	53	W
14	C	26	J	42	Q	54	X
15	D	31	K	43	R	56	Y
16	E	32	L	45	S	61	Z
21	F	34	M	46	T	62	SP
23	G	35	N	51	U	63	;

C

	1	2	3	4	5	6
1		mom	eat	drink	toilet	bed
2	I, me		you	she	he	we
3	P.T.	time		sick	dog	please
4	rain	snow	lake		yes	thank you
5	Mary John	bath	sad	happy		no
6	home	ice cream	T.V.	phone	why	

D

12	mom	24	sick	36	I, me	52	Mary John
13	dad	25	please	41	you	53	rain
14	eat	26	thank you	42	she	54	snow
15	drink	31	T.V.	43	he	56	happy
16	dog	32	phone	45	we	61	sad
21	P.T.	34	bath	46	yes	62	why
23	toilet	35	time	51	no	63	lake

Figure 28.

When considering two movement encoding systems, there are two points which should be kept in mind. First, as we shall see in the subsequent discussion, the two encoding elements need not be numbers. For children who have trouble sequencing numbers, other techniques can and have been used. Secondly, when using two movement encoding systems, it is dangerous to use double numbers (e.g., 11, 22, 33, 44, 55...). Using these double numbers usually leads to confusion on the part of the individual trying to decipher the child's message, and frustration on the part of the child. This confusion and frustration usually results in one of the following two situations. First the child may point to his first number, (say the number "2"). His pointing may be rather erratic, but the second person (whom we shall call the teacher for now) is able to guess the correct number and say it for the child, "two." The child then continues to try to point to the "2" to indicate that he wants a second "2." The teacher may then either say, "I already have that number," or she may think that she guessed the wrong number, and that the child is actually trying to point to the number right next to it. In this case, she may say, "I'm sorry, not 'two,' number 'three.'" At this point the child may get very excited but there is little he can do to try to straighten out the confusion. Since continued pointing at a number is the technique that the child usually uses to let the teacher know she guessed the wrong number, there is no way for the teacher to tell whether or not the child simply wants a double number, or whether she has guessed the number wrong in the first place.

Or, suppose the child is pointing at the number two, and the teacher responds, "number two." The child then looks up at his chart to check the next number that he wants to use. Say it is a "4." During this delay, however, the teacher may think he is trying to indicate that he wants a second two, since he did not move off the square or point to any other square after she guessed the first number. She therefore guesses "2, 2" and again there is a problem. If there is a good rapport between the child and the person he is communicating with, and if good feedback is given after each and every number to confirm that it is a correct number, it is possible to use double numbers without difficulty. However, since the children will be communicating with a number of different people, some of whom may not interact often with them, it is usually best to avoid the use of double numbers.

We have talked about the two movement encoding system and have seen that, by using the listing, it is possible for an individual to specify a large number of vocabulary elements (pictures, words, etc.), even though he may only be able to physically point to a very limited number of squares. We have also seen that this system can be used by children who cannot spell but who rely on pictures or symbols to communicate. It can further be noted that number concepts or the ability to count are not necessary to use this technique. The child need only be able to find the picture or the symbol he wants, look at the numerals which are beside it, and then point to those numerals on the squares in front of him. In fact, he need not use the numerals at all, but could substitute any other arbitrary shapes in their place. The numerals are, however, convenient and familiar shapes to use for this purpose and can generally be used with a wide range of children. Still, there will be those children who are very young or who are severely mentally retarded so that they will find it difficult to use these number-pairing techniques. Other children will be able to use number-pairing techniques in the long run, but will have difficulty starting out with that task. Still others will have specific visual or other learning disabilities which cause them to reverse numbers or have difficulty in sequencing them correctly. For these children, other adaptations of the two-movement encoding approach have been developed.

An alternate technique makes use of color in place of one of the two numbers. With this approach, the child indicates which element of his message he wants by indicating first the color, and then a number. When this procedure is used, the vocabulary listing can be more easily constructed in one of the ways shown in Fig. 29. Each of the indication squares would contain both a number and a color. Using this technique it is possible to significantly reduce the problems associated with reversal. In addition, the child can now think of specifying his element as a two-step process rather than being a compound process involving the sequencing of two indicators. In fact, the process can be reduced to one involving no sequencing at all except on the part of the message receiver. To do this, the message receiver would ask the child what color was around the picture (symbol, etc.) that he wanted and then ask the child what number was next to the picture he wanted. In this manner, all the child need do once he had indicated he wanted to express something would be to answer simple one-response questions concerning it. If the numerals presented a problem, they could be replaced by other shapes or perhaps even simple figures of people or animals so that the task became one of specifying the color wanted and the familiar objects or caricature printed next to the picture (in the same position where the number would have been printed). There is a possibility that this last technique may be too visually confusing and that one would be better off sticking with colors and numerals, even though the numerals may be simply abstract shapes to the child.

For some children, this two movement encoding technique may be applicable except for the fact that they are physically unable to point to any number of squares, either with their hand or with a headstick of any kind. For these children, use of the eyes may be an appropriate signal source. One technique which has been developed for using eyes places the numbers and/or color squares around the very edges of the children's laptrays. The children then indicate appropriate numbers and colors by simply looking at them. When using this approach, it is important not to place too many of these number squares around the edge of the tray, or they will be too close together to easily tell which one the child is looking at. This technique may also be difficult for children who have poor head control or other problems which make it difficult to determine exactly where they are looking.

49

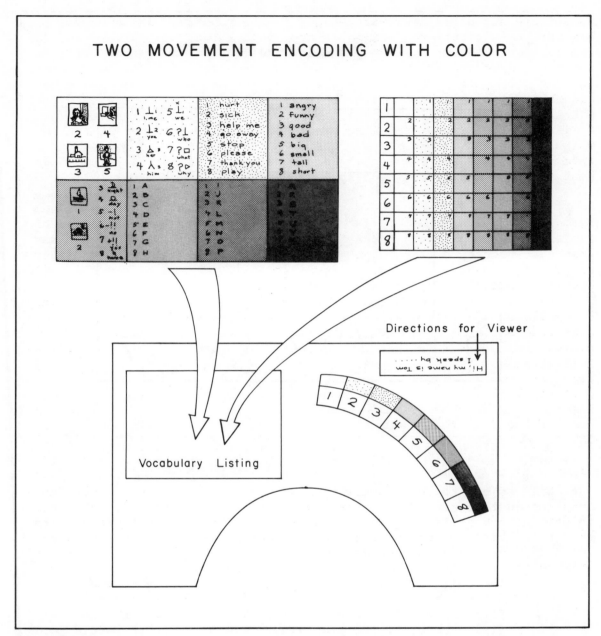

Figure 29.

One technique which can help to alleviate this problem is the use
of an adapted ETRAN chart (here called the ETRAN-N). This adapted chart
is a plexiglas sheet with a hole cut in the middle. The numbers are
placed around the outside of the plexiglas sheet (see Fig. 30). In use,
the ETRAN-N chart is placed so that the two people communicating are
looking at each other through the window (hole) in the chart. The child
looks at the numbers to indicate them in the same manner that the point-

50

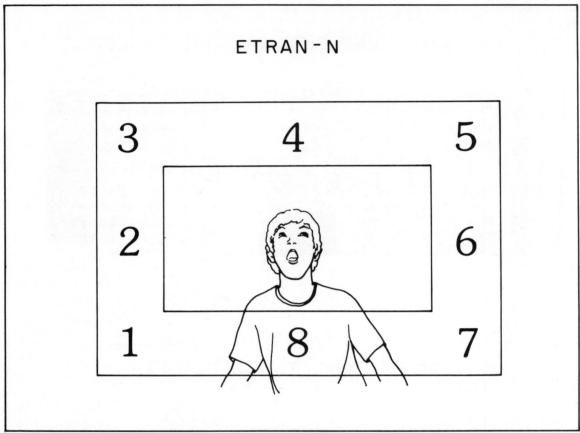

ETRAN-N

3	4	5
2		6
1	8	7

Figure 30.   ETRAN-N - an eye gaze 2-movement encoding technique.

ing child points to the numbers on his tray. Since the eyes are also
used for just looking, it is important that a procedure be established
to prevent the child's normal visual activity from being confused with
the use of his eyes to indicate the correct numbers. To do that the
following procedure is recommended:

> The child will generally start out by looking down at
> his vocabulary listing which will usually be placed in
> front of him. He would then look up and stare at the
> first number of the plexiglas ETRAN-N chart. He would
> continue to stare at the number until the second person
> would say the correct number. If the second person
> says the wrong number, the child just continues to
> stare until the second person corrects himself and says
> the correct number. The child would then look up at
> the ceiling briefly to acknowledge that that is the
> correct number and then go on to the second number.
> When the second person had identified the second num-
> ber correctly, the child would look up at the ceiling

again. The second individual should then repeat the two numbers and the message element from the chart. To confirm that the item is correct, the child would again look at the ceiling. If there was a problem, the child would look down to make sure that he had picked the right numbers and the second person should read back the numbers one at a time to figure out if he'd gotten the first one right and the second one wrong. If there is any confusion, the second person should simply say, "Let's forget that, let's do it again."

As the child and the communicator become more experienced, this process can become quite swift and some of the confirmations can be dropped to streamline it even further. In the beginning, however, the full procedure is recommended to avoid initial frustrations with the technique. In addition, the full procedure is also recommended for general use with individuals who are not as familiar with the individual in using the technique. As with the pointing system, the ETRAN-N chart can be used with color and numerals as well as with the numerals alone.

In the preceding discussion, we have been talking about the two movement encoding technique and how the original ETRAN chart has been adapted for use with the simple number encoding system. I'd now like to introduce the original ETRAN chart to you and describe its operation. Because the ETRAN chart and the ETRAN-N (the modified version) are similar in appearance and in some of their operational characteristics, there is a tendency to confuse the directions for using the two systems. The layout of the original ETRAN chart is shown in Figure 31. The ETRAN system uses no additional vocabulary listing and assumes the individual will spell out all his messages using the letters that are on the plexiglas sheet itself. The original ETRAN system is completely self-contained, and is a system for indicating the letters of the alphabet (and numbers) only!

Directions for using the chart are as follows:

Looking at the chart, it can be seen that the letters have been broken up into eight groups. Each group consists of a principal letter on the top and four "corner letters." To use the aid, the handicapped individual starts out by looking directly into the eyes of the person with whom he is communicating. He then slowly looks up to the group of letters that contains the letter that he wants. For this example, let's say he looks up at the top middle group of letters, If the handicapped individual wanted the letter "R" (which is the principal letter in that grouping), he would simply look back into the eyes of the person with whom he is communicating. The second person would then know that the handicapped individual

wanted the principal letter of the group that he
had just been looking at. Now, if the next letter
desired was a "U," the individual would again look
at the top group of letters. This time, however, instead of looking directly back into the eyes of the
second person, the handicapped individual would move
his eyes from the center group to the corner of the
ETRAN chart corresponding to the position of the "U"
in the grouping of letters. Since the "U" is in the
upper left-hand corner of the grouping of letters,
he would look at the corner of the ETRAN chart which
is near the letter "A." After looking at that corner, the handicapped individual would then look back
into the eyes of the person with whom he was communicating. The second person would then know that the
desired letter was from the grouping in the top center
and that it was specifically in the upper left-hand
corner of that grouping (since the handicapped person
looked at the upper left-hand corner of the chart before he returned his gaze to the second person). In
this manner, the individual can direct the second
person's attention to any letter or number on the
chart and can spell out his message in this fashion.

You will note that there is no upper left-hand corner letter in the
"A" grouping. This is because the handicapped individual would have the
same "double indication" problem that we were talking about earlier with
respect to the double numbers. That is, you have to look at the "A"
grouping to show that you wanted a number from that grouping, and then
would have to look from that grouping to the corner of the chart which
is only an inch away. The second person would never be able to detect
this small movement of the eyes. Thus you will notice that all four corner groupings are missing a letter which corresponds to their respective
corners.

Because this approach requires spelling, it is, of course, a more
advanced communication technique. It is convenient, however, in that it
does not require either individual to look up items on a vocabulary listing. All the items are directly on the chart itself. On the other hand,
it does require that the individual spell out everything he wants to say.
Since the numbers are provided on the chart, however, it would still be
possible to use them to encode words that would be on a vocabulary listing. Using this technique would require four motions of the eye to indicate the words since it would take two motions to indicate each number.
It should be noted that Hugh C. Neale, for whom the aid was first developed, only used the ETRAN chart with his family for a limited time. After that time, he no longer used the chart but would simply look to the
position in space where the letter groupings would be if he had a chart
in front of him. His family had used it so much with him that they
knew the position of the letters and they were all able to "use" the

chart even though it wasn't present. Mr. Neale used the chart when communicating with strangers and others who were not as familiar with the system.

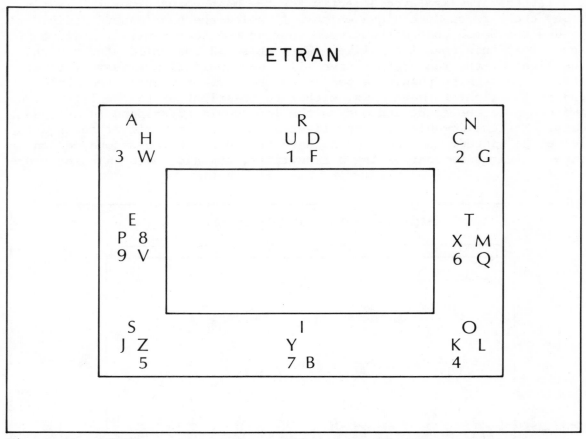

Figure 31. ETRAN - an eye gaze spelling communication system.

The remainder of the encoding techniques which have been developed much more closely fit the picture which you probably originally formed when the term encoding was first mentioned. Techniques which utilize the Morse Code, as well as techniques which utilize a series of sips and puffs on a tube are examples of such techniques. The sip and puff techniques have been used extensively with individuals who have good control over their oral musculature (and are often able to speak), but who are unable to write. The sip and puff techniques are used to control typewriters to enable these individuals to have a means of writing.

There are also individuals who have good quick control over some very small movements, but are unable to operate a larger number of switches. For these persons, codes such as the Morse Code may be quite effective means of communication. The problem with these codes is that they are generally very restrictive because other individuals do not usually know the code well enough to use it for communication. For this reason, aids have been developed which can decode the Morse Code and display the letters either one at a time or on a printout. With such an aid, the handicapped individual is the only one who need know the code, since the letters are displayed directly for the message receiver. In addition, there is one technique which will allow the handicapped individual to use the Morse Code without even knowing the code himself. Figure 32 shows what this code looks like. With this aid the child starts with the light at the top of the "tree" lit. By indicating either a dot or a dash (perhaps by pushing a paddle to the left or right), the child causes the light to move down, either to the right or to the left. Thus, two steps to the right and one to the left would correspond to dot, dot, dash. The child would move the light down the tree until it reached the letter he wanted. He would then leave it there for the second person to view. If it were controlling a typewriter, the aid would wait for a de-

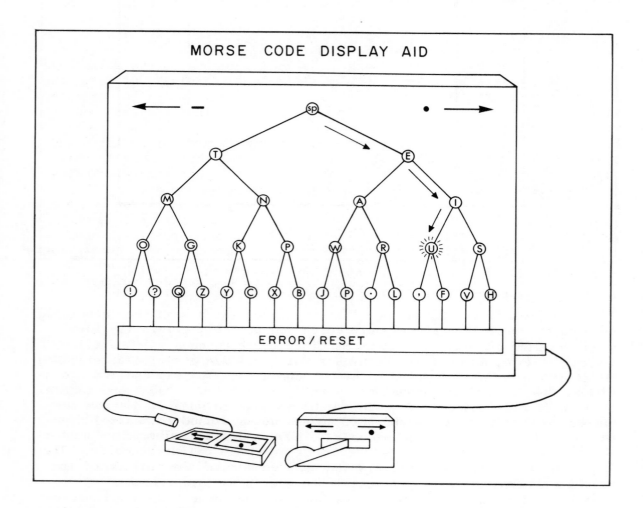

Figure 32.

lay, and, after the light had stayed in the same place for a set amount of time, it would print that letter and return the light to the top of the aid. If the child made a mistake, he could simply keep the light moving down any one of the tree branches until it ran off the bottom. He would then return to the top and come down again. To facilitate his use of the aid, it could be set up so that if the child held the paddle to the left or to the right, it would step down in that direction automatically. Thus, to signal dot, dot, dash (right, right, left), which stands for the letter "U," the child would simply hold the switch to the right for two steps and then push it to the left, let it make one step, and then release it. Using this technique, the child would be able to use the efficiency of the Morse Code without having to have to learn it himself or rely upon others learning it. [Editor's note: If one looks carefully at this tree technique, it will be apparent that it is not an encoding technique at all, but rather a directed scanning technique. It has been described at this point, however, because of its relation to other techniques which use the Morse Code].

The final technique which I'd like to describe under the topic of encoding is "successive quartering." With this technique the child indicates which letter or word, etc. he wants by successively dividing the display into fourths and indicating which fourth he wants. For example, with the chart shown in Figure 33, the child would indicate that he wanted the letter "R" by: 1) indicating that it is in the upper left-hand quarter, 2) by indicating that it was then in the bottom left-hand quarter of that section, and then 3) by indicating that it was in the upper right-hand quarter of that piece. Thus, by making three pointing motions, the individual would be able to select from any one of 64 squares. By making four motions, he would be able to pick from any one of 256 squares. If the child has more ability on a joystick than he would pointing to squares, or if he is faster using a joystick, then the joystick may replace the four squares used for the successive quartering. This technique could be used manually or it could be used with an aid which would light up the display and extinguish the various sections as they were eliminated until a single square was left lighted.

PARTIAL SURVEY OF ENCODING AIDS

Again, starting with the simple aids and working through, we begin with an encoding communication board developed by Karen Culhane at the Home de Rehabilitation, Bellevue, Huemoz, Switzerland. (Fig. 34) This board combines a color-number encoding technique similar to the one developed by Dr. McDonald (which will be described later) with the Bliss-symbolics (also to be discussed later). The vertical columns are numbered, whereas the horizontal rows are each colored a different color. The child then uses the numbers and color patches around the outside of the board to communicate.

Figure 35 shows Jack Eichler with the original ETRAN chart which was developed by him and by Hugh C. Neale, Ridgefield, Connecticut. Fig-

56

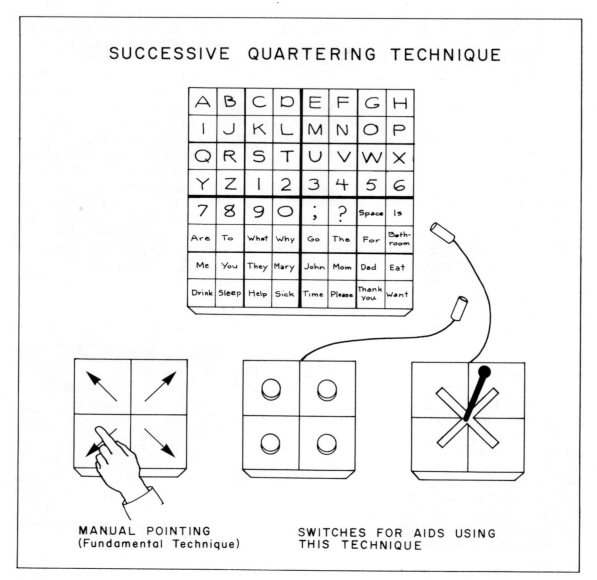

Figure 33.

ure 36 shows a version of the ETRAN-N which was developed at the Trace Center. When not in use, the ETRAN chart folds flat, providing him with a plexiglas cover laptray. A piece of plexiglas is permanently screwed down to the tray both to fill the center hole in the ETRAN and to make a flat tray when it is folded down, and to act as a protective cover over the child's vocabulary.

The communication aid shown in Figure 37 was developed at Rancho Los Amigos, Downey, California, for a mentally retarded child. The aid consists of a commonly available beeper coupled with a specifically adapted switch. Depending upon the abilities of the children, the beeper could be used for either a very small set of messages, using one, two, or three beeps, etc., or the child would be able to pick from a number of lists and then signify by the number of beeps.

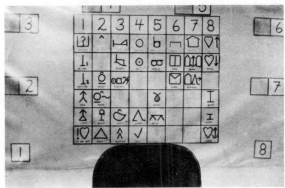

Figure 34.
Encoding Review - fundamental 2-movement encoding technique using colors and numbers.

Figure 35.
The ETRAN eye gaze communication chart - a fundamental encoding aid.

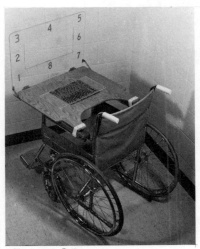

Figure 36.
The ENTRAN-N - a 2-movement eye gaze encoding technique.

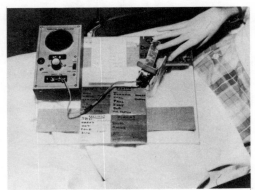

Figure 37.
The Ranchos Beeper, a simple electronic encoding aid.

The Cybertype,® (Cyber Corp., Washington, D.C.) is an example of both a row-column and a two-movement encoding aid. This aid is also part of the Cybercom® family discussed under scanning aids. Two keys are used to print each letter in the fourteen key models of the Cybertype.® When only 7 keys are used, the same code applies except that the two keys are operated in succession. Many different interfaces have been developed for the Cybercom aids.

The Comhandi, developed by the National Resource Council of Canada,

---

®Cyber Corp., Washington, D.C.

is one of the few aids designed to operate in a variety of operational modes. The Comhandi can be operated as a scanning aid, using the panel shown in the upper right-hand corner of Figure 38, as an encoding aid, using some of these switches also shown there, (in addition to a variety of other switches which have been developed for the aid) and as a direct selection aid, using the teletype keyboard with or without a keyboard.

The MC6400 Communicator is a very compact electronic communication aid developed by Medicel, Incorporated, Burlington, Vermont. (Fig. 39) The aid, which is entirely enclosed within the small package to the right, can decode the Morse Code which can be input from a variety of switch forms, and display it on the screen of a television. The unit provides for high visibility and correctability and has a printer option if typewritten copy is desired. The Medicel unit is also able to take a keyboard for input and be used as a direct selection unit.

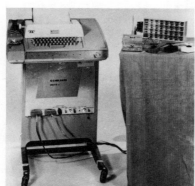

Figure 38.
The Comhandi, an independent aid which can operate as a scanning, encoding or direct selection aid. Shown here with some of its different interfaces.

Figure 39.
The MC6400, a Morse code based independent communication aid.

POSSUM Controls, Ltd., Aylesbury, England, has several encoding typewriter controllers. The one shown in Figure 40 is a unit originally developed by Hengrove, which uses a four-level sip and puff encoding system. Other models offered by POSSUM can be operated by chin and foot switches in addition to the sip and puff technique.

Both the Versicom (see Fig. 27) and the Auto-Com (Fig. 66), developed by the Trace Center, are capable of operating in a variety of encoding formats. Most encoding techniques which require a display can be implemented using the Versicom. Encoding techniques not requiring a display could be implemented on either the Versicom or the Auto-Com.

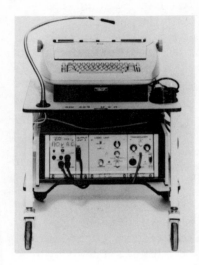

Figure 40.
The Hengrove/Possum Sip and Puff Typewriter
System, an independent encoding aid.

ENCODING AIDS - SUMMARY REMARKS

In summary, the basic advantage encoding techniques have over the scanning approach is the potential for greater speed for some individuals. These encoding techniques, however, may require a greater degree of control on the part of the user. More complex movements, or more responses per message element, are usually required. In addition, some encoding schemes must be learned by the child before he is able to use the aid or technique. Clinicians who have used the encoding technique with their children have indicated that the process of learning the simple encoding systems was much faster and easier for the children than they had at first expected.

A second very large advantage of the encoding system is the ability to access large vocabularies in an efficient manner. Using only the numbers from one to ten, and a three-movement encoding scheme, a child can access over 700 vocabulary elements in just a few seconds. This would require very fine motor control for direct pointing and would be very slow using the scanning techniques. Thus, encoding techniques may provide a faster means of communication and a means of accessing relatively large vocabularies, but they may also require greater physical control and usually require higher cognitive abilities than either the scanning or direct selection approaches.

THE DIRECT SELECTION APPROACH

The direct selection approach is the simplest and most straightforward of the three. It is, therefore, the easiest to implement with both young and mentally retarded children. It also has the potential for the greatest speed of the three approaches. Unfortunately, it usually also requires the greatest range of motion and fine motor control.

As we shall see, however, there are techniques which can be used to overcome the range of motion problem, as well as techniques which can eliminate the need for fine motor control. There is a limit to these techniques and there are a great number of individuals who are unable to use the direct selection approach. For those who can develop the skills necessary to use one of the approaches, however, a quick, efficient, and straightforward communication system results.

Overview of the direct selection techniques

Because with the direct selection approach you simply point directly to the various elements of one's message, there is not the great diversity of techniques which are found in the other two approaches. There are, however, four general categories which I would like to make a few comments about. These categories are guarded or expanded keyboards, light-spot operated aids, range of motion expanding techniques, and erratic motion interpreting techniques. I will address these four topics starting with the most straightforward approaches, and those which require the most control, and move toward the techniques which have been designed to work with individuals having more severe motion problems.

The first category is that of expanded and/or guarded keyboards. Because typewriters are both inexpensive and versatile output devices, many efforts have centered around trying to make the typewriter keyboard more usable to the severely handicapped. The simplest technique for doing this is simply to provide a keyboard guard or mask for the typewriter. This keyboard usually takes the form of a metal or plastic plate which has holes punched in it corresponding to the keys of the typewriter. The plate is then placed above the keyboard so that the individual must push a finger down through the hole in order to actuate a key. With such a guard in place, the handicapped individual is able to rest his hand over the keyboard and apply force on the plate to help steady himself. He can then slide his hand around on the plate without actuating any of the keys. When he wants to type a letter he simply pokes his finger, or perhaps a dowel which he is holding in his clenched fist, down through the hole to actuate the keys on the typewriter. Although this is a very simple technique, it surprisingly is not very widely well-known. This is truly unfortunate, because it is very inexpensive and can allow even some fairly severely involved individuals to have ready access to the typewriter for communication and/or writing. Keyguards for IBM and Smith-Corona typewriters are available directly from the companies although in some cases it is difficult to get hold of someone who knows about the policy. For more information on this, you can consult the Annotated Bibliography of Communication Aids distributed by the Trace Center.

In addition to providing keyguards, many researchers have also expanded their keyboards in order to make them accessible to even more severely handicapped individuals. With the exception of one or two experimenters who developed mechanical linkages to accomplish this, the researchers generally used solenoid banks positioned over the keyboards and remote keyboards which then controlled the typewriter electrically. This, unfortunately, raises the price of the aid quite rapidly above the cost of the typewriter alone. They are still among the less expensive independent communication aids, however.

The second category of direct selection aids that are of particular interest are the light-spot operated aids. With these aids, researchers have provided individuals who have good head control with a rapid and efficient means of pointing even though they may have limited control over the rest of their bodies. These aids usually consist of a fairly high-powered light beam which is attached to the head (or occasionally to some other part of the body). The individual then directs the spot of light to an array of photodetectors which have the alphabet printed alongside of them. By training the lightspot on the photodetectors, the handicapped person is able to print out his message. The largest problem with the technique is the fact that high levels of ambient light interfere with the system. Some of the aids have to be used in darkened rooms and cannot be used in sunlight. Since most of the aids are stationary, however, it is usually possible to avoid situations where ambient light is a problem.

The third group of techniques I'd like to discuss are the range of motion expanding techniques. With these techniques, a very small movement is electronically expanded and displayed for the user, usually on a backlit display. A typical example would be an aid which provides the user with a very small joystick which he can either operate with small movement of a finger or with his mouth. (See Fig. 41) As he moves the stick, a lighted square on a panel moves around in correspondence. The position of the lighted square on the panel would directly correspond to the position of the joystick. In this manner, the individual who has a very small but well controlled range of motion would be able to directly "point" to a fairly large number of letters, words, etc. on the backlit display.

An extreme example of range of motion expanding would be the technique developed by a research group in England. With this technique, the electrical signal generated by the flexing of a muscle (EMG) was used to control the position of a lighted square on a matrix. Two muscles, one from each arm, were used to control the square. The one arm would control the up and down motion of the square, while the other arm controlled the left and right motion. In this manner, the individual did not really have to move his arms at all, but only begin to tense or relax his muscles in order to direct the lighted square to the items on the display. This aid, called the GMMI, is further described in the survey of aids.

The fourth category is that of erratic pointing interpretation techniques. The most common mechanism for interpreting erratic pointing

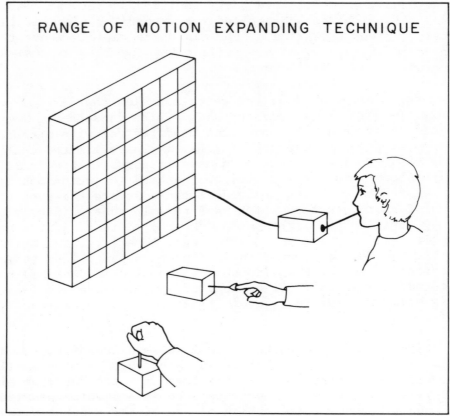

Figure 41.
In ROM expanding techniques the position of lit square
is directly determined by the position of the joystick
(or other signal).

motions is the human himself. The second person functions as such an interpreter whenever he is working with a severely handicapped individual on a communication board. An automated technique which seeks to imitate this process has also been developed. This technique uses a combination of delayed activation proximity sensors, and a hard, smooth surface to produce an "auto-monitoring" effect which is very similar to the process used by a second invididual when he is watching a handicapped individual on a communication board. Erratic pointing motions of severely athetoid cerebral palsied children have been used successfully with aids utilizing this technique.

PARTIAL SURVEY OF DIRECT SELECTION AIDS

The most common direct selection aid is, of course, the communication board. (Fig. 42) As can be seen from these examples, communication boards can take a great variety of different forms. Even within the same center (Figs. 43 through 48) communication boards for different children can take vastly different forms. It is also interesting to note the dif-

Figure 42.
Manual communication board, a fundamental, direct selection aid.

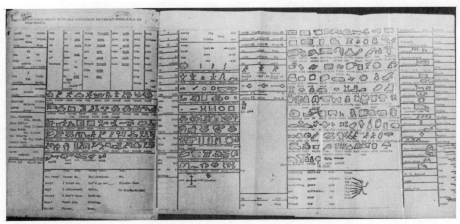

Figure 43.
Picture/Word board - University of Iowa Hospital School Nonoral Communication Project.

ferent forms that a communication board used for a single child can take. Figure 45 was the first formal communication board for the child who is now using the communication board in Figure 46.

The communication board shown in Figure 49 is the thirteenth edition of a board designed by F. Hall Roe, a cerebral palsied individual

64

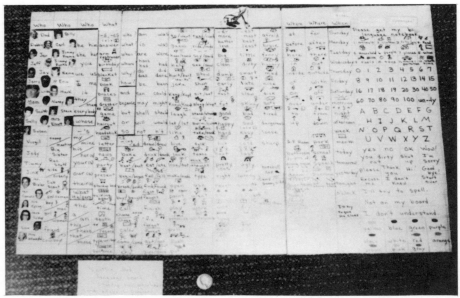

Figure 44.
Picture/Word Board with alphabet - Iowa Project.

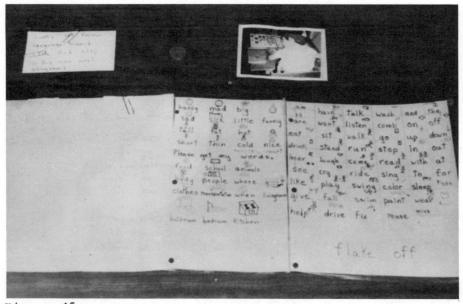

Figure 45.
First formal communication board (second step of program)
for one boy using headstick - Iowa Project.

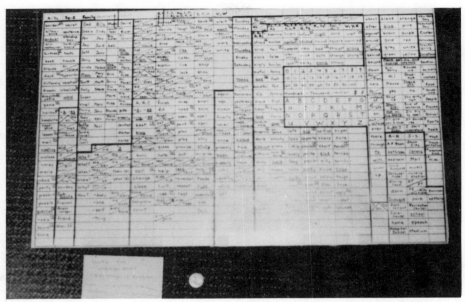

Figure 46.
Later communication board (fifth stage) for the same boy as in Figure 48 - Iowa Project.

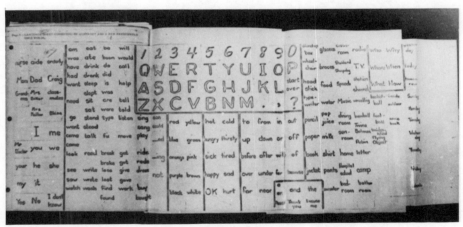

Figure 47.
Communication book with foldout pages - Iowa Project.

who has been using communication boards since he was about twelve. This last board was designed by him when he was in his fifties. These pre-made boards are distributed as a service to the handicapped by the Ghora Khan Grotto (a Masonic organization), St. Paul, Minnesota.

The communication board shown in Figure 50 is one produced by the

66

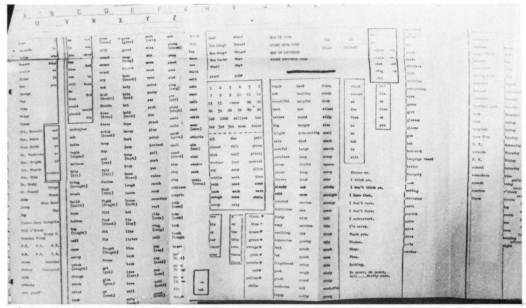

Figure 48.
A communication board prepared on a typewriter - Iowa Project.

I CAN HEAR PERFECTLY	PLEASE REPEAT AS I TALK (THIS IS HOW I TALK BY SPELLING OUT THE WORDS)	WOULD YOU PLEASE CALL
A AN HE	AM ARE ASK BE BEEN BRING CAN	ABOUT ALL
HER I IT ME	COME COULD DID DO DOES DON'T	AND ALWAYS
MY HIM SHE	DRINK GET GIVE GO HAD HAS HAVE	ALMOST AS
THAT THE THESE	IS KEEP KNOW LET LIKE MAKE MAY	AT BECAUSE
THEY THIS WHOSE	PUT SAY SAID SEE SEEN SEND SHOULD	BUT FOR FROM
WHAT WHEN WHERE	TAKE TELL THINK THOUGHT WANT	HOW IF IN
WHICH WHO WHY	WAS WERE WILL WISH WON'T WOULD -ED	OF ON OR
YOU WE YOUR	-ER -EST -ING -LY -N'T -'S -TION	TO UP WITH

A	B	C	D	E	F	G	AFTER	AGAIN
H	I	J	K	L	M		ANY	EVEN
N	O	P	Qu	R	S	T	EVERY	HERE
U	V	W	X	Y	Z		JUST	MORE
1	2	3	4	5	6	7	ONLY	SO
							SOME	SOON
8	9	10	11	12	30		THERE	VERY

SUN. MON. TUES. WED. THUR. FRI. SAT. BATHROOM	PLEASE THANK YOU GOING OUT	$¢½(SHHH!!)?
	MR. MRS. MISS	
	MOTHER DAD DOCTOR	START OVER END OF WORD

Figure 49.
The F Hall Roe communication board (notches are for hanging board between wheelchair hand push handles).

Ontario Crippled Children's Centre as part of its Symbol Communication Research Program. These Blissymbols will be discussed in greater detail later in the workshop.

A rather interesting direct selection aid is the Slip 'n Slide communication board shown in Figure 51. This aid is of particular interest because it is one of the very few non-electric aids which allow a child to assemble a complete sentence by himself. With the Slip 'n Slide, little blocks containing pictures, symbols, words, or letters of the alphabet are placed in the track around the outer edge. The child can then select any block he chooses and move it around into the center slide where he can line the blocks up to form his message.

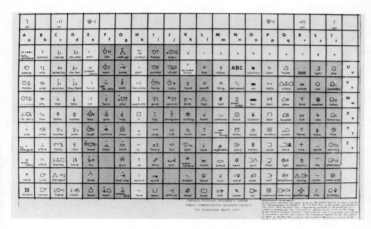

Figure 50.
A Blissymbol communciation board - one of available preprinted formats.

Figure 51.
The Slip N Slide, a simple direct selection aid which can allow independent construction of sentences.

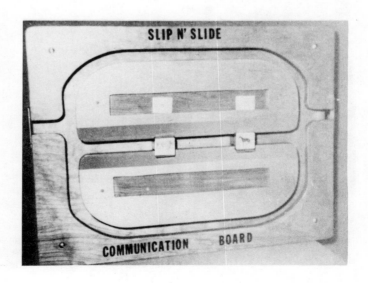

Moving to the independent aids, we have a picture of one of the
IBM typewriters with keyguard, armrests, and paper roll. (Fig. 52) IBM
makes all these items available at low cost (the keyguard costs $5).
IBM also has a special program whereby it sells the used typewriters at
the trade-in cost to handicapped individuals. With this procedure,
handicapped individuals can secure the IBM typewriters for as little as
$100 to $150, depending upon the condition of the machine.

Figure 52.
IBM typewriter with standard
modifications available - a direct
selection independent aid.

Palmstiernas Mekaniska Verkstad, AB, in Stockholm, Sweden, has produced several expanded and miniaturized keyboards for controlling typewriters. Figure 53 shows a collage of four of their expanded keyboards
being operated by different parts of the body. Figures 54 and 55 show
two of their miniature keyboard arrangements as well as the typewriter
fitted with a solenoid unit. PMV systems will also control IBM typewriters in addition to the Facit shown in the picture.

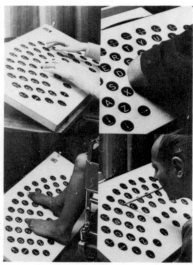

Figure 53.
PMV expanded keyboards for typewriter control -
direct selection independent aids.

An expanded recessed keyboard is also available from Possum Controls in England. (Fig 56) This keyboard also has a built-in adjustable delay to further reduce accidental triggerings.

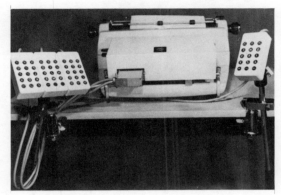

Figure 54.
PMV "minimum" keyboard.

Figure 55.
PMV miniature modular keyboard shown with typewriter controller.

Figure 56.
POSSUM expanded, recessed keyboard - a direct selection independent aid.

Two examples of light-spot operated typewriters are shown in Figures 57 and 58. The system shown in Figure 57 was developed at Delft University of Technology, Delft, The Netherlands, and is called the LOT (light-operated typewriter). The OCCUR, which is shown in Figure 58 was developed by the National Research Council, Radio and Electrical Engineering Division, Ottowa, Canada.

The aid shown in Figure 59 is the muscle potential range of motion expanding aid which was discussed earlier. By using the muscle potential in his two arms, the user is able to move the lighted square around on the display to choose the letters he wants typed. The aid can also be controlled using a joystick or other more conventional switches. This aid, called the GMMI, was developed at the Warm Springs Laboratory, Herts., England.

Figure 57.
The LOT lightspot operated typewriter - an independent direct selection aid.

Figure 58.
The OCCUR lightspot operated communication aid.

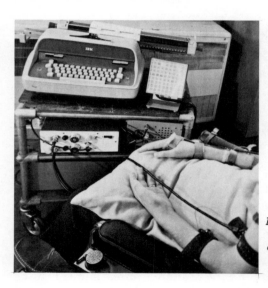

Figure 59.
The GMMI - a range of motion expanding direct selection aid, shown here with the muscle potential (EMG) input.

Several aids which have been specifically designed for the deaf also have application for the severely physically handicapped. One of these is the TVphone shown in Figure 60. This aid is a typewriter keyboard base aid which prints out on a normal television screen. In addition, it can be used with a telephone to communicate with other TVphones or teletypes. This aid could, of course, be fitted with a keyguard to facilitate its use by the more severely physically handicapped.

Figure 60.
The TVphone - a telecommunications
aid for the deaf which can be
modified for the physically
handicapped.

The first portable independent aid in this survey is the Light-writer developed by Toby Churchill, Cambridge, England. (Fig. 61) The unit has a seperate battery pack and the 32-character electronic display is removable so it can be placed conveniently for either or both user and the person with whom he is communicating.

Figure 61.
The Lightwriter - a portable
independent direct selection aid
with removable electronic display.

Another somewhat smaller fully portable communication aid has been developed for the deaf in the United States. This unit, called the MCM, is distributed by Micon Industries, in Oakland, California. (Fig. 62) The unit is completely self-contained and has a special low power 32-character display which was developed especially for it. In addition, the aid has a telephone cradle so it can be used to communicate to other similar aids over a phone line.

A rather unique approach has been taken by researchers at the University of Southampton, England. (Fig. 63) This aid, which was designed primarily for the mute, has a 5-character display which fits in the shirt pocket like a brooch and has a separate keyboard. The aid is able to get by with such a small display because it, unlike most alpha-numeric displays, floats the words across the display gradually rather than having them jump one whole letter position at a time. (Fig. 64) Because of the position of the read-out display, the aid has been named "The Talking Brooch."

Figure 62.
The MCM - a portable independent direct selection aid primarily designed as a telephone communication aid for the deaf. Modification for the physically handicapped available.

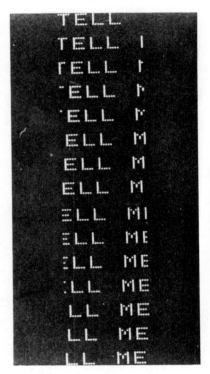

Figure 63.
The Talking Brooch - a portable direct selection aid originally designed for mute individuals.

Figure 64.
Illustration of the walking display of the Talking Brooch.

Probably the most compact and portable of all of the independent communication aids to date is the Canon Communicator which was developed as a joint effort between Canon Incorporated in Japan and researchers in the Netherlands. (Fig. 65) The Canon Communicator is designed to strap to the wrist and has a small strip printer as its output form. To facilitate use with people having some muscular problems, special keyguards have been designed, which are shown in the background of the picture. Canon has also been experimenting with a slightly larger version which has built-in battery supply and a typewriter arrangement for the keyboard.

The Auto-Com (Fig. 66) is a portable communication aid which utilizes the auto-monitoring technique described earlier. The aid has an optional 32-character LED display, in addition to its standard strip-printer output, which makes the aid completely correctable and portable. The aid is capable of printing single letters or whole words, phrases or sentences with a single pointing motion. The vocabulary as well as the arrangement of the words and letters on the surface of the aid can be selected and changed by the user to meet his specific needs.

The Versicom described earlier (Fig. 27) is also capable of operating as a portable, range of motion expanding, direct selection aid.

Figure 65.
The Canon Communicator - a portable
independent direct selection aid
shown with one of its keyguards.

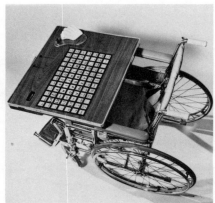

Figure 66.
The Auto-Com - a portable
independent communication
aid using auto-monitoring
techniques.

DIRECT SELECTION APPROACH - SUMMARY REMARKS

The major advantages of the direct selection approach are that it is straightforward and no learning of a technique is required. This approach also provides good direct feedback and can be used with very low level children. In addition, the potential speed of this approach is quite high, limited only by the pointing speed of the child.

The major limitation of the aids in this category is that they generally require a greater range of motion or finer motor skills on the part of the child. Thus, the direct selection approach provides a relatively fast, fairly simple and straightforward means of communication for the child who can develop the range of motion and/or control necessary to use a letterboard or keyboard.

COMBINATION TECHNIQUES

Many times these specific approaches in and of themselves won't quite meet the need of a particular child. In these cases, one can sometimes combine the characteristics or advantages of two of the approaches to better meet the needs of the child. For example, scanning and encoding techniques could be combined to form a scan/encode system like the one in Figure 67. This system would provide a very simple one-switch control for a severely physically involved individual, but, because it uses the encoding technique, would allow for quick access to a fairly large vocabulary.

Figure 67. Combination Scan-Encode Technique.

As another example, a combination approach might be necessary for a child who can point to 30 squares or so, but who is advanced, and would like to communicate faster than having to spell out every letter. For this child the combination approach shown in Figure 68 may be what he needs. In this approach, he is provided with the alphabet and a number line which he can use for encoding. In this manner, the child has access to a large number of words for speed in communication but, when he needs to spell out a word, he has direct access to the alphabet so that he can spell out the word more quickly. This same approach could, of course, be implemented in an independent aid, and is similar to the approach used in the Auto-Com.

COMBINATION TECHNIQUE

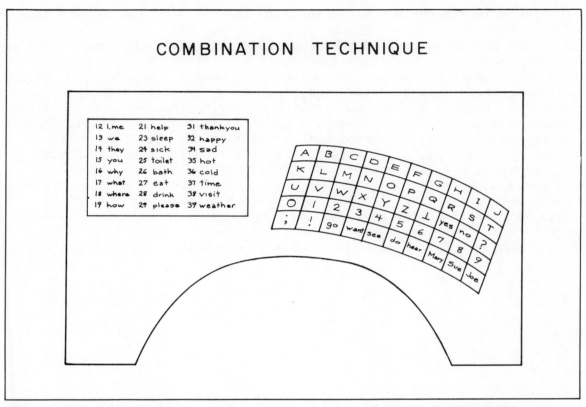

12 I,me	21 help	31 thankyou
13 we	23 sleep	32 happy
14 they	24 sick	34 sad
15 you	25 toilet	35 hot
16 why	26 bath	36 cold
17 what	27 eat	37 time
18 where	28 drink	38 visit
19 how	29 please	39 weather

Figure 68. Combination of Direct Selection and Encoding Techniques.

SUMMARY AND CONCLUSIONS

From these discussions, it has become apparent that there are a large number of different techniques, each with its own advantages and disadvantages. There are no easy guidelines which can be generated to help guide you in trying to select particular approaches for a particular child. You may want to start with the direct selection approach if the child has those abilities since it seems to hold the greatest potential, speed, and simplicity. And, if the child is able to develop enough skill to use a typewriter, you will have opened a very inexpensive and powerful means for him to express himself. Even for those children who will not learn to spell the straightforwardness of the direct selection approach may be very important in helping the child learn to communicate earlier.

A large percentage of severely handicapped individuals, however, will not be able to use any of the direct selection approaches, particularly not in the beginning. For these individuals it is important to provide them with an appropriate communication system even if you are also working on developing pointing skills. Some communication system should be set up immediately with the child so that he has a viable means of interaction while work proceeds on the development of additional skills.

In reviewing the present literature in this area, it is also apparent that much more work is needed on the development of very simple techniques and in development of techniques for very young children. Through the techniques which have been discussed, however, we hope to have given you some ideas as to how you might provide a severely handicapped child with "a means to indicate" the pictures, words, or symbols which he can then use to express himself and respond to his environment. Once he has a means to indicate, we must work to provide him with a means of representing his thoughts: a symbol system which he can use to relay the elements of his thoughts to others. That will be the subject of the next speakers, Dr. Eugene McDonald and Ms. Shirley McNaughton, who will be discussing application of symbol systems with some of the techniques we have been discussing. While their discussions will be framed principally around the pointing communication board, it should be remembered that the symbol systems they will be discussing can be applied with other techniques if the child is unable to use a pointing board.

CONVENTIONAL SYMBOLS OF ENGLISH -   (Eugene T. McDonald)

I am going to be talking about the development of symbols in English. We are going to be discussing visual symbols and symbols in English grammar as a background for developing some types of communication boards.

There are many different forms of visual symbols. One widely used form is pictorial symbols. As you know, travelers are now being aided a great deal by the use of universal symbols in road signs. You can see a pictorial sign in a foreign country and know that you shouldn't turn left or you shouldn't make a U-turn even though you can't read the language. They are also beginning to use some readily decipherable pictorial symbols to identify the men's and ladies' rooms. These pictorial symbols allow information to be communicated without requiring the knowledge of a specific language. For this reason, this type of symbol can be quite useful in developing communication systems for young children.

Photographs, too, can carry meaning and are quite useful in working with these children. When writing a book on cerebral palsy I wanted to mention the fact that we begin communication training with some children by using photographs to get them started. The editor, however, protested because he felt that young children can't identify pictures. I wrote back and said "That's nonsense, I know they can. We see them do it all the time." He wrote back saying "No, perhaps you see a few who can identify photographs, but it would be a misrepresentation to suggest that this can be used routinely as a training procedure."

I had a delightful experience a few Sundays ago when my daughter called me saying that somebody wanted to talk to me. It turned out that my two year old grandson had found a photograph of me that morning and had carried it around all day, bugging his mother to get me on the telephone. Several times she found him with the telephone in his hands trying to talk. Finally, to satisfy him she picked up the phone and called me. All he said was "Pop pop Mike talk, Pop pop Mike talk." He repeated that throughout the call.

I want to make three points about that story: First, of course, I want to brag a little about my grandson; second, a two year old found and identified a photograph; and third, he had a drive to talk. I think that the need to talk is a drive that the psychologists, whose union card I carry in my pocket, haven't included in the drives that they mention. They talk about sex drives, they talk about hunger drives and things of that sort. I think there is also a communication drive that is very, very strong. People want to talk. We should expect non-vocal children to have this need to communicate. We ought to stimulate this drive and take advantage of it. If we do not provide non-vocal children with a means to communicate when they are young, this drive may slowly be extinguished and later intervention attempts will have limited success.

Verbal symbols

There are verbal symbols which we use visually. The 26 letters of the English alphabet are very familiar to us; but there are some problems in using these to communicate. Consider, for instance, the sequence, g-h-o-t-i. How many of you know what it is? This was a word created by George Bernard Shaw to show how illogical, how unphonetic our spelling is. To decipher 'ghoti,' write down the word "enough" and underline the "gh." Now write down the word "women" and underline the "o." Finally, write down the word "nation" and underline the "ti." Using that information, what is the word? Fish. Ghoti is fish. It can also be noted that the letter "a" represents some 7 different sounds. So we create a very difficult learning situation for some children when we expect them to develop spelling skills in order to communicate.

Levels of English grammar

The letters of the alphabet are combined into words, the words into phrases, the phrases into sentences. Sentences have been analyzed in many ways by linguists who agree that there are several levels of language structure. The lowest symbol level is the phonological level which is comprised of the sounds of our language. I want to elaborate on this point a bit because some misunderstandings have developed concerning phonology. We should make a distinction between phonology and orthography, and between phonology and articulation. Today one hears, "We are not dealing with articulation problems; rather, these children have phonological problems. The reason they have difficulty in talking is because they don't know the phonological rules." This may be true of some children, but as we shall see it is not true of all children. Phonology is the lowest level language structure consisting of speech sounds. Orthography is the spelling, the representation of these sounds by letters. Articulation is a motor act. It is a physiological act. It is the process of making maneuvers to and from target zones in the supralaryngeal area of the vocal tract. It is related to but separate from phonology.

There are many children who cannot talk, who cannot articulate, but who have perfectly developed phonology. If we can give them an opportunity to express themselves in another modality, they will demonstrate highly refined language structure that they understand and can use. Let's not confuse these terms phonology, orthography, and articulation.

The second level of language structure is morphology. A morpheme is the minimum unit of meaning. It may consist of just one speech sound or a short sequence of phonomes. The third level, called the syntactic level, can become elaborated into sentences of great complexity. The semantic level has to do with the meaning which our sentences convey. In developing language with non-vocal children it will be necessary to give attention to helping the child develop language structure. However, professionals of all disciplines tend to get on bandwagons. As soon as people began applying transformational grammer to the teaching of language, many jumped on this bandwagon and started trying to teach children transformational processes before they were ready to learn them. The approach with the young non-vocal child should be simple in the beginning. We can become more complicated as the child demonstrates that he is ready for more complicated kinds of structures.

Several procedures have been developed to teach language structure to children. Among these, the psycholinguistic approaches have become quite popular. This approach is described in an excellent booklet published by the University Hospitals at the University of Iowa with the title, "Non-Oral Communications System Project, 1964/1973." This is a report of several years work in developing non-oral communication systems with cerebral palsied children and includes a discussion of a psycholinguistic approach to developing language. It is available on order from Campus Stores at the University of Iowa. Another very excellent source is the book "Language Acquisition Program for the Severely Retarded" by Louise Kent. I would recommend both of these references for your further reading.

We use a relatively simple but effective approach to developing language structure which is based on an adaptation of the Fitzgerald Key. The Fitzgerald Key was developed for teaching language to the deaf and the manual is subtitled "Straight Language for the Deaf." It breaks language down into categories such as who, what, where, verbs, modifiers, etc. We arrange the child's words in columns as illustrated in Figure 69.

Figure 69. Communication Board Using the Fitzgerald Key

0 1 2 3 4 5 6 7 8 9 10							
YES. HI.	HOW ARE YOU?	I DON'T KNOW.		PLEASE.	THANK-YOU.	GOOD-BYE.	NO.
WHO	VERB			WHAT	WHERE	WHEN	
I MOMMY DADDY SANDY LINDA BOY GIRL YOU TEACHER THERAPIST HOUSE-MOTHER	HAVE PLAY GO AM READ SEE MAY LOVE LISTEN IS WANT ARE WILL EAT LIKE GET	A NOT IN FOR THE WITH AT TO AND	BIG MY LITTLE SICK GOOD BAD HAPPY SAD	BALL COOKIE PRESENT FUN CAR PUZZLE BED WORDS STORY LETTER GAME CAKE CANDY MAT BOOK DRINK	HOME PLAYROOM BATHROOM UP SCHOOL OUTSIDE ROOM P.T. STORE INSIDE DOWN SPEECH DINING ROOM	NIGHT YESTERDAY TOMORROW WEEKEND SUMMER EASTER CHRIST-MAS THANKS-GIVING TODAY	RED YELLOW ORANGE GREEN BLUE PINK PURPLE BROWN BLACK WHITE

In the "who" column this child had I, mommy, daddy and names that were meaningful to him. He has a verb column – play, go, etc. Next there is a column of "little words" – a, big, little, and things of that sort. The last columns contain "what," "where," and "when" words.

We usually color code the chart making each column a different color. When teaching we use colored chalk or colored crayons to write the words in the colors that correspond to the categories. With this approach the child can construct sentences with good structure. He can say, "I have a ball" by pointing to different words in the categories. He can say "I want a puzzle" or "I like..." (whatever he wants to say). He can proceed from a simple lexical level to a point where he can construct sentences. [Editor's note: For a more detailed description of this technique see "Communication Boards for Cerebral Palsied Children," Journal of Speech and Hearing Disorders. Feb. 1973, 38, 73-88].

APPLICATION OF SYMBOL SYSTEMS WITH THE COMMUNICATION BOARD

Let's take a look now at the application of these concepts in developing a communication system for the child. For the most part I will be relating my comments to the application of pictorial and orthographic symbols to the communication board. Many of the principles however, would apply to the use of other symbol systems as well.

When we first begin helping the young child learn to communicate we make our language boards very simple. Sometimes we have only two pictures on it. We have found that many children are most eager to communicate their need to go to the toilet. It's interesting that we often work and work and work at toilet training our children but fail to help them develop a way to signal when they have to go. Instead they have to wait until someone asks "Do you want to go to the toilet?" This means that the other person is programmed or trained instead of the child. Many children have learned quickly to point to a picture of a toilet when they want to go to the bathroom. Someone once said to me that in her institution the children did not want to tell when they had to go to the toilet because they had learned that one way they could get attention was by soiling their pants. Then they got the attention of the attendants. That comment tells us more about the environment than about the children.

Another picture that these children want early is one which will enable them to communicate that they want something to drink or eat. In figures 70-72 we see some examples if early communication boards. On the first one we see a picture of a cup and a TV. Initially the TV indicated that the child wanted to go down to the playroom to watch TV. This picture soon expands however, into the concept of play or recreation in general.

We also use actual photographs of things in the child's environment. For example, faces of a person smiling or frowning. The child can point or look at these to indicate when he is happy or displeased about something. It is extremely important to give children, very early in their communication training, ways to show that they don't like what is going on or that they are not happy with a situation. We take some of these pictures with a Polaroid camera while the child observes. This helps the child see that the picture represents part of his environment. This is illustrated in Figure 71. Often we begin this training with pictures of a child's parents, and then the child himself. A young child probably wouldn't have as many pictures in the beginning as we have in this example, but when this boy came to us he was able to handle that many pictures.

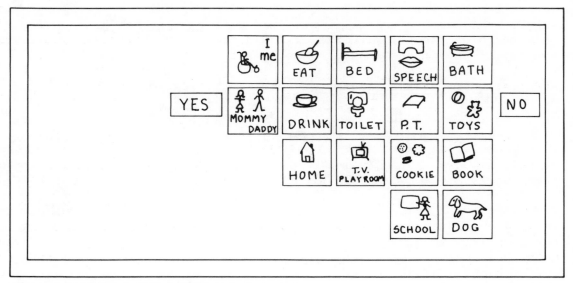

Figure 70. Early Communication Board

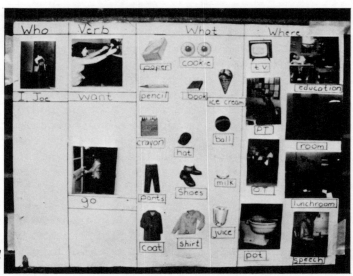

Figure 71.
Early Communication Board
Showing Use of Pictures

In some boards we combine drawings and words. The board in Figure 72 was made for a very interesting little boy who began with just a couple of pictures which he was soon expanding. He is now learning to use "daddy" for "man," and "mommy" for "lady." He is expanding nurse to doctor or sick.

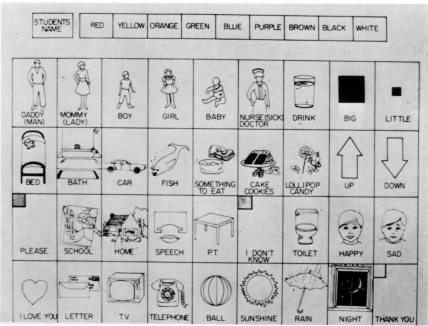

Figure 72.
Early Communication Board Using Drawings and Words

We find almost universally, that as soon as non-vocal children begin communicating with us, they want to say "I love you." I remember meeting a young man, 17 years of age who never had an effective way of communicating. We very quickly whipped up a simple communication board with which we could converse. I asked him if he had anything in particular that he would like to put on the board. He said "love" so I teased, "You have a girlfriend and you want to tell her you love her." He said, "Yes," Then he pointed to me and indicated that he wanted to tell me that he loved me too because I was helping him to talk. The point I want to stress is that these boards must not be restricted to cognitive material only. One of the first things that this young man wanted to communicate was his feelings toward others. Most children have this desire. We must take into account the importance of allowing non-vocal children to express their emotions, both positive and negative, and devise communication systems which will allow them to express their feelings.

A more advanced communication board is shown in Figure 73. It was developed for a boy named Jimmy who is now learning that "me" and "I" are the same as Jimmy. His 'who' words also include mommy, daddy, boy

and girl. Note that this board contains an alphabet, which is arranged
in the format of a typewriter keyboard. When the occupational therapist
believes a child will eventually be typing, we arrange the alphabet in the
form of a typewriter keyboard so that he can begin learning these posi-
tions quite early.

Figure 73. Picture/Word Communication Board with Typewriter Alphabet

The word content of these boards is individualized. We plan the
content with the child, with his parents and with the staff members who
work with the child. In some cases the child may need different boards
for different situations.

Some boards combine photographs and drawings and we arrange them
in the manner of the Fitzgerald Key to help the child to progress from
the lexical level to a structured language level. Early in the picture
stage we put words under the pictures. Eventually we will fade out the
pictures leaving the words. We do this by using flashcards to teach the
youngsters to match pictures and words. As soon as the child has a sight
vocabulary which is sufficiently large, we eliminate the pictures. This
approach can be used with the Fitzgerald Key organization and line drawings.

Another item which children in our program want very early is a
way to tell people that they have a letter so we often use a symbol on
the child's board which means, "I have a letter." Some parents keep in
touch with us about what items have been added to their child's language
board so that they can be sure to use these words or structures when
writing to their child.

Some children cannot point to very small areas so their wordboards or pictures are spread out more, such as on the board in Figure 74. In other cases the boards are more elaborate and the words are closer together. You will note that some of the areas of the board in Figure 70 are not filled. This is due to the fact that some children have trouble pointing to certain areas on their boards. For this reason we don't arrange everything in a purely rectangular or square form. Rather, the positioning of the materials on the board is determined by the child's physical capabilities.

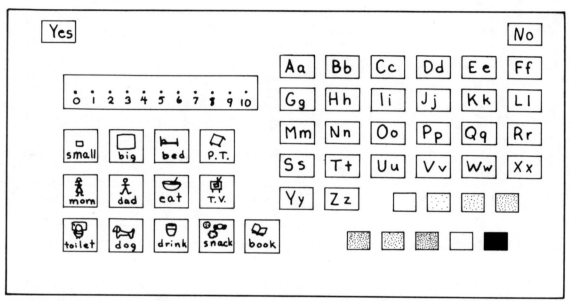

Figure 74.   *Expanded Communication Board to Facilitate Pointing*

In this section I've talked briefly about traditional symbol systems and how they can be implemented on communication boards. A little later, in the Application and Results session, I'll be going into more detail about the application of communication boards as well as some of the other considerations involved in developing a communication system for a severely handicapped child. Shirley McNaughton will now introduce and discuss another symbol system which is being used with these children.

BLISS SYMBOLS - AN ALTERNATIVE SYMBOL SYSTEM
FOR THE NON-VOCAL PRE-READING CHILD - (Shirley McNaughton)

In this afternoon's discussion I hope to introduce you to the
Bliss Symbol system and to show you the similarities and differences
between Bliss Symbols and English words. One of the main objectives
of the discussion will be to present some of the advantages and disadvantages of Bliss Symbols and to discuss why we are using the Bliss
Symbols instead of written English to initiate communication programs
with our children. A very common question we are asked is, "Why don't
you teach your children to read instead of teaching them the symbols?"
The basic reason we have gone the symbol route is that we think it
is important that the child be able to communicate as soon as possible.
As we will demonstrate later, the Bliss Symbols seem to be easier to
pick up than English and the children are communicating sooner. Once
they have communication we can work on reading and other skills.

Before we go farther, I would like to give you a little background
on the Bliss Symbols. Blissymbolics, also called Semantography, is
a symbol system developed by Mr. Charles Bliss as a bridge between
meaning and traditional orthography. Mr. Bliss was very concerned
about international understanding and was attempting to create an easily
learned modern language for communication between all peoples. The
symbols were based upon his experience in China during the war. With
these symbols he sought to do the same thing for the world that the
Chinese written language has done for the people in China: allow people
of different spoken dialects to communicate using a common symbolic
language. We discovered Bliss Symbols through our efforts to find
a communication vehicle for non-vocal, non-reading children and we
thought this system might have a potential for use to the young handicapped children. We have adapted this system somewhat in our programs.

The Bliss Symbol Program at the Ontario Crippled Children's
Centre is a new program. It started in October of 1971. We are very
excited about what we have seen happen in our Centre. We have seen
it spreading to other centers in the United States, Canada and overseas.
We feel that it is something that people who are interested in non-vocal
communication will want to look at. We're not saying it is for every
child and we are not saying it fits in every environment. But I think
it's an alternative that you should know something about and give consideration to for some children. When you first look at Bliss Symbols
I think you have to have the same kind of adventure feeling that you
have when you dive into a swimming pool. You have to say to yourself,
"I'm going to get into it and find out what it's like," rather than
stand back and say, "It looks too complicated, it must be hard to learn."
It becomes apparent when you watch the young children using Blissymbolics
that it really isn't difficult at all once you get into it.

86

It is important to note that on every display a child uses, <u>a word always appears under the symbol</u>. We're making it as easy as possible for people who do not know the system to be able to communicate with the child. Thus, the system is <u>not</u> closed as are some signing systems, and anyone who can read can communicate with the child. On the other hand, people who learn the symbols can have a much richer form of communication with the children. As we go through the examples I think you will see how the children can communicate on a greater number of topics and use the symbols in more versatile ways when they are working with people who are familiar with the symbols.

The system itself is entirely visual. We have wondered why the symbols are so easily learned by the children. There are many points of view on this. Here is one interpretation. It is from an article from Bob Scott of the Photographic Art Department, Ruerson Polytechnical Institute, Toronto - an art teacher looking at why symbols seem to be easy for children to learn. He says, "The primary function of storing visual information by configuration is manifest in the children's drawings (where outline is more important than interior details), and also in children's ready understanding of cartoon figures as opposed to high definition photographs. It is precisely these qualities that characterize Bliss Symbols and allow for their easy assimilation by beginners in the 'new' language." Now, no one is claiming that Bliss Symbols are self evident, that when you first see a symbol you know what it means. But once you've been given the explanation of the symbol it is very easily learned and remembered. This is due in part to the many cues to the meaning of the symbol that can be seen in the symbols.

Before we introduce the symbols and discuss them in any great depth, I would like to have you take a short test to demonstrate to yourself the relative ease of learning Bliss Symbols compared to what it might be like to learn English. The test only takes a few minutes and is the best way I know to get a comparison of learning Bliss Symbols vs. what it might be like to learn English.

To try this test, you need only a blank piece of paper and a pencil. Now put the numbers 1 through 12 down the left edge of the paper and the numbers 13 through 24 down the center of the page. You are now ready to take the test.

In this test you will be seeing two sets of symbol representations, along with the English translation of them. One symbol set will be the Spence Symbols and the other will be the Bliss Symbols. The first set of symbols has been designed by Murray Spence, Assistant Co-ordinator, Special Education Programmes, North York Board of Education, in Ontario, Canada. He uses them to provide teachers of early reading programs with the experience of relating to a new medium and attempting to derive meaning from it. Each symbol represents a letter of the English alphabet; the symbols are sequenced to form words on the basis of the sound(s) each symbol represents. The relationship between each symbol and sound is as consistent as English letter-sound relationships!

The second set of symbols are Bliss Symbols with the component parts representing meaning, either directly through a pictorial symbol, or indirectly through an arbitrary or abstract symbol.

Procedure for the test is as follows:

1. Study the Bliss Symbols for <u>one minute</u>, <u>without</u> taking notes. Look for shape-meaning correspondence.

2. Turn to the Spence Symbols and study them for <u>one minute</u>, <u>without</u> taking notes. Look for sound-shape correspondence.

3. Engage in a new and completely different activity for 10 minutes.

4. Return to the test page. Allow yourself <u>one minute</u>; write as many words as you can, doing the easiest ones first.

5. Tally your score from the answer page.

Study for one minute without taking notes .

(Hint: Look for shape - meaning correspondence)

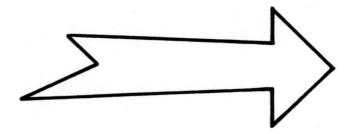

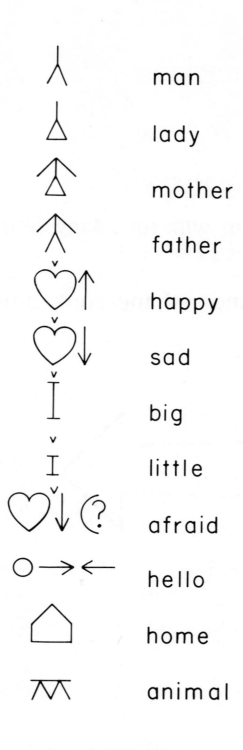

	man
	lady
	mother
	father
	happy
	sad
	big
	little
	afraid
	hello
	home
	animal

BLISS SYMBOLS

Study for one minute without taking notes.

(Hint: Look for sound - shape correspondence.)

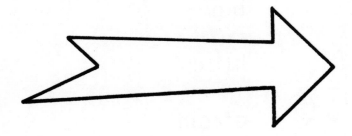

⋮ (symbols)	man
⋮ (symbols)	lady
⋮ (symbols)	mother
⋮ (symbols)	father
⋮ (symbols)	happy
⋮ (symbols)	sad
⋮ (symbols)	big
⋮ (symbols)	little
⋮ (symbols)	afraid
⋮ (symbols)	hello
⋮ (symbols)	home
⋮ (symbols)	animal

SPENCE SYMBOLS

Now break for ten minutes of unrelated activity.

After ten minutes:

Allow yourself one minute.

Write as many words as you can.

Do the easier ones first.

Your score is the total number correct.

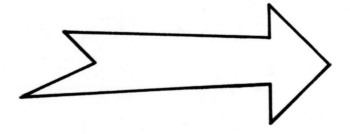

1.

2.

3.

4.

5.

6.

7.

8.

9.

10.

11.

12.

13.

14.

15.

16.

17.

18.

19.

20.

21.

22.

23.

24.

TEST PAGE

ANSWER PAGE

1.	lady	9.	mother	17.	animal
2.	little	10.	animal	18.	sad
3.	hello	11.	big	19.	father
4.	happy	12.	father	20.	afraid
5.	man	13.	happy	21.	lady
6.	sad	14.	hello	22.	house
7.	home	15.	man	23.	little
8.	afraid	16.	big	24.	mother

When you have completed the test consider the following:

Which symbols did you want to translate first?
Which symbols were easier to retain?
Which symbols appeared visually simpler?
Which required the least effort to analyze?
Which symbols made you think about meaning?

If your score was <u>over</u> 3 for the Spence Symbols, you did better than the majority of workshop attendants to whom I have given this test. If your score was <u>under</u> 9 for Bliss Symbols, you did more poorly than the majority of those trying this test.

Compare your experience in processing the Spence Symbols to that of the young child learning to read. (Keep in mind that the comparison is not entirely valid. The young child brings much knowledge of English letter shapes to his learning-to-read experience. He reads street signs, cereal boxes, people's names, etc., long before his formal reading instruction begins. You, too, however, bring experience of another kind to the task of reading Spence Symbols).

Allowing that the two situations differ in some ways, I hope that the contrast, for you, between learning Spence Symbols and learning Bliss Symbols provides you with an appreciation of the contrast, for the young child, between learning English words and learning Bliss Symbols.

INTRODUCTION TO BLISS SYMBOLS

The Bliss Symbol system is composed of about 100 elements. These various elements are combined to form the symbols. Bliss began with numbers and mathematical symbols which are international and added symbols he devised himself. The symbols are based upon meaning and therefore symbols which deal with a similar topic will have common components.

Let us first take a look at the symbols which represent people. The number 1 person (see below) is the child--I, me, or mine. Since symbols stand for concepts, and not specific words, the young child can use the symbol for "I" to mean "mine," the possessive form, or to mean "me," the objective form.

"You" is the second person, number 2, and it is quite apparent to each child that he or she is always number 1 in this world! That fellow who can't be seen directly is number 3. The concept of numbering persons is not as difficult as it might initially appear and our children pick it up quite readily.

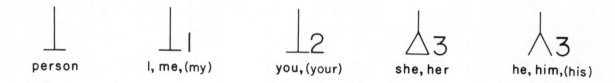

The multiplication mark is used over any symbol to convert it to the plural. The children learn that symbol as "much," or "many."

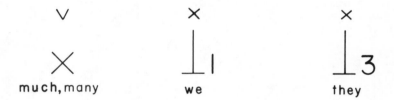

The symbols for man and woman are very simple. The roof symbol denotes protection. So the woman who protects, or the woman who lives in your house, is your mother. The man who protects is your father. In Mr. Symbol Man, Mr. Bliss gives his rationale for the component parts of man and woman.

The brother is that male person in your house who is number 2, (never number 1!) and the sister is the female number 2, (never number 1!) You will see as you look at the different symbols that some are pictorial while others are more arbitrary. The pictorial ones are usually introduced to the children first. After they get the idea of symbols representing meaning, more abstract symbols can be introduced.

sister   brother

The inverted V represents the "action" symbol. It is used over
another symbol to denote action associated with that symbol and to
change it into its verb form. For example, when used over a part of the
body such as the mouth, it changes the meaning from "mouth" to "speak."
The one children like best is when you "make action with your brain,"
and then you "think." We had an incident early in the program with a
young child saying that she was sad. When asked why, she replied,
"because my guinea pig cannot think." That's the kind of insight you
can get from these children.

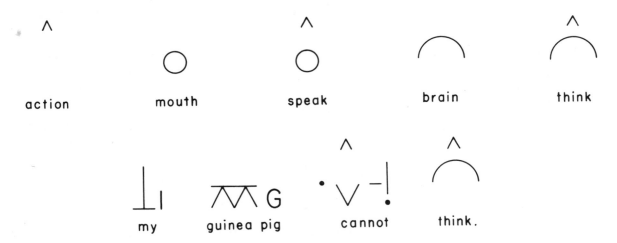

action   mouth   speak   brain   think

my   guinea pig   cannot   think.

We debated on whether we should put the action sign over legs
for "walking" and "going," as is suggested by Mr. Bliss in his original
system, and decided that we would maintain this extended meaning even
though most of our children are in wheelchairs. They do have a wheelchair, however, and they "make action with their wheelchair" when they
are independently going somewhere, rather than being pushed.

walk, go   wheelchair

There are three special indicators. The action symbol (the inverted V) converts a symbol to a verb. The "thing" symbol (a little square over the symbol) converts a symbol to a noun. The evaluation symbol (an upright V over the symbol) is used for adjectives and adverbs. Mr. Bliss chose the shape to denote adjectives and adverbs because it is unstable and tips easily from side to side. I demonstrate with a drinking cup or an ice cream cone for the children. It will not stand stable and Bliss was saying that any evaluation is open to discussion of the person. I might say it is quite hot in this room and a lot of people might say it is quite chilly, while someone else might say it's just right. Our opinions vary back and forth and an easy way to remember the difference between the adjective and the verb is to think about that shape.

thing

making
descriptive

opening

to open

open

All the emotions are based upon the heart. When you make action with the heart you feel something. "To want" something involves the heart and action symbol plus the action for flame or heat (to burn with desire).

heart

to feel

to want

The heart is used in a lot of adjectives as well. When you are "feeling up," you're "happy;" "feeling down," you're "sad." If you are "feeling afraid" (sad about the future which is unknown), you add the symbol for future and a question mark to the symbol for "sad." If you don't know if you're "feeling up or down," you're "upset." "Excited?" Add an exclamation mark. Anger is represented by two thrusts directed towards the heart. The multiplication sign indicates much anger.

happy

sad

afraid

upset   angry

One problem we had was that of giving the child the swear word he wanted. The symbol for "feeling" and "mouth," along with the symbol for "negativeness with intensity" were chosen for this purpose. When the children are younger we translate the negative word as "yuk." If it's an older student we sort of wink when they point to it. We don't have to say it but we know what they're thinking when they point to it. We have left words off these symbols to facilitate generalization.

"yuck"

An "eye" symbol in the "open" symbol means "awake;" in the closed symbol, "asleep." A "question mark" in the open symbol indicates a question being asked; in the closed symbol it represents the answer. Freedom comes from being open. You're free and unrestricted. "Closed in emotions" indicates "oppression."

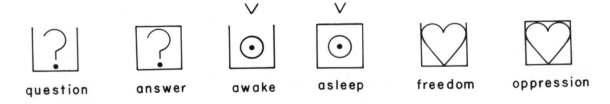

question   answer   awake   asleep   freedom   oppression

The accuracy in writing symbols is very important. Symbols can take on a new meaning if they're placed in a different position. The same line placed at the bottom of the space becomes the earth symbol. If it's at the top it's the sky. If you have both lines you have that space between the sky and the earth--the world. Water in this position is water in general. At the skyline, it's clouds; at the baseline and there is much of it, it's a lake. If you have two multiplication marks in front of it, you have the ocean. Many different meanings are derived by combining other symbols with the symbol for water. Water coming down in the direction of the arrow is rain. If it's in the shape of a star it is snow. Water under the sky is fog.

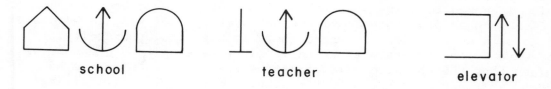

earth　　sky　　world　　water　　cloud　　lake

ocean　　　　rain　　　snow　　　fog

CONSTRUCTION OF SYMBOLS

When putting symbols together or making up a symbol the classifier comes first. For example, in the symbol for "school," the symbol for "building" comes first, and the symbols for "give" and "knowledge," which describe what kind of building it is, come after the building symbol. For teacher, it is a "person." What kind of person? A person who gives knowledge. The typewriter is a machine for writing. The elevator is a room that goes up and down. A dessert is a food that makes you happy. An exception to the classifier first rule would be when the multiplication sign is used for much, as in lake, "much water."

school　　　　　　teacher　　　　　　elevator

We have not had the difficulty in classifying that we had anticipated. We thought some children would not be able to see the symbol for animal and have it relate to all animals. Most children in our program, however, have been able to generalize in this way.

One of the things that symbols cannot do easily for the children's usage is to discriminate between a cow, horse, pig, goat or sheep. Bliss provides for this distinction by adding numbers and distinguishing body parts, but using these would add greatly to the number of symbols on a display. The general symbol for animal is more functional and versatile for the children. To indicate specific animals, descriptors can be used along with the general animal symbol. At the beginning stage we used pictures of the individual animals with words accompanying them. As the children learn how to classify things we remove the individual animals and give them the general animal symbol. If the child can give his mother the idea of animal, then from that point the child

can indicate what type of animal by giving her clues..."it's yellow, orange or brown; it's big, it's little; it starts with a D or a C or a P..." He can describe it to her using his other symbols so it isn't essential that he use up his limited board space having the exact symbols for each animal.

When looking for a new symbol we use Mr. Bliss's Semantography book. It is an excellent resource book. It has a dictionary and whenever we want a new symbol we check there first. If you don't find the symbol you want there or if you need to make up a new symbol, it is important to check with the Blissymbolics Communications Foundation in Toronto before making regular use of it. The BCF is trying to catalogue new symbols and promote standardization to facilitate communication between symbol users.

TECHNIQUES FOR EXPANDING VOCABULARY USE

The children's vocabulary has been expanded through an emphasis on homonyms, antonyms and synonyms. Using these techniques, it is possible to give the children the capability of communicating on the greatest variety of topics even though their physical abilities greatly restrict the number of symbols which they can point to. Teachers in the primary classes are making use of these terms. They are teaching the children the meaning of the terms and how these strategies can be used to talk about things for which there are no symbols on their displays. An example that a teacher used in one primary class was to take the symbol for vehicle, "car," and have the children devise a symbol for "tow truck." The child is asked to think about things that would describe the vehicle classifier so that others could figure out what type of vehicle he was trying to talk about. Here is where there is a golden opportunity to become aware of the concepts that the children have. These are some of the things that the children said about the tow truck: "My uncle had one once." "It has six wheels." "It goes to a garage." "It carries cars." "It's big." "I like it." "It's a toy." To help the children determine which of these concepts would best convey the meaning of "tow truck" to someone else, the teacher had them decide what were the essential characteristics that other people would need to know in order to understand what the child was trying to communicate. She went through the various descriptions and said "Is that going to help someone else know what you mean? Will it help to know that your uncle has one? Would it help to know it is a toy? Would it help to know it carries cars or that it goes to a garage?" The children selected the ones they thought were important. They were the ones that then became part of that class's tow truck symbol.

ROLE OF THE TEACHER IN SYMBOL USE

When the instructer is working with Bliss Symbols we feel he has the responsibility to set a model for the children. One of the disadvantages of the system is that the children have so few models in their environment for them to emmulate. We feel that one responsibility of the instructor is, therefore, to know the system and know its potential. Hopefully she can be a little ahead in knowing what the system is capable of but she is never going to be ahead of the child in what he starts to do with it because the children end up being more creative than we are.

The teacher has quite a hard role; she wants to encourage the child to be creative but she still wants to give him some idea of order, syntax, and how to clarify his ideas. Our teachers use symbols in many ways: on the blackboards, in messages to other children, in worksheet instructions, through letters and through little books. The instructors go through various levels in responding to a child's symbol output. At the very beginning they ensure that the child's response is reinforced. To check if we have the right meaning, we confirm everything. When a child points to a symbol we verbalize the meaning and we repeat it. But, as soon as we know that the children know the meanings, we stop doing this. We wait until the child has indicated all the symbols, and then we give him the full sentence. This way we hope that the child is seeing how we are able to translate the symbols into a total sentence or a total idea. If we misunderstand we ask the child to tell us what symbol was misinterpreted and we go back to that part of the sentence and try to clarify it. It is essential for me when I am relating with the symbol children to write down what they are saying. I find it hard to retain 8 or 10 symbols in sequence. I like to get them all down and from that whole unit I get the message.

With some children we get to the level where the child "says" something and we just respond. This is the nicest of all. The child puts together a sentence and we respond with something like, "Oh, you're going home. Great! When are you leaving?" It is the most gratifying experience of all to be able to engage in normal conversation.

Regarding the model of symbol output presented by those communicating with the children, for the children who are now pointing, I think it is fairly straightforward a decision (certainly it has been at our Centre), to use in general the model of English word order. Teachers use it when writing on the blackboard or writing symbol messages, and have asked us to use it as an example for the child. We are not drilling them in it, however; we're not forcing it upon them. We hope it will become within their area of confidence but we don't want the children to feel that they have to use it all the time. And, of course, most of the the time, people are speaking to the children. The presentation of symbol models has to be planned--for the major part of the child's input is received through the speech of those with whom he relates.

ADVANTAGES AND DISADVANTAGES OF BLISS SYMBOLS

Through our program we've been able to isolate a few of the advantages and disadvantages of the Bliss Symbols. As with any new program it is open to constant inspection and change, but on the whole we feel that our program has had a positive impact.

One of the principal advantages of the Bliss Symbols is that they are easily learned. This is in fact one of the principal reasons why we have gone to the Bliss Symbols. Another very important advantage of the symbols is that they seem to be more generalizable. When the children only have a limited number of words or symbols which they can fit on their tray and point to, this becomes very important. The children are able to use the Bliss Symbols to communicate on a much wider variety of topics than with an equivalent number of words. Another advantage is that the symbols contribute to the child's total development, whether it is social, emotional...his self-image. The children see themselves as capable, active persons, able to become involved in their world.

The attitude of other people, on the whole, becomes positive. Many come to the children to see what they are doing. They are impressed that these symbols--that appear to an adult at the beginning to be difficult--are being handled capably by the children. It changes the concept they have of the children's intellectual capabilities. They begin to realize that the thinking child can be a creative child. The children certainly get more attention directed toward them.

There are some children who have visual difficulties. In this case it is a much more difficult teaching task, but it seems to be the minority of the children who have these severe visual problems. They do occur, however, and special displays and teaching procedures must be developed to accommodate the special needs of these children.

Generally, most of our children have been able to learn the symbols quite readily. It has certainly made learning to read easier. We tested six of the children (who had received no intensive reading program) at the end of the third year. Three of the children had learned 70% of the sight words (words printed under the symbols) in the 400-symbol set. They had lived with these words in print, they had been looking at them, and finding their own way of recognizing those words. These words were then used as a base for their sight vocabulary. Within the reading program, we are transferring from symbols to words by gradually increasing the number of words in symbol sentences. First the children read Bliss Symbols; gradually they begin to read conventional orthography.

And now for some of the disadvantages. One of the principal disadvantages of teaching a child with Bliss Symbols is that they are not used by other people in their environment. This causes a problem in providing adequate models for the children. They don't see the adults around them using the symbols for everyday communication so it is hard for them to find the easiest and quickest way to do things. They have to develop skills themselves and from each other. This is a problem which is also faced by children on wordboards in that the people around them generally communicate with a much different and larger vocabulary set than the children have on their wordboards. Thus, the children may have difficulty in picking out the easiest and quickest way to express themselves with the limited word set they have at their disposal. The problem of providing a model can appear with any different symbol system but perhaps is even more evident with the Bliss system.

Some people feel threatened by the symbol system. But there are very few people who over time don't come to accept it. For some parents the introduction of symbols--and this would hold true for wordboards and any alternative communication system--is seen as a confirmation that the child will never develop speech. We had one child who was withdrawn from our program because the parents wanted to place a complete emphasis on speech and speech training. No alternative communication system was acceptable to them, and we had to abide by the parent's decision.

Another disadvantage to the Bliss Symbols is that there is presently no way to provide the children with a printout. Unlike aids which use the standard words and can therefore use standard strip printers, etc., aids which are used with Bliss Symbols do not have any printout. Without such a printout the teacher must wait--and have the entire class wait--for the child to get into position to point to the symbols. With a printout the child could be preparing an answer while the other children were giving their answers. The teacher could then respond to the child in a normal fashion. [Editor's note: Research into the development of a printout capability for the Bliss system aid is presently being done at the University of Wisconsin under the auspices of the Blissymbolics Communication Foundation, Toronto.]

Another disadvantage of the Bliss Symbols, that is also common to communication boards, is that we don't have as much eye contact as we would like. We're dealing with a communication board that is in front of the child, and he must therefore look down. It doesn't mean that we don't look at the children and they don't look up when we communicate, but the communication board just doesn't provide as much eye contact as we would ideally like to have.

We developed our program because we wanted the young non-speaking physically handicapped child to be able to do what the typical young child does with speech; he plays with words, questions persistently, elaborates simple things into long narratives, comments with approval on his own behavior and criticizes the behavior of others.

Symbols don't provide the perfect substitute for speech, but they certainly do provide many of the experiences that speech does. We wanted something that would be easily learned and automatized. Symbols have this capability. The child can get going with what he wants to say and think about meanings rather than having to devote time and energy to remembering what a word looks like and what it means. The child is free to communicate.

SUMMARY

In this short presentation I tried to give you a basic introduction to the symbols and to illustrate some of the reasons why we have implemented the system with the children in our Centre. A little later, in the Results section of the workshop we will be discussing further how we have applied these symbols at the Centre. For more specific information on the symbol system you should consult the book, Semantography, or write to the Blissymbolics Communication Foundation, 862 Eglinton Avenue East, Toronto M4G 2L1, Ontario, Canada. A very interesting and enjoyable film is also available documenting Mr. Bliss and his symbols. In the film there is a very good 20-minute segment showing the use of the symbols with some of the children at the Crippled Children's Centre. The film, titled Mr. Symbol Man, is available from the National Film Board in Canada.

APPLICATION AND RESULTS

DESIGN AND APPLICATION OF COMMUNICATION BOARDS -
(Eugene T. McDonald)

ENTRY SKILLS NECESSARY FOR SUCCESSFUL UTILIZATION OF COMMUNICATION BOARDS

Attention to visual stimuli and verbal symbols is a basic skill children must possess in order to function with a communication board whether it uses pictorial or verbal symbols. Even if a child has not developed attending skills it doesn't relieve us of the obligation to work with this child. We ought to help him learn to attend so that he can learn to communicate. We often start with objects from his immediate experience. We take off his shoe and sock, and name them as we put them in his hands. We allow him to feel them, see them, and move them in his hands as we continue to tell him what they are called. Then we put a sock in one hand and a shoe in the other and ask him to show us which one we name by looking at it or holding it out to us. (See Fig. 75).

Figure 75.
Learning Symbolic
Representations

Figure 76.
Communication Board for
Ambulatory Individuals

Figure 77.
Use of Ambulatory Communication
Board in Sitting Position

From objects we go to symbolic representations. Unless the child can understand that the picture or drawing has symbolic value he won't be able to use a communication board. (See Fig. 75.)

The child must be able to store and retrieve meanings associated with pictures and drawings. Some children demonstrate a handicapping lack of ability to store and retrieve meanings. Clinicians say frequently, "We teach him a meaning today and when he comes back tomorrow he has forgotten it." We speak of the difficulty the child has in remembering things. Sometimes the difficulty isn't a problem in remembering, or a problem in storing. Perhaps the child hasn't developed an adequate retrieval strategy. Before jumping to the conclusion that the child doesn't have the ability to store information in long term memory, we should try to teach him retrieval strategies by techniques such as categorizing materials for him. Providing opportunities for him to use materials in different settings will give him additional methods of entering them into his long term memory.

To use a communication board which includes only two pictures the child must be able to recognize the pictures. This involves gross visual discrimination. A higher order of visual discrimination is required as an entry skill for using a wordboard. Before constructing a wordboard we develop a small sight vocabulary. We combine photographs or line drawings and words. Eventually we fade out the drawings as the child recognizes the words by sight.

For more elaborate language boards reliance on a sight vocabulary is too limiting. The child must develop some word analysis techniques. Initially we use configuration cues but as the child advances in reading ability we try to develop some kind of phonic approach. We often use the Phono-Visual system which was developed for teaching the deaf. It is systematic, and teaching materials are available. By using it frequently we develop a core group with experience in using it so we always have some people available to teach newcomers.

Ability to indicate a picture or word by pointing or signaling (either manually, with a headstick, or by indicating with eyes) is essential to communication board use. The signal must be accurate and consistent enough that the observer can know what the child means. Haphazard or gross signaling results in the observer's guessing or putting ideas into the child's head rather than getting them out. Unambiguous pointing or signaling is so important to effective communication that we urge therapists to insist that the child signal in as definite and unambiguous a manner as is possible.

It would be difficult to exaggerate the importance of a need or desire to communicate. Probably children are born with a drive, need, or desire to communicate. Man, by nature, is a communicating being. This need or desire to communicate can become repressed. Some of the children we see seem to demonstrate that some of their desire and certainly some of their need to communicate has been lost or repressed. They have had their needs anticipated and met so often that they have become happy with that kind of existence. They don't have to struggle to communicate in order to have their basic needs met. More programs are needed in which we can begin working with the parents and the children from birth to help parents learn some ways to encourage children in their efforts to communicate; to avoid making the child a dependent person, to help him realize the social utility of some kind of expression.

PHYSICAL CONSIDERATIONS IN COMMUNICATION BOARD USE

There are three physical areas to be considered in preparing a child to use a communication board: ambulation, vision and posture. Most of our non-speaking children are non-ambulatory, they come to us in wheelchairs; however, many become ambulatory. This change requires a shift from a language board built into a tray on a wheelchair to a language board the child can carry.

To illustrate we developed a communication board with a young girl and constructed it to fit on her wheelchair. About the time she became a skilled communicator, the physical therapists got her up on crutches. The conflict which arose in the girl was very interesting - did she want to walk or talk? The problem was solved by making (from oaktag) a folding board which contained essentially the same information as the wheelchair board. She carried the light weight board by a string around her neck and when she wanted to talk she would sit down, open the board and be ready to communicate. See Figs. 76 and 77.

Another little girl was ready to begin pushing a walker; however, she was reluctant to use a walker until she had a communication board she could use with it. One was made with a string on it so that she could stop, steady herself, and pull the board up to a position where she could point and communicate.

Posture must also be considered. When evaluating a child it is important to develop seating adjustments which will help the child make better use of his eyes, hands and mouth. This can be a controversial procedure. One might argue that if a child is stabilized or supported he won't develop independent control of his head and trunk. A counter view is that it often takes a long time for a child to develop the ability to sit properly with support. If educational work, language development, feeding and so on are postponed until he has independent sitting the child will have lost many learning opportunities during the formative years of his life. A compromise is to seat the child with good support for educational activities, speech training and for feeding. The rest of the time he can be positioned as other therapists deem appropriate.

As I mentioned, most of our non-ambulatory children are in wheelchairs. For feeding and some other special activities wooden relaxation chairs and other special chairs are used; however, they are unwieldy and inconvenient to move any distance. A modified wheelchair gives the child greater mobility and, if properly adapted provides good support and positioning. After studying a child, inserts for the chair are made of plywood and foam covered with vinyl. If, when sitting, the child is bent over all the time, as is the child who is very weak or who has slow flexor patterns, he will spend much time looking at his belly and will not learn very much. To learn, children must get their eyes in position where they can take in their environment. It is important for us to get their bodies into a position which allows them to see what's around them. Figures 78, 79 and 80 show some of the inserts which are used for this purpose. Figures 81, 82 and 83 show one of our children before and after positioning with these inserts.

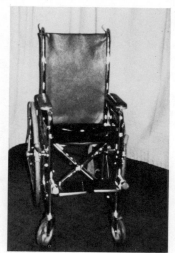

Figure 78.
Wheelchair Without Inserts

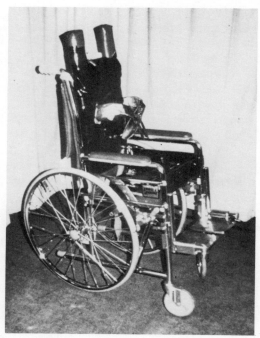

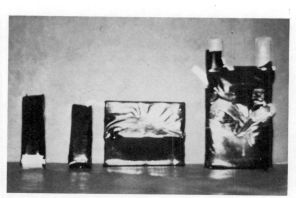

Figure 79.
Inserts Used for Positioning

Figure 80.
Wheelchair With Inserts in Place

110

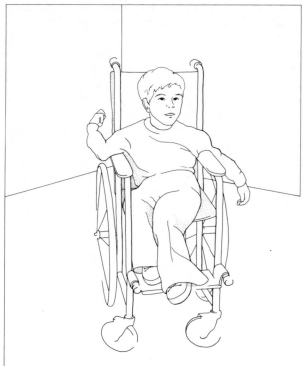

Figure 81.
Child's Position in Wheelchair
Prior to Use of Inserts

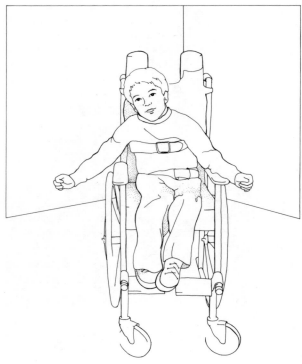

Figure 82.
Positioning of Child with Inserts
in Place

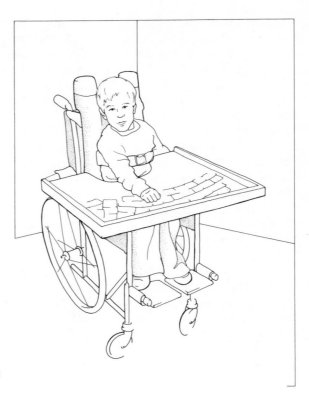

Figure 83.
Child in Position with Lap-Board in
Place

Another physical consideration is vision. It is extremely unfortunate that there are so few places in the country where good visual care
is available for the multiply handicapped child. Developing a vision
program can be a real problem. Suppose, for example, there are three or
four ophthalmologists in a community and only 30 or 40 handicapped children. These children usually get divided up among the ophthalmologists
and no one doctor sees enough of these children to feel comfortable
working with them. The result is that we often get what is even less
than a routine ophthalmological examination. Better results are obtained when members of the therapy and teaching staff provide descriptions to the ophthalmologists of what they have observed regarding the
child's problem and how it interferes with his functioning.

There are many things therapists and educators can and should
observe regarding the child's visual functioning. Children who have
neuromuscular problems which effect control of the extremities often
have neuromuscular problems with their ocular motor functions.
Strabismus, or squint, is very common. When one eye turns in and one out
the child sees double and the human brain does not tolerate diplopia. If
the child has double vision, he will suppress the vision in one eye. If
he does this long enough he will lose the vision in that eye. The child
who is seeing double may also have a difficult time attending to the
kinds of visual stimuli we want to present in his communication board.

When a child has difficulty identifying pictures, you can have the child respond while you hold a card in front of one eye and then in front of the other. If he does better seeing with one eye than with the other you have some helpful information for the eye doctor. Another problem found in some children is hemianopsia, a loss of vision in one half of the visual field. The loss would be on the nasal side in one eye and on the cheek side in the other. If you are working with a child from the side, and it is his blind side, you may get the impression that he is dumb, he is not seeing, or that he is not responding to visual stimuli. The problem is that you are not in his visual field. If he has difficulty with head control and is a very slow reactor, he may have trouble getting his eyes around to where he can see the material. Teachers and therapist should work in front of the child so they can observe him carefully to see how he tries to use his eyes, or turn his head, or manipulate his body to bring things within his visual field.

There are also problems of vertical imbalance, where instead of deviating in the lateral plane, the eyes deviate in the vertical plane, causing visual problems for the child. A very simple procedure for detecting deviations is to hold a little fountain pen flashlight about 30 inches in front of the child's eyes. When the light falls in the center of the pupil of one eye it should fall in the center of the pupil of the other eye as well. If it falls up too high or to the side, that is an indication that the child's eyes are probably not functioning in a binocular way. This observation warrants referring the child to an ophthalmologist.

We had in one of our residential centers a very interesting little girl who "went all to pieces" everytime she tried to handle visual material at nearpoint. Her eyes appeared to fly off in several directions and she became quite hyperactive. She was unable to keep herself integrated. Instead of working with her at nearpoint, we got some large pictures and displayed them for her at about 20 feet where her visual axes were parallel. She could identify pictures at this distance and behaved much more normally. We gradually moved the pictures in closer and closer and now she looks at things on a language board with the visual material arranged around the edge of the tray.

INDIVIDUALIZATION OF CONTENT ON COMMUNICATION BOARDS

As I describe some of the communication boards we have developed, I want to stress the individuality of these boards. Each is made for a specific child, taking into account his unique physical capabilities and his communication needs. It is not advisable to use a commercially prepared board when introducing this mode of communication to a child. It is better to prepare the board with the actual participation of the child. It is also advisable to involve his teacher, his clinicians and his parents so that he sees the board as something that has grown out of his communication with his community rather than as something that is imposed on him.

While the content and format of the communication board must be designed for an individual there is some commonality in what children want to express. In addition to wanting such things on their boards as symbols to express feeling happy, feeling angry or "I love you" children want to use the social lubricants as well - How are you? please, thank you. To give the child a chance to express his feelings or show awareness of the feelings of others we include words of emotional tone in the child's early boards. The children are also given symbols to express "yes" and "no" on their boards. The negative is an important concept for the children to develop and children need a way to express the negative. It is nice to go through life accentuating the positive, but life isn't always that way so we should give these youngsters the means of expressing negative feelings as well as positive ones.

INDIVIDUALIZING BOARDS FOR PHYSICAL PROBLEMS

Children with specific disabilities often require communication boards which are tailored for them. In setting up a beginning language board (Fig. 84) for a young boy who could point only on one side of the board without getting a great deal of tension, we placed the materials on his "good" side. We wanted the physical task to be as simple for him as possible. If we put the material on the other side of the board as well it turned out to be quite stressful for him. Besides reducing the number of responses we could make and frustrating him in the process, placing the material on both sides of his board would also make it more difficult for other people to know what he was saying.

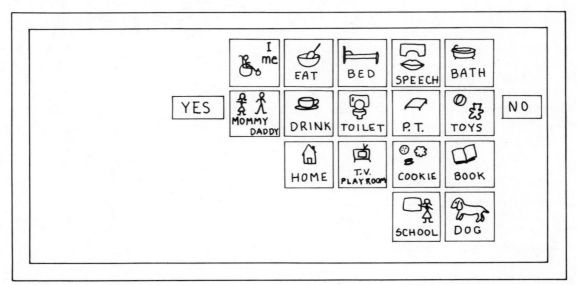

Figure 84.
Placement of Material to Accommodate Child's Range of Motion

Another example of individualized placement involved a highly motivated, bright child who had for some time been struggling with a

board containing materials displayed over the entire rectangular area
of his tray. Everytime he looked on one side of his board his arm
would go into extension, making it very difficult for him to point to
the symbol he wanted to indicate. We hit upon the idea of putting all
the materials on the other side of the board because he can point while
looking in that direction (Fig. 85). In order to get more material for
him we prepared another display of words and hung it over the side.
When he wants to get these words he can pull on a stick causing this
additional display to flip up where he can use it. He is to push this
display back over the edge when he is through.

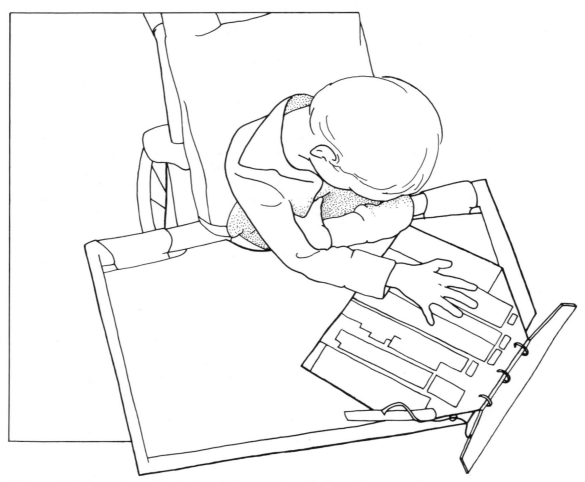

Figure 85. Range of Motion Placement with Flip-Up Display

For a young girl who apparently had trouble crossing midline we
arranged the display so that she could point to one section with one hand
and to another section with the other hand.

For a child who uses a headstick we arranged the display in an arc

(Fig. 86). He had no previous training of this type. He is severely dysarthric and can produce only one unintelligible syllable on exhalation. His oral motor control is so poor that he can't make any articulatory maneuver with sufficient precision to produce recognizable sounds. Upper extremity control was not good enough for accurate manual pointing. He learned to use this board in about three weeks, pointing with a head-stick. His parents were thrilled, and began writing him letters using words from his language board. That got him going even faster. His mother wrote us at Christmas saying that it was a very good Christmas for them. It was the first time their son had been able to communicate to them what he wanted for Christmas and to talk about what he wanted to give his brothers and sisters. His mother said the language board had changed the entire climate of the home because the family could now talk to him.

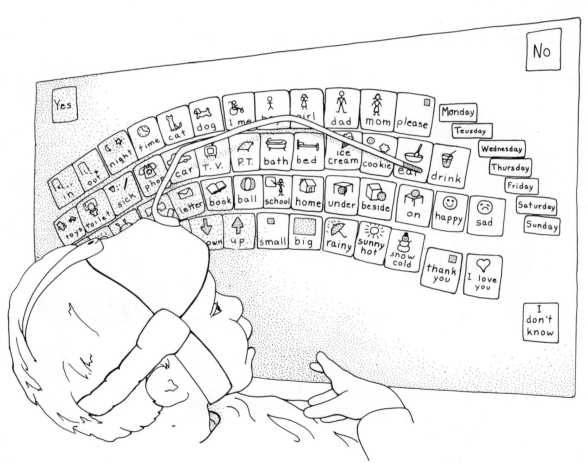

Figure 86. Placement of Words to Facilitate Use of Headstick

A two-movement encoding system was developed for a child who had very severe upper extremity involvement which precluded manual pointing. Poor head control precluded use of a headstick. The board is in the form of a matrix with the columns identified by numbers (1, 2, 3, 4, 5) and the rows by colors (Fig. 87). The child is taught to look first at a color and then at a number to indicate what column he wants. For children who don't recognize colors and numbers the columns and rows can be coded with shapes or pictures of animals. This technique may be used with the alphabet for spelling or with numbers for arithmetic lessons. The colors and numbers are located on the rim of his tray (Fig. 88). With this system a child can signal effectively with gross movements. Once the child has established a pattern of signaling color (row) first and then the number (column) it is easy for him to encode his messages. As vocabulary increases other displays are made and the child indicates which display he wants to use (Fig. 89). He may have one for use in school, another at home, and another for use in the recreation room.

Another two-movement encoding system where numbers only are used

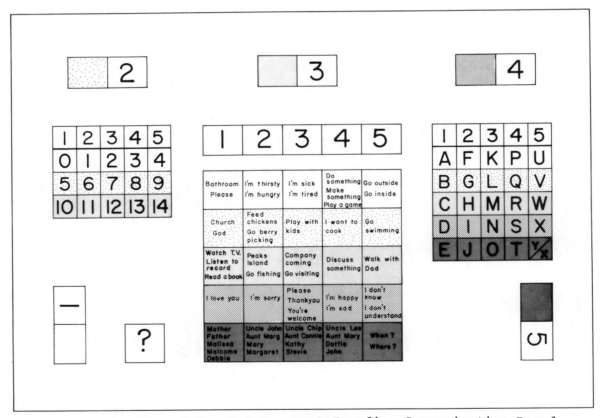

Figure 87. A Number Color Two Movement Encoding Communication Board

Figure 88. *Use of Eye-Gaze to Indicate Encoding Elements*

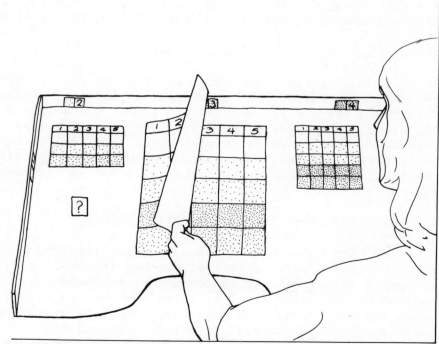

Figure 89. *Use of Multiple Displays to Increase Vocabulary*

to identify the item may be used by a child who can use a large vocabulary but does not have the precision necessary for accurate pointing to a large number of the items. Each of the entries is numbered and the child indicates which one he wants by pointing to the appropriate numbers. If the child wants a word not on his listing, he can use a number coded alphabet displayed around the edges of his board to spell a word.

CONSTRUCTION OF COMMUNICATION BOARDS

Communication boards are made so that they fit on the child's tray. Material on the board may be covered with clear contact paper to protect it or it may be protected by a piece of plexiglas cut to fit into the child's tray. The cover is sealed with tape around the edges. Thus protected, the material won't be soiled if the child spills or drools on it. The board serves as a tray for eating, a desk for working and as a communication board. If a child flails a lot while pointing we train him to slide his hand across the surface. To increase the tactile sensation of the hand on the tray we sometimes roughen the surface of the plexiglas a bit to heighten the tactile sensation. Another helpful procedure is to put a red mark on the nail of the pointing finger with crayon or magic marker and have him try to put the mark on the symbol to which he is pointing. Another helpful technique is to identify a "home" position where the child is most quiet and place a piece of flannel or moleskin at that position. The child is trained to come back to that position between pointing. It is surprising how some children who are flailing around will become more quiet with this kind of training.

The dynamics of a communication board

Communication boards must be dynamic; content must be changed as the child develops. You cannot make a board for a young child that will meet his needs for the rest of his life. The boards may require changing every few days as a child develops new vocabulary or has a new experience that he wants to talk about. Not only must the boards be individually created, they must undergo continual modification as the child's language development progresses and as his needs to communicate expand.

INVOLVING OTHERS IN THE COMMUNICATION PROCESS

We have stressed that communication involves more than one person. We may 'commune' with ourselves, we may 'commune' with nature, but if we are going to communicate there must be somebody else involved. For communication skills to develop it isn't enough to make a communication board for the child. The environment must be structured to afford opportunities for interpersonal relations. Attendants must be involved in what we are doing with the child and they should learn how to use the boards with the children.

We must create a climate of understanding and acceptance with the parents. In a survey of the parents of the 50 most recent children for whom we have created communication boards we found that most of the parents had an initial reluctance to accept the board. Once they observed how much language the child is able to use when he has a board, the initial reluctance disappears.

Also consideration must be given to demonstrating the use of the board to teachers, therapist and other children. That such an approach can make a significant change in a child's life is dramatically illustrated by the following experience.

A five year old boy was enrolled in our program at the Home of the Merciful Saviour. This type of child is not unfamiliar to therapists. Nothing seems to work with them and everyone is tempted to give up. His case demonstrates how tenacity coupled with ingenuity can sometimes find answers to insoluble problems. The boy of this illustration had carried, for about four years, the label of 'severaly mentally retarded.' Several people who had seen him in various outpatient clinics thought there were signs that he was not functioning as a severely mentally defective child. They felt he had potential which was being masked. He was referred to the Home, where his behavior during the first few weeks led to anything but optimism. We decided to approach him through visual and tactile modalities instead of talking to him and found that when we put objects in his hands he could easily match them with things that were placed before him. We observed him play with the pictures of a language lotto game as he assembled it even putting the TV antenna on the roof. His behavior when no one was talking to him showed that he had a pretty good grasp of his environment. People working with him were advised not to talk to him but to work with him through visual and tactile modalities only. Previously non-ambulatory, he began walking in three weeks. The therapists put a blue shoe on one foot and a yellow shoe on the other foot. They put blue and yellow marks down on the floor and showed him how to put the blue shoe on the blue mark, the yellow shoe on the yellow mark and so on. In the dormitory where he had been 'unmanageable' and 'disruptive' the personnel quit speaking to him and began using a communication board which we devised. He soom changed from an unmanageable child to a child who not only was manageable but one who adjusted to other people and who could demonstrate his potential as a learner.

While not all cases will yield such favorable outcomes, there are many techniques through which the non-speaking child can express himself in socially acceptable and educationally productive ways. It is our responsibility to find and develop an appropriate means of communication for each non-speaking child.

BLISSYMBOLS AND THE MENTALLY RETARDED -
(Deberah Harris-Vanderheiden)

I would like to share with you an experience that we have had at the University of Wisconsin which was very exciting and which we feel is significant and encouraging. About a year ago some Trace staff members were responsible for implementing a communication program for five severely mentally retarded and physically handicapped children at Central Wisconsin Colony in Madison, Wisconsin. Some of these children had been enrolled in institution school programs prior to the time that we started the Bliss Symbol program, while others had not had any prior structured educational experience. Since several of the student researchers who were to implement the program hadn't had any previous experience with these severely handicapped children, we knew there were going to be some real barriers in trying to develop an effective communication program for these children.

BACKGROUND ON THE RESIDENTIAL ENVIRONMENT

Many pilot communication development programs are carried out in rather ideal situations and are well staffed with teachers and clinicians who are enthusiastic and well versed on the procedure before it is implemented. This program was carried out at a large institution where the staff was very busy with prior caseloads and some were initially skeptical about the use of Bliss Symbols. A good portion of the programs in the institution are carried out by direct care staff on the wards, and this means that if any program is going to be successful it has to demonstrate its value to the ward staff. This is difficult at times because these special programs must be carried out by the aides in addition to their primary concerns of clothing the children, feeding them, and providing for their "basic" care needs. To further complicate the matter, developing communication skills in non-vocal children generally would mean more work for ward aides since they would then have to respond to requests and questions from the children in addition to their regular workload.

The situation was therefore one in which the staff was willing to let us try, but the program was going to have to prove itself in order to be continued. Thus, our independent venture into the use of a new and different communication system put us on the line--which I suspect may not be too dissimilar from the position that many of you may also be in when initiating a new program at your school or institution.

SELECTION OF THE CHILDREN FOR THE COMMUNICATION DEVELOPMENT PROGRAM

At the time we started the program there weren't any guidelines available on how to select a child for a Bliss Symbol communication development program. We identified six things which we thought would be basic skills and used these to select five children for the program. The first thing that we thought important was the ability to establish eye contact with the child. The second thing we looked for was whether or not the child could demonstrate object permanance. This was something that we felt was fundamental for the development of communication skills. The third item that we felt was important was that the child be able to attend to task for at least five minutes. When we first started the program some teachers said that we would be lucky if we could get some of the children to look at us and that we would be even luckier if we could get the child to communicate or sit for even ten minutes with us. Later we found that by alternating time-on-task with time-off-task, the children were able to sit through two hour sessions with intermittent 15-minute breaks.

The fourth criterion was that the children be able to follow oral directions. This was assessed by asking the child to do basic things like put your hand up, put your hand down, look up at the ceiling, etc. The fifth criterion was that the children be able to demonstrate in some manner the desire to communicate. This was very subjective. We spent about a week observing the children on the wards and watched them in a number of different environments and in a number of different interactions with people. We watched for any attempts by the children to express a thought or a desire, or to interact with those around them.

One additional prerequisite for this program was that the children chosen were not currently able to produce any intelligible sounds or functional speech. A lot of children had some sounds, but if after working with the children for a week we couldn't understand anything they were trying to communicate vocally, we judged the child as not presently having speech which was functional for communication.

SELECTION OF THE COMMUNICATION INTERVENTION APPROACH

When we first sat down to develop a communication intervention program for these multi-handicapped children, we had not decided that use of Bliss Symbols was the approach we were going to use. Several other approaches were considered before the decision to use the Bliss Symbols was made.

One of the first things we looked at was manual signing. These children were cerebral palsied and very involved motorically, however, and we found that finger spelling and manual signing were impossible motor tasks for them. Next we considered picture boards, wordboards, and letter boards. Communication boards of some sort were currently being used with other children at Central Colony and it turned out that many of the children in this program had tried picture boards or wordboards in the past. They hadn't been successful, however. For this reason we decided not to try the picture and wordboards again, but we did keep them in mind as future possibilities for the children to work on once they had developed some basic communication skills.

We finally decided on Bliss Symbols for a variety of reasons. One was that the children were non-vocal and really needed a means of communication which would be functional for them <u>immediately</u>. These children were becoming very frustrated and we thought it important to provide them with a means of communication before they began to cope with their frustration by giving up attempts to communicate. The second reason was that we thought using Bliss Symbols rather than pictures would increase the generalizability of the child's limited symbol set and allow him to say more things with the few symbols he might acquire. An advantage that Bliss Symbols had over signing and gestural systems was that the English word is always written beneath every symbol. For this reason the system would not be a closed system because anyone in the child's environment who could read would be able to interact with the child. No knowledge of the Bliss Symbols was required. This was considered very important since if these children could be provided with an effective means of communication, there was a possibility that they might be able to be placed in other educational programs.

THE ROLE OF SPEECH IN THE PROGRAM

Our stated objective for the program was to develop an auxiliary or augmentative means of communication which could serve as a supplement to the child's present attempts at vocal communication. We never disregarded speech for the children and it was worked on throughout the program. When we pointed to a symbol we encouraged the children to vocalize each symbol for us. We also found that when the child would co-vocalize with his pointing we were sometimes able to understand the vocal word once having been given the visual cue. The children tended to vocalize more once they began to use the symbols. They would supplement their vocalizations by pointing to the symbols, thus taking the pressure off having to rely upon their vocalizations alone to get their ideas across.

IMPLEMENTATION OF THE PROGRAM

One of our first tasks was integrating and involving teachers and ward staff into the program. We were only physically at Central Colony twice a week and we therefore had to depend very much upon the staff for program carryover. The ward aides didn't get very involved in the beginning, but they became more involved as the program progressed.

To facilitate interaction and involvement of the teachers and ward aides we would leave a copy of a report describing what we had done after each teaching session. The report described everything we did: the objectives of our teaching session, what the child had learned, what he hadn't learned, and what should be worked on for the rest of the week. We found in the beginning that some of the teachers were not very involved, but later when the children would come back after our teaching session and start asking questions, pointing to the symbols on their trays, etc., the teachers became more actively involved. We found that after about the third week of leaving a report of session results, teachers would pick it up and scribble some notes back about how they had used Bliss Symbols in the classroom as they became more and more involved in the program. In addition, we held a planning session prior to the initiation of the program and explained the Bliss Symbol system and the proposed program. In this manner, teachers and ward staff knew what the program goals were and were able to judge its progress for themselves. They were also given a notebook to write down anecdotes about the children and their use of the symbols and to record their feedback to us. We asked them for symbols that they felt the child should learn, what curriculum the child was involved in, what he was learning at school, and what the ward aides were working on with him in the ward. Again, we didn't get many symbol suggestions in the beginning. But, after the children began using the symbols for awhile, the teachers and aides would say, "She needs a symbol for workshop because she goes to workshop in the afternoon," or "She needs a symbol for break because we want her to ask for her break," or "She needs a symbol for drink because she should be the one who asks for a drink instead of us always having to give her a drink when everybody else gets one."

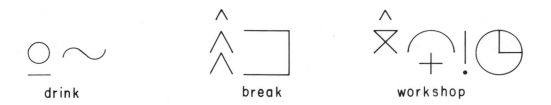

drink   break   workshop

Another thing that we initiated was an <u>idea exchange letter</u> between all the teachers and ward personnel. In this newsletter the staff could write down things that they liked about the Bliss Symbols and things that they didn't like, as well as how they were using the symbols with their children. The newsletter was designed to stimulate inter-communication among the teachers themselves. We didn't take part in the newsletter at all ourselves except to get the ball rolling. The newsletter worked very well. We would get one teacher who said I am using the symbols in such and such a way in my curriculum and I have incorporated these symbols this way. The next week some other teacher would put in a paragraph saying that she had tried that but it really didn't work because of some problem but they had adapted something else. The exchange letter turned out to be very helpful.

IMPLEMENTING THE PROGRAM WITH THE CHILDREN

We could only meet with the children twice a week for approximately eight weeks and we had only a two-hour session with them each time.

This gave us a total contact time of approximately 32 hours with the child, and an average total teaching time of approximately 20 hours.

When working with the children the first thing we wanted them to do was to identify the symbols. We wanted to determine whether or not they could discriminate the symbol for "want" from the symbol for "like" or the symbol for "like" from the symbol for "please."

to want   like   please

We generally started with concrete symbols. This seemed to work out very well. The very first symbols that we actually introduced, however, were "yes" and "no." We used these because every one of the children had an effective means of saying "yes" and "no" and understood these concepts. We therefore started out by pairing their manners of indicating "yes" and "no" with the symbols for "yes" and "no" to get them used to the idea that the symbols had some meaning behind them and that it was a meaning that they could understand and could express. Essentially what we did was to supply them with a means of expressing things that they already knew the meaning of and used frequently.

yes   no

Next we wanted to determine whether or not they could comprehend use of other symbols. This was the first real test to assess whether or not they really understood "drink." We used the symbols "eat" and "drink," matching them with something to eat and something to drink. They caught onto that fairly well and teaching them the meaning behind the symbol for toilet was very easy.

We would then introduce other symbols and initiate their use by having them respond to questions. We would say things like "How would you tell me you wanted something to drink? How would you tell me you wanted something to eat? How would you tell me you wanted to go to the bathroom? How would you tell me you were sick?"

We took pictures of the teachers and ward personnel, put them on the children's lap trays, and then paired them with the appropriate symbols for teacher, ward mother, etc. To incorporate the people in the environment with the Bliss Symbols we also posted the symbols on doors, windows and everything in the environment that we could label with a symbol. These symbols weren't necessarily all taught to the children. They were there to give the children a model so that they could see that Bliss Symbols could be used to label things in their environment. (Fig. 90)

Figure 90. Labelling Objects in the Environment to Model Blissymbol Use

To reinforce the children's use of the symbols we tried to insure that the children would be responded to if they tried to communicate. We didn't want to have them ask for something to eat or to drink and not be reinforced for this communication. In the beginning this was a little difficult but then the ward aides began to notice what they said was a change in the children's personalities; that these children were becoming "real people" to them and not just children to take care of. They also started becoming fascinated with the symbols and the fact that the children were able to use them. As the attitudes of the ward aides changed, they began to enjoy talking to the children and used the symbols quite extensively.

CASE STUDIES

Child A. Child A was 11 years old and medically diagnosed as "mentally retarded with spastic quadruplegia and microencephaly." Prior to the program, Child A's teacher described her communication as "limit-

126

ed to slightly differentiated sounds and indistinguishable utterances."
She felt that Child A's lack of communication was the largest obstacle
to her educational achievement at present.

Figure 91. Child with Blissymbols on Lap-Tray

Child A was met with once a week for approximately one and one-
half hours. Sessions were broken down into (a) review, (b) practice,
(c) test, (d) teaching, (e) review, (f) test. Within the 10-week program, Child A learned 15 symbols and utilized them for respondent communication. She is now able to correctly point to symbols in response
to questions and will occasionally use symbols spontaneously to initiate
a conversation or express a thought. She will put two symbols together
to form certain thoughts and ideas correctly upon request, and in oc-
casional self-initiated responses, i.e., want drink, want toilet.
(Fig. 91) At the end of the 10-week program, Child A's teacher expressed the following:

"At first I was very skeptical, but I am impressed with the
favorable results. The children are catching on and at last
they can be understood. Although their communication with
Bliss is still limited, I am very positive that eventually
they will have total communication skills."

[Editor's Note: Sixteen months later, the child now uses over 100 symbols in both respondent and spontaneous communication. Her messages are usually around 2-4 symbols in length.]

Child B. He was 16 years old and was the oldest of the children in the program. He has cerebral palsy, is confined to a wheelchair, and cannot express himself vocally. Child B differentiated objects and symbols by slowly pointing with his left hand. An asymmetric tonic neck reflex inhibited this child's ability to look at the desired symbol when he was pointing. It was necessary to remind him to hold his head up when pointing and he was not asked to respond until he was in proper position.

It usually took Child B two to three sessions to learn a symbol completely. During the 10-week session he learned to discriminate symbols "yes," "no," "hello/goodbye," "more," and "toilet." Although he progressed more slowly and learned fewer symbols than the other children, he demonstrated that he was able to use the symbols meaningfully. During one of the final sessions, Child B, who had just returned from a 3-week hospital visit, saw his Bliss teacher and excitedly pointed to "hi." Later in that session, after receiving a sip of milk as a reinforcer, Child B emphatically pointed to "more." These were some of the child's first attempts to communicate with others without using gestures. (Fig. 92)

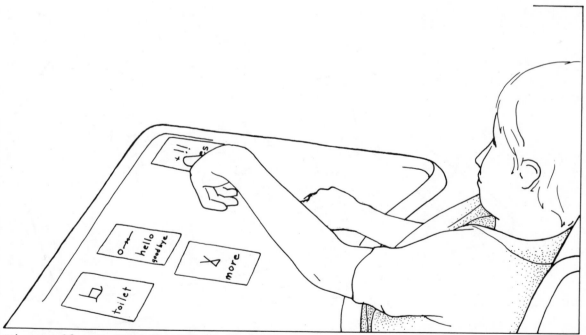

Figure 92. A Child's First Symbols

128

[Editor's Note: Sixteen months later, the child's vocabulary is approximately 25 symbols. His communication is presently still largely respondent, although he does initiate some spontaneous communications. His average message length is 1-2 symbols].

Child C. For this 14-year old cerebral palsied child with a medical diagnosis of "severely mentally retarded" the Bliss program was implemented over an 8-week period. Prior to the program her intelligible expressive vocabulary was limited to yes, no, hello, bye. Her teachers were not certain about the level of her receptive language because of the child's limited expressive abilities.

According to her Bliss teacher, Child C learned 16 Bliss Symbols

Figure 93. Vocabularies Slowly Expanded as the Child Masters More Symbols

in this pilot program which she used appropriately in communicative situations without prompting. Program test results have indicated that she is responding to the symbol rather than the word and can select a known symbol from two or three unknown symbols. This child experiences visual confusion when a variety of unknown symbols are presented, but is able to effectively utilize a small number of symbols for respondent communication. (Fig. 93)

[Editor's Note: Sixteen months later, this child now has 125 symbols which she uses for spontaneous and respondent communication. Her average message length is 2-4 symbols].

Child D. Child D was a 12-year old with cerebral palsy. Test results were not available to confirm the medical diagnosis of "mental retardation," and it was believed, at the conclusion of the program, that this child might be more appropriately considered as "physically handicapped and educationally retarded." Prior to the program her speech was unintelligible and she communicated with others through yes-no responses and "twenty questions." The vocabulary selected by the

Figure 94. Symbol Size and Position Determined by Child's Pointing Ability

Bliss teacher for inclusion in Child D's program included:

1. Basic human needs (eat, drink)
2. Basic human emotions
3. Holophrastic words
4. Question words
5. Significant persons in the child's environment

The teaching format for the 10-week period consisted primarily of a test-teach-retest format. At the end of the 10-week period, Child D had learned 50 symbols and was combining them in up to 4 symbol sentences for expressive communication. Pairing of her pointing response with a verbal approximation of the symbol was encouraged. (Fig. 94)

[Editor's Note: Sixteen months later, this child has moved from Bliss Symbols to reading and a sight word vocabulary which she uses to communicate. She is also now starting to use a typewriter with a keyboard guard].

Child E. Child E is an 11-year old, also considered to be mentally retarded. She has recently been assessed with the PPVT, the Boehm Test of Basic Concepts and the Northwestern Syntax Screening Test.

Child E quickly learned the Bliss Symbols and during the second teaching session she pointed out the message "sick-time-bed," indicating

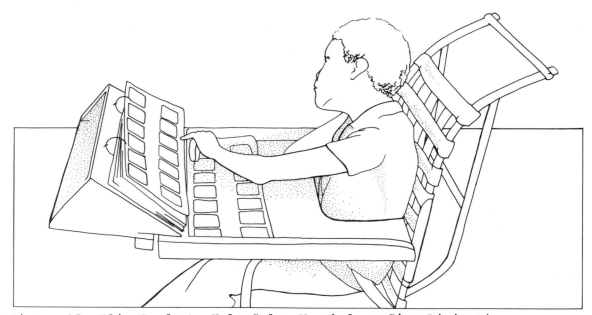

Figure 95. Flip-Cards to Help Solve Vocabulary Size Limitations

that she was sick and wanted to go to bed. The aides returned her to
her ward, whereupon she began laughing and giggling, for she wasn't
sick at all. She was merely playing a joke on her teachers using her
new communication system. It was the first time she had ever been able
to control the actions of others in a direct manner. During the following session Child E learned the symbol for "I'm sorry," and has had the
opportunity to use it quite frequently since then. Child E learned new
symbols rapidly and, by the end of the program, was using approximately
75 symbols. She uses the symbols for both respondent and expressive
communication, (Fig. 95)

[Editor's Note: Sixteen months later, this child has a symbol vocabulary of over 200 symbols which she uses for spontaneous and respondent
communication. She uses the "to make action" symbol to specify verbs
and constructs her own symbols when necessary. She is currently using
an OCCC electronic scanner, due to her limited pointing skills].

RESULTS OF THE 10-WEEK PROGRAM

        Informal evaluation by Central Colony staff indicated that the
Bliss Symbol program was extremely successful. Children who were on a
five year old cognitive ability level were expected by the staff to be
able to pick up only a couple of concrete symbols. Yet at the end of
the program some of them were using 80 symbols and 4 symbol combinations to express themselves. Children who were on a 2-year old level
were not expected to be able to learn the symbols, but these children
learned from 7 to 30 symbols and used them for respondent communication.

SYMBOL COMMUNICATION PROGRAMME AT OCCC -
(Shirley McNaughton)

In the previous presentation you heard Debbie describing a program
that was implemented with severely and profoundly mentally retarded
children. The children in our programs have approximately the same
range of physical handicaps but they have a higher mental capability,
most of them in the normal or near normal range. As a result the approaches and techniques we were able to use with these children are
more advanced and the progress is much quicker.

In this presentation I will first be talking about ways in which
we implement the symbol systems with the children in our programs.
I will then be presenting some examples of communication that the
children have done with the Symbols. Finally, I will present a summary
of the various symbol programs which are being conducted in the United
States and Canada.

STARTING A CHILD ON SYMBOLS

The first thing we work on with a young child beginning to use
symbols is the concept that symbols have the same function as speech.
We give the child symbols he can use immediately. The minute he is
given a symbol he uses it in conversation with the teacher. Then we
start to develop as many symbol meanings as we can to build up a working
vocabulary. We begin with symbols that are of interest to the child.
Sometimes it's "happy" "sad" "yes" or "no". One little girl was learning symbols at home with her mother and wanted "vacuum cleaner" and
"dishes." We tried to tune in to where the child is at and to begin
with those symbols. Even the more difficult ones may be used in this
initial stage if that's what's meaningful to the child.

Next we want the child to start to realize that symbols represent
a range of meaning, not just a specific word. Then we try to help
him develop speed in using the symbols purposely. We continue working
with the child to develop an understanding of the entire system, the
strategies he can use,.different levels of usage, and to learn to converse with a wide range of persons.

We first start with the basic symbols which are on separate 2" x
3" cards and are quite large and which some children are able to move
around with their hands. We then introduce the 100 level. (Fig. 96)
This level gives them a few feelings, the strategy of opposite, plurals,
and the action symbol to create verbs. They are also given some nouns,
some verbs, some additives, and two pronouns. We start to show them
some of the characteristics of the symbol system. For example, direction

makes a difference; if an arrow goes up it means you're happy, down
you're sad.

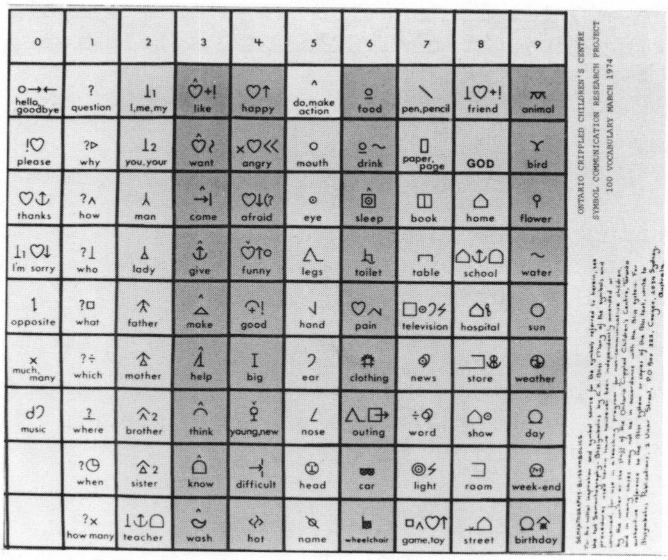

Figure 96. Blissymbol 100 Display

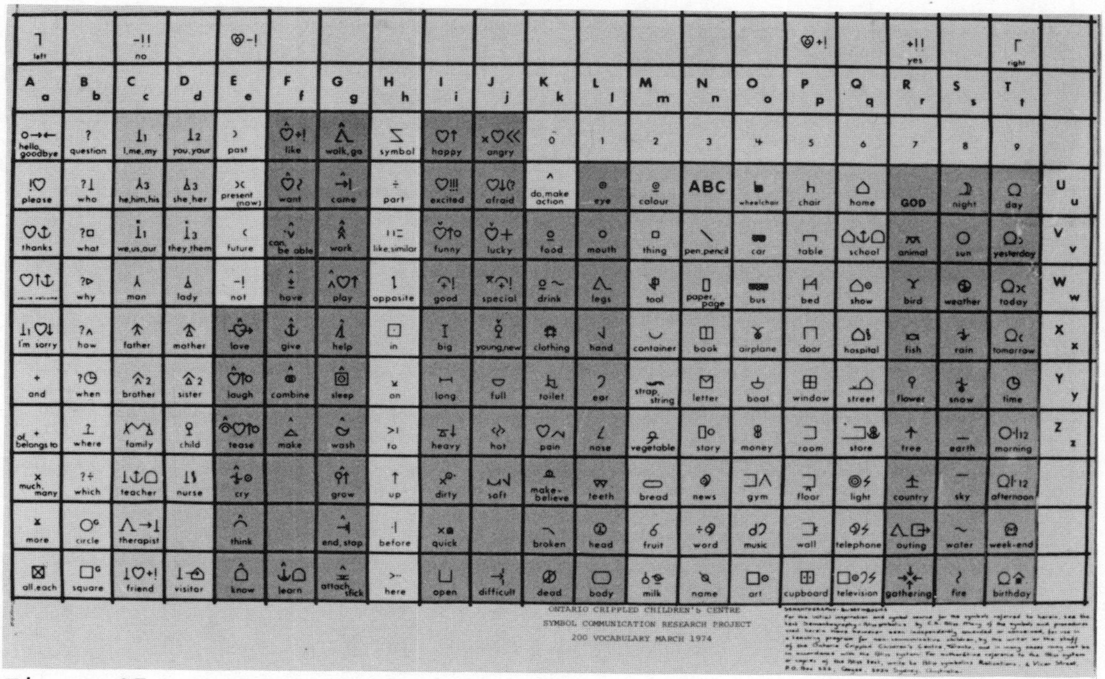

Figure 97. The Blissymbol 200 Display

At the 200 level we have added numbers and adjectives. The tense system has been put in and the negative has been added. We also include a few prepositions and adverbs, the conjunction "and" and the strategy "it's like something." The 200 level also includes the "combine" symbol. The 400 level gives the child more symbols with additional subordinating conjunctions, articles, multipliers, and a fourth geometric shape. (Figs. 97 and 98)

CHILD DEVELOPMENT WITH SYMBOLS

We have seen children developing in all areas through symbol use. In the beginning of the program we knew where the children were in their concepts and as the program has progressed we have watched their concepts expand and develop.

Socially the children were able to interact with a wider range of people through symbols, including people in their immediate environment, strangers, and speaking and non-speaking peers. This has had many, many ramifications.

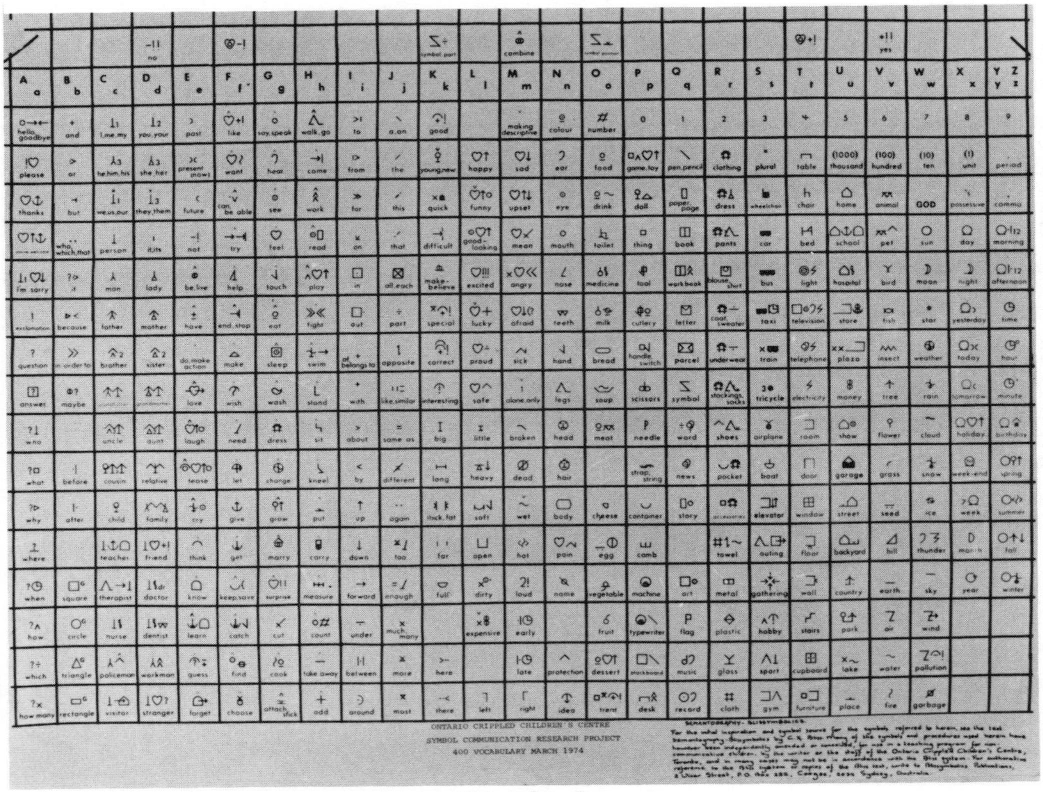

Figure 98. The Blissymbol 400 Display

In the area of emotional development we hear parents saying that now the children don't have to have a temper tantrum, they don't need an unsocial way to indicate displeasure. The children can analyze their own feelings and express themselves. They are able to say "I feel upset right now," or "I'm upset because so and so is doing something." They have a much better understanding of themselves.

We are not saying that symbols will be the only form of communication for these children. We are saying that right now symbols are a substitute for the speech they don't have and we hope that symbols will help the children develop until they are ready to use words. We don't know whether the children will want to retain the symbols or not; we don't know exactly what symbols are doing for them. Perhaps these children will have visual images of their world that we would never dream of...seeing the world and expressing things in a very different way. As our program goes on, we hope to learn more about how the children conceive of their world and how this affects them as they grow older.

We are thinking of the possibility of integrating the mentally able children into regular schools. They would not be able to go into regular classrooms because of their physical disabilities, but they could be placed in classrooms where they would be surrounded by speaking children and where they will be able to go to the same schools as their brothers and sisters. (Editor's note: Two OCCC symbol children were integrated into Special Education classes, regular schools, September, 1975.)

Some of our children will be going to schools for the retarded, some to orthopedic schools. There is one teacher who is teaching symbols to all her non-speaking children, regardless of their ages or reading abilities, because she feels that many of them are going to be living in institutions before their lives are finished. She wants them to be able to relate to everyone in that institution. We have cases of young people who could use wordboards, but who are going to a residence where they would not meet anyone who could read their wordboard. This teacher wanted her students to be able to communicate both with the symbol readers and the word users. Since the Bliss Symbols have both the symbol and the word, her children would be able to do this.

EXAMPLES OF COMMUNICATION THROUGH BLISS SYMBOLS

I can provide you with facts and figures on the various Bliss Symbol programs which have been implemented, and I will give you a few brief ones at the end, but I think you can understand the impact of the program much better if you can see some of the conversations and thoughts that the children are relating through the symbols.

The following symbol examples have been taken from the OCCC Symbol Communication Programme Year-End Report 1974. They have been substituted for the examples shown at the Workshop in order to up-date the samples of symbol output. (Pages 137-143.)

PROFILE OF CURRENT REPORTED SYMBOL PROGRAMS IN THE UNITED STATES AND CANADA

As of June, 1974, 40 out of 60 invited settings responded to a survey conducted by the OCCC Symbol Communication Programme. This represented 150 symbol-using children. Results reported at that time indicated that 38% of the settings were retarded, 4% were opportunity classes (slow-learning elementary school classes), and over 50% were academic classes in orthopedic schools or opportunity centers.

Since one very strong argument that has been voiced against symbol use has been that it might discourage vocalization, we included this aspect in our study. The results showed that in 63% of the people who responded there had been no change in vocalization, while 35% noted an improvement. The two children for whom vocalization was reported to have decreased were both adolescents for whom vocalization had been non-functional.

We discovered that 43% of the symbol instructors were also making use of the alphabet which is on the larger Bliss symbol vocabularies and showing the children how to transfer and how to make use of the symbols along with the alphabet. For a more complete description of the results of this survey, please see Appendix A.

The program at the Ontario Crippled Children's Centre consists of two parts. The first is the classroom aspect which involves 20 children. The primary level class is composed of 12 children and 2 teachers, while the other class of 8 children and 1 teacher is at the kindergarten level. The children range in age from 5 to 13 and have varying degrees of physical disabilities. Half of the children point while the other half are either using electronic equipment or are getting a lot of help from the adults in the room. One very great advantage we have at the Crippled Children's Centre is a relatively large number of teachers' aides and volunteers.

The other half of the Crippled Children's Centre's program has to do with interaction and support of outside programs. We offer a resource workshop twice a year. These workshops run three days and are offered in the spring and again in the fall. In addition, we offer Bliss Symbol teaching guidelines and have Bliss Symbol displays which we have had printed so that they will be available to others.

We are members of the Symbol Coordination Committee. The Symbol Coordination Committee is composed of a group of instructors who have banded together to keep informed on the use of symbols and their development. This Committee publishes a newsletter four times a year made up solely from contributions from symbol instructors around the country.

The children are now making use of the newsletter as a pen-pal service, too. [Editors Note: The Symbol Coordination Committee disbanded in 1976 when the Blissymbolics Communication Foundation was established. The Foundation has assumed the activities previously carried out by the committee, including the Newsletter.]

CONCLUSION

Although the Bliss symbol program is a new one, I think it has already proven to be very effective in providing a communication outlet for non-vocal physically handicapped children. What the eventual outcome of this program will be we won't know until we are able to study symbol-using children as they grow older and more fully develop their potential. What we have seen so far indicates to us, however, that the program is fulfilling its initial purpose...to help non-speaking children to communicate as soon as possible.

(1)   KINDERGARTEN CHILD

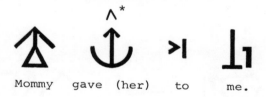

Mommy   gave (her)   to   me.

Barbie

Barbie   is sleeping.

138

(2)   <u>INTERMEDIATE CLASS</u>

Two examples of symbol output for each child using
200 Vocabulary

A) Exceptional utterance   B) Typical utterance

<u>Child 1</u>. A)

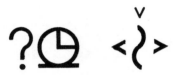

   I   have (a) treehouse to sleep in

when (it's) hot.

B)

Dalmation <u>fire dog</u>

<u>Child 2</u>. A)

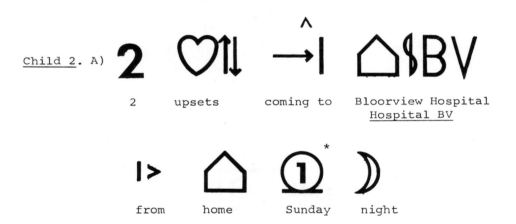

  2   upsets coming to Bloorview Hospital
                         <u>Hospital BV</u>

from   home   Sunday night

B)

Traffic <u>gathering (of) cars</u>

(3) <u>Examples of Combined symbols created by Children using 200 Vocabulary</u>

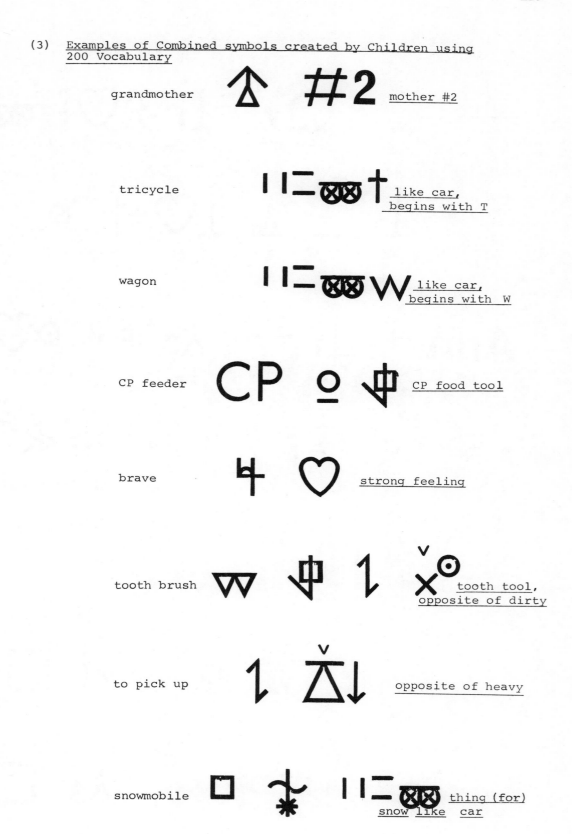

grandmother		<u>mother #2</u>
tricycle		<u>like car, begins with T</u>
wagon		<u>like car, begins with W</u>
CP feeder		<u>CP food tool</u>
brave		<u>strong feeling</u>
tooth brush		<u>tooth tool, opposite of dirty</u>
to pick up		opposite of heavy
snowmobile		<u>thing (for) snow like car</u>

(4) <u>ADVANCED CLASS UTTERANCES</u>

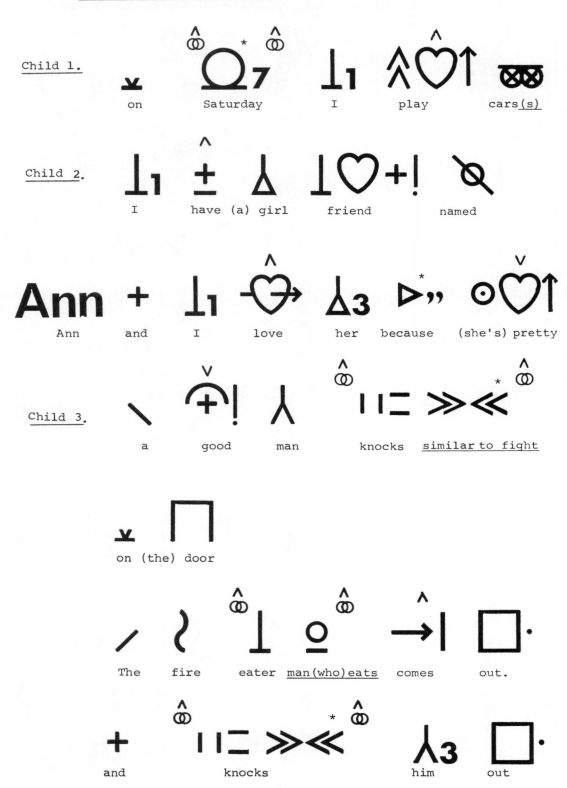

Child 1.

on   Saturday   I   play   cars<u>(s)</u>

Child 2.

I   have (a) girl   friend   named

Ann   and   I   love   her   because   (she's) pretty

Child 3.

a   good   man   knocks   <u>similar to fight</u>

on (the) door

The   fire   eater   <u>man (who) eats</u>   comes   out.

and   knocks   him   out

(5). A SYMBOL POEM

10 9 8 7 6 5 4 3 2 1 ⸮

Blast off!
fire

I'm pretending I'm going on the moon

I'm going here and there and here and

there and here and there

10 9 8 7 6 5 4 3 2 1 ⸮

Blast off!

CONTINUED .....

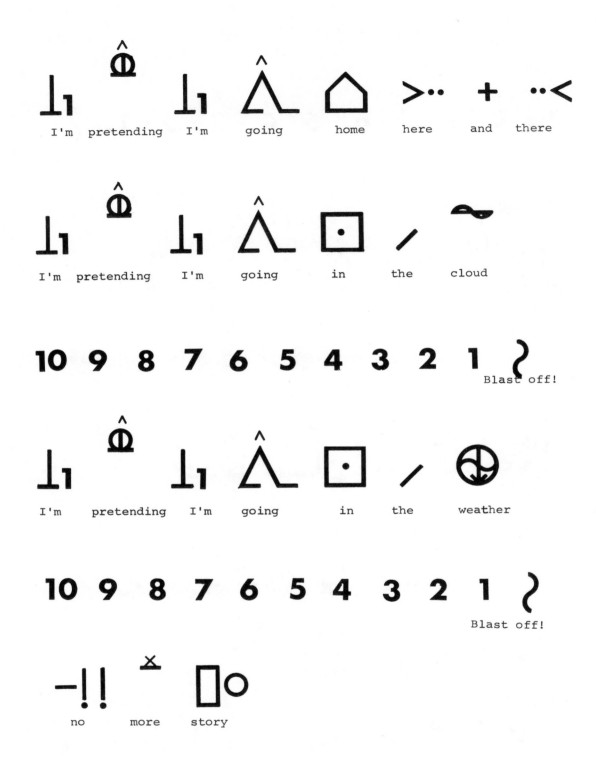

I'm pretending I'm going home here and there

I'm pretending I'm going in the cloud

10 9 8 7 6 5 4 3 2 1 }
Blast off!

I'm pretending I'm going in the weather

10 9 8 7 6 5 4 3 2 1 }
Blast off!

no more story

(6). <u>NORTHWESTERN SYNTAX SCREENING TEST</u>

Examples of variety of responses on one item

Northwestern Syntax Screening Test

Expressive

THE DOG IS IN THE BOX

THE DOG IS ON THE BOX

Silvano ⊡ ∪

          in   container

       ⴸ   ∪

        on   container

Kari D⩚ ⊡ B∪

      dog   in   box <u>container begins with B</u>

<u>animal begins with D</u>

     λ3 ⴸ B∪

     he   on   box   <u>container begins with B</u>

Terry D ⊡ ∧

    D (dog) in (thing which) protects

    ⊡ D −! ∧

    In (dog)   not (thing which) protects

FIELD EVALUATION OF THE AUTO-COM - (Deberah Harris-Vanderheiden)

Many people have had questions concerning what types of children could use the Auto-Com, where it's been used before, etc. I'd like to spend a little time now explaining how the Auto-Com has been used by describing a field evaluation that we are conducting at this time. In addition to providing specific information on the Auto-Com, the results of this program can also serve to demonstrate the general effects of providing children with an effective means of communication. Similar results should be obtainable with other aids that can provide the same function for a child as the Auto-Com has for the children in this study.

DESCRIPTION OF THE AUTO-COM

The Auto-Com is similar both in appearance and operation to a traditional language or letterboard. With both of these methods a child communicates by pointing to the components of his message which are displayed on a hard, smooth surface, normally a laptray or a lapboard. With a traditional communication board (see Fig. 99), a second person is required to monitor the child's erratic pointing, to memorize or record the components of the message (letters, words, etc.) as they are indicated by the child, and to determine the child's total message.

Figure 99. Communication Board Used by Advanced Student Prior to Auto-Com

144

As most of you are aware, this process is time-consuming and demands absolute and total attention of the message receiver. The Auto-Com, however, was developed to allow a child to communicate without needing a second person to record or monitor message elements. A special electronic circuit within the board monitors the sporadic movements of a motorically involved child and determines the correct letter automatically. As the child selects the letters by pointing to them, the Auto-Com prints them out on a display. In this manner the child is able to compose the message entirely on his own and a second person is needed only to respond to the child as he would to a vocal question or comment.

In actual operation, the Auto-Com is very simple and in cases that we've experienced, it has only required 3-5 minutes of instruction for the child to understand its operation. To use the Auto-Com, a child indicates his choice by using the same gross motor pointing ability as he would with a regular language board. The only difference with the Auto-Com is that now he uses a magnet instead of a finger or a hand to point to message elements. The Auto-Com watches the pointing motions of the magnet, and, if the child is concentrating his pointing motions in the area of a letter or word, the Auto-Com prints that letter or word out onto the strip printer or TV screen. The Auto-Com can handle erratic pointing motions, and has been used successfully by severe athetoid cerebral palsied children. The timing is adjustable so that the aid can also be used by spastic children who have much slower pointing motions. (Fig. 100)

Figure 100. The Portable Auto-Com with Wordmaster

146

The surface display of the Auto-Com consists of a letter/symbol
matrix of approximately 84 words and squares. The matrix that we currently have on the board includes the alphabet, numbers, symbols, punctuation marks, and control squares which allow the children to utilize
output options, such as televisions or teletypes. (Fig. 101) The Wordmaster option allows the aid to print out whole words or sentences
with a single pointing motion of the child. Also, the Auto-Com is
portable and fits on the child's wheelchair as a laptray so that it
can be the child's voice in whatever environment he may be in.

Figure 101. Television Display Used with the Auto-Com

I'd like to comment here that the Auto-Com we are using now is
a portable model (Fig. 102). The children in the study all started with
an earlier "stationary" model which printed only one letter at a time
(no Wordmaster) and had to be used with the TV monitor which plugged
into the wall. (Fig. 103) Later three of the children were able to get
portable versions of the Auto-Com which contained the Wordmaster capability and the miniature strip printers. (The portable models could
also print out on the TV screens for stationary school work). The
results of the study we will be discussing will include children on
both types of Auto-Coms.

Figure 102.
Portable Auto-Com on Wheelchair

Figure 103. The Stationary Auto-Com with Television Display

148

POPULATION USED IN EVALUATION

The previous communication methods used by the students in the evaluation program included gestures, gross pointing, limited vocalization, and occasionally letter or word boards. In some cases, children had tried guarded or masked typewriters but none of the students had the physical skills needed to effectively use this type of aid for communication. The student population in the evaluation program was composed of three male and four female students ranging in age from 7 to 19 years. This figure reflects the student population at the end of the first year of the evaluation program. As stated previously, there were originally nine children in the study. One child developed his pointing skills accurately enough to be able to use a guarded typewriter. He had been sharing his Auto-Com with one other very involved child. The school staff and the Trace Center staff subsequently determined that it would be more beneficial if that child would use the guarded keyboard and allow the more severely involved child to use the Auto-Com on a 100% basis. One other child in the program had developed severe scoliosis, became involved in a lot of surgery and was unable to use any type of communication aid. This reduced our student population to the seven students reported here. Five of the seven children in the program were educationally assessed as average or near average in intellectual ability, while two appeared to be in the EMR range. However, there really weren't any formal assessment results available for the children. This assessed level was mostly arrived at through vocabulary tests and teacher evaluation. Educational environments in which the Auto-Coms were placed also varied. They consisted of special education resource rooms, public high schools with resource home rooms for handicapped children, multi-handicapped segregated classrooms, and an institution for mentally handicapped individuals in southern Wisconsin.

The results of the Auto-Com evaluation program have been, for the most part, documented in a descriptive case study manner. As I think you can understand, we found it extremely difficult to try to go through an experimental/control group type of evaluation. In addition, our purpose at this point was not to get extensive statistical analysis of effectiveness of the aid. Instead we were trying to field test physical features of the aid, obtain teacher and child reaction to the aid, and collect information on actual use and integration of the aid in classrooms on a day-to-day basis.

Teachers were the primary observers and data collectors for the program. Since each program was carried out on a long distance basis from Madison, we relied very heavily on mail and phone correspondence with teachers and periodic visits to schools.

RESULTS - EFFECT OF THE AUTO-COM ON STUDENTS' EDUCATIONAL PROGRESS

Teachers have reported that the Auto-Com has greatly facilitated the students' acquisition of and progress in educational skill areas, especially in the areas of math, sentence structure, vocabulary and reading skills. Teachers and other professional staff working with the students felt that students made progress in these areas because the Auto-Com provided them with their first consistent and dependable means of responding to and communicating with people in a learning environment. This really was felt by everybody to be an initial step to effective, productive educational participation for the students. As was typical of most cases, prior to receiving the Auto-Com most of the students' classroom interactions were restricted by their limited ability to initiate communication with others in their environment. Teachers felt that the acquisition of basic skills was really hampered by the amount of time the teachers would have to spend with students in order to elicit and record their responses. In order to work with the students, the teachers had to stop working with others in the classroom and come over and spend an inordinate amount of time on a one-to-one basis with the non-vocal handicapped child. As a result, the teacher spent more time giving directions and recording responses than in productive use of instructional time with the child. Teachers commented that they have enjoyed the Auto-Com because it enables students to take an active role in classroom activities, providing these students with a means of producing their work independently. One of the major factors in the successful integration of the Auto-Com in the classroom has been the use of the visual TV display in classroom discussions. With the aid the children could write their answers to questions on the television screen and the teacher could look at their comments and include them in the class discussions without having to have someone spend ten or fifteen minutes assembling the child's message as he pointed it out. Also, because the children were given totally correctable visual feedback, they could work on their own, completing exercises and solving problems independently for the first time.

Teachers felt they were much better able to accurately assess what the children knew in basic skill areas. Through assessing children using the Auto-Com, some teachers discovered that their students hadn't learned basic concepts which they had presumed that the children knew. This accurate assessment of their abilities resulted in curriculum changes for most of the students. Changes for the most part were concerned with gearing material toward the students' demonstrated abilities rather than their assumed abilities. Because the children were able to work independently for greater amounts of time, teachers felt that they were able to develop much more detailed curricula and expose the students to a greater diversity of materials. For some of the students, independent work became a challenge and teachers commented on marked improvements in motivation and quality of their work. In the basic skill areas, the Auto-Com was shown to be especially functional in acquisition and development of math skills. Prior to the Auto-Com, the students were not able to perform arithmetic manipulations. Someone else always did the work for them and they saw only the final product. Using the correctable TV display students were able to write out the entire arithmetic problem and teachers remarked that many of the students began to understand mathematical processes and concepts for the first time. In one case a student was noted to place ones or marks across the top of the TV screen. It was later discovered that he used these for counting purposes in much the same manner as manipulative children count on their fingers.

Improvement in spelling, sentence construction, and in vocabulary development was also noticed. Teachers felt that the Auto-Com enhanced the children's development in these areas because it let them see their letters form words, and their words form sentences. One of the children who had previously been communicating through a letterboard said that she had never had the opportunity to see her expressions written out. Someone would write down what she was pointing to and respond to it, but would not necessarily see the need to show the student what she was writing as she went along. Now she could actually see what her expressive output looked like as she assembled it.

A few comments on the effect of the Auto-Com on the student's communication skills are important here. Initially, the Auto-Coms were primarily used for doing work in the classroom, but in all cases they were used increasingly for expressive communication and social communication purposes as the children's spelling skills increased. It was the feeling of both parents and teachers that increased use of the Auto-Com for social communication had an important effect on the student's vocalization. One of their primary concerns before using the aid was that the child who had very limited speech would stop vocalizing once provided with a communication aid. However, teachers and parents noted that students' vocalizations increased once they began to use the Auto-Com. They felt that use of the Auto-Com allowed the child time to complete his sentences and thoughts without feeling the pressure of having someone waiting for him to speak. This decrease in pressure helped the children to relax and communicate clearer unambiguous thoughts at their own rate. They became aware that transmission and understanding of their messages wouldn't be solely dependent upon the intelligibility of their vocal word approximation. Thus they spoke, and in a more relaxed manner.

In addition to enhancing classroom interaction and skill acquisition, use of the Auto-Com affected the students' interaction with parents and siblings. The Auto-Coms were used at home to communicate with family members, to write letters and notes and to complete homework tasks. Prior to the Auto-Com, completion of any of the above required that a family member stop his activity and devote full attention to the child as he attempted to express his thoughts. By decreasing the need for cessation of ongoing activity, the Auto-Com allowed a more relaxed family atmosphere and students became more active in family activities. Parents especially commented that the children's increased communication ability allowed siblings to see that this child could do things by and for himself. This, and the privacy which the aid allowed, resulted in what one parent expressed as an "intangible effect on the children's self-esteem." Parents also noted that when the child's communication no longer depended upon the presence of a second person to log his thoughts, the student felt freer to communicate personal thoughts and opinions and to disagree with others. Some teachers and parents said that they really didn't think they knew the students until their personalities emerged through their communication skill and use of the Auto-Com.

SUMMARY

The Auto-Com was shown in this program to enhance the students' acquisition of a progress in basic skill areas. It enhanced their personal and motivational development, including self-confidence and independence. One of the primary goals of this program was to investigate the effect of the Auto-Com on students' acquisition of basic education and communication skills. We found that these students, who previously were unable to do much more than observe classroom activities, started to become active participants in their educational programs and really produced evidence that they are quite able to think, learn and communicate. In nearly all cases, increased communication ability gave students personal satisfaction and motivation to learn.

There were three primary features shown to be significant to successful results of use of the Auto-Com: 1) the independence which the aid provided, 2) the ability to communicate through a visible correctable TV display, and 3) the ability to transport the aid to virtually any environment. We found from teacher feedback that these three features would be key features for successful use of communication aids of any sort.

Finally, while the Auto-Com was the aid used in this study, we feel very strongly that many of the same results could have occurred with other comparable types of aids. The results of the program seem to be results of providing the students with an effective, consistent, dependable means of response, and an independent means of relating their thoughts and feelings.

SOME REMARKS ON ASSESSMENT

FACTORS INVOLVED IN AN ASSESSMENT - (Deberah Harris-Vanderheiden)

First of all, if anyone is waiting for pat answers, I don't think we're going to be able to give you any right now. Assessment is something that each and every one of us is concerned with, but there just hasn't been enough work done on developing assessment techniques for this type of severely handicapped child. For this reason most of you will be required to develop your own assessment batteries. These will most likely take the form of adaptation of existing materials and procedures in combination with informal assessment techniques. Before we get into discussing what some of these might look like, let us first take a look at what is involved in an overall assessment program.

What's involved in assessing a non-vocal child from a communication standpoint?

In an overall comprehensive assessment I would consider physical, educational, communication and language skills components.

Under physical skills, one should include response mode, posture/seating, hearing, vision and vocal skills. Assessment of the child's response mode(s) is of course very important since much or all of the rest of the assessment procedure depends upon it. Posture and proper seating are often overlooked but should be studied carefully since the child's physical skills may be seriously hampered by poor seating or greatly improved with improved seating and posturing. Hearing and vision should be checked to insure that the child's input media are optimum and, of course, the child's vocal skills should be closely tracked and worked on throughout any communication intervention program.

Jo Ann Schurman, from the University of Iowa, has put together a test relating specifically to assessing a child's physical skills for developing alternate communication programs. It goes through a basic assessment of pointing skills, visual acuity, visual tracking, perceptual skills and so on.

Under "educational skills," the question most asked by teachers working with the child are: Does he have basic readiness skills, what are his current math and reading comprehension skills? What can I expect from the child in these areas? In addition to these one would also want to look at his communication skills. How is he expressing himself now? How effective is this expression in obtaining appropriate or desired responses? How does he express himself at home, with his peers, with others in the classroom?

152

Finally, under "language skills" one will want to know what his expressive and receptive skills are and what cognitive milestones he has achieved thus far.

Who should conduct the assessment?

This concern goes back to the basic question of who is involved in and who is primarily responsible for providing an augmentative communication system for the child. Is it the speech clinician, the classroom teacher, the occupational therapist or the physical therapist? Actually, it doesn't fall into any one of these particular realms. It falls into ALL of them, and all of these people need to be involved in assessment of the child. Occupational therapists, physical therapists, speech clinicians, educators and, most importantly, the child's parents should always be involved in assessment procedures; they're the ones who have lived and grown with the child and they know the level of his present communication. They know what they can and cannot expect from him, and they can offer a lot of valuable information on what's happening in the home and what types of things you can expect them to carry out at home. You can also learn just how involved the parents are going to be in the programming and remediation process.

What kinds of practical questions are we to answer?

We have identified previously some of the areas that should be included in an assessment procedure. Before getting too far into the procedure, however, let's take a quick look at some of the practical questions that this procedure will have to speak to if it is to be truly useful.

As far as the teachers/clinicians are concerned, they will be looking for answers to questions like: what skills does he know now, how should I teach him, through what modality should I teach him (i.e., is he a visual learner, an auditory learner), what can I use as a communication modality for the child, what types of educational programs should I use with him, what skills (both educational and communicative) can I expect him to acquire in the immediate future and what should I be heading for on a long range basis?

Parents are going to have questions similar to: what does the child really know now, what can I expect of him, what can I work on at home that is realistic? Occupational and physical therapists will be concerned with questions such as: what response modes are currently available to the child and how effectively can he utilize these for communication? How can the child be interfaced to communication aids, what are his current physical skills, how can his posture and overall tone be improved for classroom functioning, is he in need of any adaptive or assistive equipment?

These questions from various persons who will be involved in the assessment process need to be incorporated into or answered from the assessment procedure. Where formal assessments do not exist, informal assessment measures will need to be developed.

What's available now?

Currently most assessment teams are relying on informal testing measures, as only a few standardized tests exist which are applicable to or modifiable for non-vocal severely motor involved children. Standardized assessments, as a general rule, are not applicable for the stated assessment needs as they have not been designed for this population, nor have children of this type been included in populations upon which these measures have been normed. In addition, a major drawback in use of standardized tests concerns their ability to provide answers to questions such as the above. Results from standardized measures usually yield global descriptions of a child's current level of functioning, and important answers to specific assessment concerns cannot be obtained from such measures. Standardized tests may, however, be useful for obtaining some types of general information if the child can physically take the test.

One of the most useful trends occurring in the educational field is the development of criterion reference testing and diagnostic teaching. In criterion reference testing, the assessor takes a skill area such as communication skills or language skills and breaks it down into the component skills or tasks that are involved in that particular skill area. The child is assessed in each and every component or pre-requisite task for this skill area. Imagine this as sort of a skill hierarchy. Assess each one of the tasks involved in mastering a skill and at the end of the assessment procedure you have a complete profile of the child's skill abilities and deficits. As a result, teachers, clinicians and parents will know specifically what they should be working on with the child and what he already knows.

There are a couple of criterion referenced tests that are now available and hopefully we'll be seeing more and more of these types of tests. One is the Key Math by American Guidance Service. Some parts of this test have to be physically adapted for the children, but it's set up in a criterion referenced manner. A non-vocal motor impaired child can be given this test if you take the sections that a child would normally answer vocally, write them out as multiple choice items, and set them up something like the Peabody Individual Achievement Tests with flip cards. Work on this has been done by the Trace Center at the University of Wisconsin-Madison. A second example of a criterion-referenced test is the Silent Reading Diagnostic Test by Hoyt & Barlow. This is an older test, but it specifically assesses silent reading skills in a criterion referenced manner.

Finally, direct observational assessment can be quite useful. Putting the child in an environment and observing how he actually behaves and interacts when performing certain skills can often be more valuable than the global information obtained from standardized tests.

ASSESSMENT AT OCCC - (Shirley McNaughton)

I'd like to make a few comments on how we handle assessment at the Ontario Crippled Children's Centre. We are well aware of the scarcity of assessment materials and the lack of objective techniques for testing non-vocal physically handicapped children. We really rely on the expertise and know-how of professionals in the various areas...occupational therapy, physical therapy, psychology and education. The child is seen by at least four people: the occupational therapist, speech therapist, psychologist, and a teacher. If equipment seems to be one of the assessment goals, we include a rehabilitation engineer as well. We usually see the child for two days. Sometimes, if we feel there is a need for a longer stay, we will have the child stay for a week. If the child is going to be with us for other reasons, we intersperse the assessment over a three-week period.

Our occupational therapist is the first person we like to have see the child, so physical assessment is the first thing we do. We want to have the child at his best functional level before anyone else even sees the child. Seating becomes one of the most important things, and we find dramatic changes after the therapist has had time to seat the child properly and get him in his most functional position for either hand, head or foot use.

Next, our speech pathologist and psychologist consult together with the child. They collect general history background information and the speech pathologist assesses the child's level of functioning speech, using the Reynell Receptive Language Test. She also tries to make a prognosis as to possibility for speech and ascertains the present means of communication. The psychologist assesses the present level of intellectual functioning. For some children she uses the Columbia Mental Maturity Test. Visual acuity is tested by the psychologist by presenting visual material to the child. This is often done through materials that are at the child's current communication level, (i.e., pictures, symbols, words) or through standardized testing if the child has the physical capabilities. When I see the child, I look at his play level if he is a pre-school child or do a reading assessment if he is at the academic level. I look at his school report, and then I talk with him. I base most of my recommendations on: how effectively I can communicate with this child, where things break down, whether the child gets upset because of breakdown, or whether it doesn't bother him at all.

If it is a pre-reading child, I may introduce him to symbols. I can tell a lot by the way he responds to these symbols. Some children start to use twelve symbols in a half-hour assessment. We look at a book together. We work with two symbols using a yes/no response...who is in the picture, how they feel, and what he thinks they are doing. I can tell if he is able to relate back instantly through another form of communication which has just been introduced to him.

Making recommendations at OCCC

To make program recommendations we gather information and together the team looks at the child's total physical and mental situation, and at the resources in the child's home community. Sometimes recommendations are made in the form of choices for the parents. Parental attitude is very important and it enters into any decision that would be made. One member of the team sits down with the parents and discusses possible directions for the child in order to determine which ones are realistic for the family. We select the team member that has the greatest involvement with the child. If it is an intellectual consideration that's primary, then the psychologist is chosen. The two things we look at primarily are: 1) the desire to communicate and 2) the child's developmental level. If we are considering symbols, we look at the child's ability to relate to pictures. We don't recommend symbols for every child who comes to the Centre. We take a very careful look at many factors: general history, present use of a communication device, how much support can be given to a child, willingness on the part of the people who are referring him to learn something new. We may recommend a language board. Sometimes we recommend that a child remain with the system he has because he has invested many, many years of learning to spell and is using a spelling board. If the child is satisfactorily relating to his environment, we recommend he continue to use his present system. If the child is already reading, it is a very strong possibility that we would pursue reading for him. We keep as open as we can, depending on the child's setting. We try to look at the child's total situation and to make decisions that we feel are best.

Conclusion

Assessment is an area that we're very interested in and for which we know we don't have all the answers. Our communication program is three years old and we're learning as we go. We're trying to collect information from each child who has been referred to us. The child's environment becomes very important in the kinds of recommendations we make.

INFORMAL ASSESSMENT TECHNIQUES - (Eugene T. McDonald)

We use standardized tests in our assessment, but we don't feel that we get all the information we need for the child from such instruments. One standardized test, The French Pictorial Test of Intelligence, has been especially useful. This test uses pictures and requires no verbal response from the child. He can indicate the picture he selects in response to a question by pointing or moving his head or eyes. The Haeusserman Test has also proved useful in evaluating the developmental level of pre-school children who are cerebral palsied. To assess language development we use The Zimmerman Pre-School Language Test, The Utah Language Scale and the Northwestern Syntax Screening Test.

In many cases we get more useful information from a task analysis approach than from standardized tests. We ask ourselves, "When we present the child with a task, what must he do to process the information we give him? What must he do to organize a response? And what must he do to respond?" We urge staff members to think through the answers to these questions and to consider what the anticipated response will be as well as what some alternative responses might be. This approach makes better observers of staff personnel.

A very crude task analysis might take this form: In order for a child to point to an appropriate picture when it is named, he has to be able to fix his vision on the picture, he has to be able to identify it, and he has to be able to make an association between the visual input and some information he has in his auditory store so he can make a movement with his eyes, or respond in some way. Suppose he can't perform this task. We might then show him some pictures to see if he can match them. This becomes a very different task. He now no longer has to make that association between the verbal or the auditory and the visual. If he can perform this we can rule out defective visual functioning as the reason for his not succeeding with the former task and proceed to analyze other parts of the process. In this way we attempt to break down the tasks that we present to the child and identify those parts of the task with which the child is encountering difficulty. We often get more information from procedures such as these than we do from a Stanford-Binet or a WISC (Weschler Intelligence Scale for Children).

Diagnostic teaching also furthers assessment. After identifying some of his problem areas we try to teach a child a specific skill. We develop some strategies which focus on developing his strengths. If the child succeeds with one task we may present additional tasks in the same modality or we shift to another modality or use other types of tasks. As a standard procedure we follow the philosophy that even though there has been considerable psychological evaluation done on the child before he comes to us and during his pre-admission visit, judgment on potential for skill acquisition is postponed until we find out how the child responds to teaching of skill tasks.

We see assessment as a continuing thing. We think that it is criminal when children are taken to centers where they are seen by psychologists for an hour and then some number such as an I.Q. is assigned the child to follow him around from clinic to clinic, from school to school, for many years of his life. We think that is makes much more sense with these multiply handicapped children to get them involved in a program where you can work with diagnostic procedures over a period of time, and adjust them until you find a method by which the child can process information and learn.

Until we have very clear evidence from a number of approaches that the child is unable to process information at a level where he can begin communicating, his failure to do so is our fault. We may have not structured the learning tasks in such a way that the child can succeed.

CONCLUDING REMARKS

CONCLUDING REMARKS - (Gregg C. Vanderheiden)

We have tried to present an overview of the topics and concerns involved in providing supplementary modes of communication to individuals whose speech and/or writing is severely impaired. Due to time restrictions, we have concentrated our discussions on those aspects which are not well documented elsewhere. As a result, supplementary reading will be necessary to get a complete view of the area. One very good starting point for such explorations would be "Communication Assessment and Intervention Strategies" edited by Lyle Lloyd and published by University Park Press, Baltimore, MD.

A few points have been brought up during the workshop which I would like to reemphasize in closing. One is the need for cooperative interdisciplinary effort. When dealing with a multihandicapped child, there are many aspects which need to be considered in developing a fully functional mode of communication and interaction. The expertise of all the professions of occupational therapy, physical therapy, speech, language and special education are needed. Of special importance is the cooperation and active participation of the parents. A large portion of the child's communication and social life is in the home and the tremendous potential of the parents as a resource to the communication development program for this child should be fully utilized.

The second point which should be emphasized is that the communication systems for these children should be dynamic. As the children grow and develop, their communication needs will change and expand. At the same time their skills may also be improving, allowing them to take advantage of more efficient or more flexible communication approaches. To meet these growing needs, their communication systems will need to be continually updated and revised to take advantage of any new capabilities either in physical or language skill areas. Because of the importance of effective and efficient communication to development, much attention should be paid to this throughout the child's developmental years.

Finally, speech training and non-vocal communication programs should be carried on in parallel. Just as providing a non-vocal channel should not be put off to work exclusively on speech, speech training should not be stopped when a non-vocal approach is adopted. If the child is unable to communicate through speech, another approach (non-vocal) which the child can use to communicate immediately should be developed. Then, with the child able to communicate and interact, more efficient communication techniques, including speech, can and should be worked on. For many children, speech may never be physically possible. But new training techniques and the use of bio-feedback are increasing the chances of developing at least partially functional speech in some of these children.

160

WHERE DO WE GO FROM HERE?

In these presentations, we have talked quite a bit about specific techniques and aids and have talked about some of the considerations that go into a communication development program. There is, however, much more involved in setting up such a program for a non-vocal multiply handicapped child than we have been able to cover here. With this workshop, we have tried to take a first step toward providing practical information to the teacher/clinician/parent working with the handicapped child. Until more comprehensive information is available, however, it will be necessary to rely very heavily upon one's own expertise and creativity. In these efforts, interaction with other clinicians, teachers and researchers will also be helpful. A cooperative inter-national newsletter is being fostered by the Trace Center to facilitate such interaction. But growth in this field will be largely dependent upon the documentation efforts put forth by teachers and clinicians working in successful communication development programs.

The time is right, the need is there, and the resources are be-coming available. If efforts can be coordinated, I think we will be seeing trememdous advances in this area during the next few years.

APPENDICES

SURVEY OF SYMBOL-USING CHILDREN

JUNE 1974

This preliminary survey of Ontario Crippled Children Symbol Communication Programme users was conducted for the purpose of obtaining information re the present extent and effect of symbol communication for non-speaking physically-handicapped children.

I. SURVEY RESPONSE

Total number of settings invited to
            participate.........................60
Total number of settings responding........40
Percentage of responding settings to total
            number of settings invited..........66%
Total number of symbol-using children
            reported............................150

II. TOTAL NUMBER OF SYMBOL-USING CHILDREN REPORTED

Age levels of symbol-using children:

```
            0-5 yrs........14........9.3%
            6-12 yrs.......83.......55.33%
            Teen...........40.......26.66%
            20 yrs & over..12........8.00%
            not stated......1........ .66%
            Total         150       99.98%
```

III. LENGTH OF TIME ON SYMBOLS: of symbol-using
                                  children
```
      (i)   6 mos. & under............59...39.33%
      (ii)  over 6 mos., under 1 yr...54...36.  %
      (iii) 1 yr. to 1 yr. 11 mos.....30...20.  %
      (iv)  2 yrs. & over............. 6... 4.  %
      (v)   not stated................ 1... .66%

            Total                     150   99.99%
```

IV. <u>DEGREE OF DISABILITY</u>: of symbol-using children

      (i)   mild....................... 5.... 3.33%
     (ii) moderate...................40...26.66%
   (iii) severe.....................54....36. %
    (iv) needs electronic equipment.47....31.33%
     (v) using electronic equipment. 3.... 2. %
    (vi) not stated................. 1.... .66%

            Total   150   99.98%

V. <u>VOCABULARY LEVEL</u>: of symbol-using children

      (i)   30 symbols & under........23....15.33%
     (ii) 31-99 symbols.............38....25.33%
   (iii) 100-199 "   ....39....26. %
    (iv) 200-399 "   ....19....12.66%
     (v) 400-& over   ....30....20. %
    (vi) not stated   .... 1.... .66%

            Total   150   99.98%

VI. <u>LEARNING CAPABILITY</u>: of Symbol-using children
                                 as described by teacher

      (i) Trainable retarded-drill...36....24. %
     (ii) Trainable retarded -
           learns quickly..........29....19.33%
   (iii) slow learner...............26....17.33%
    (iv) average....................16....10.66%
     (v) learns quickly.............42....28. %
    (vi) not stated................. 1.... .66%

            Total   150   99.98%

VII. <u>PROGRAMME PLACEMENT OF SYMBOL USING CHILDREN</u>

      (i) retarded...................58....38.66%
     (ii) opportunity................ 6.... 4. %
   (iii) academic...................80....53.33%
    (iv) other...................... 3.... 2. %
     (v) no programme............... 3.... 2. %

            Total   150   99.99%

VIII. <u>MAXIMUM UTTERANCE LENGTH</u>: of symbol-using
children

   (i) 1 symbol......................26....17.33%
  (ii) 2 " ....24....16. %
 (iii) 3 " ....22....14.66%
  (iv) 4 " & over.................66....44. %
   (v) not stated.................12.... 8. %

       Total   150   99.99%

IX. <u>LEVEL OF SYMBOL OUTPUT</u>: of symbol-using children

   (i) 1 single symbol.............25....16.66%
  (ii) 2 or 3 symbols
      (not sentence form).......46....30.66%
 (iii) single sentence.............23....15.33%
  (iv) full syntax................. 3.... 2. %
   (v) random order, over 3 symbols ..... .66%
  (vi) type not stated (*)........52....34.66%

       Total   150   99.97%

X. <u>PARENTAL ATTITUDE</u>

   (i) opposed to symbols......... 1.... .66%
  (ii) no support.................20....13.33%
 (iii) some support...............65....43.33%
  (iv) strong support.............29....19.33%
   (v) not applicable.............33....22. %
  (vi) not stated................. 2.... 1.33%

       Total   150   99.98%

XI. <u>TEACHERS RATING OF SYMBOL-USING CHILDREN'S
COMMUNICATION ABILITY</u>

   (i) excellent...................20....13.33%
  (ii) good........................42....28. %
 (iii) fair........................60....40. %
  (iv) poor........................27....18. %
   (v) not stated................. 1.... .66%

       Total   150   99.99%

(*) This question had a low response due to the inad-
vertant omission of the symbol level summary sheet
which should have accompanied the questionnaire.

164

XII. TEACHERS RATINGS OF VOCALIZATION CHANGE IN
SYMBOL-USING CHILDREN

       (i) less vocalization............ 2.... 1.33%
      (ii) no change....................94....62.66%
    (iii) some improvement.............36....24. %
     (iv) marked improvement.......... 9.... 6. %
      (v) not stated.................. 9.... 6. %

                               —   —

      Total   150   99.99%

XIII. USE OF THE ALPHABET BY SYMBOL-USING CHILDREN

              Yes......................65....43.33%
              No.......................82....54.66%
              Not stated.............. 3.... 2. %

                            —   —

      Total   150   99.99%

XIV. ARE SYMBOLS USED BY THE CHILD AS A SUBSTITUTE OR
COMPLIMENT TO ANOTHER MODE OF COMMUNICATION?

       (i) substitute...................117....78. %
       (i) compliment.................. 31....20.66%
           not stated................. 2.... 1.33%

                            —   —

      Total   150   99.99%

XV. CHILDREN WITH WHOM SYMBOLS WERE ASSESSED AS INEFFECTIVE

    a) Total number of children - 18

    b) Age distribution of children for whom symbols were ineffective

Under 5..................	5	....27.77%
6-12 years..............	2	....11.11%
Teen....................	-	....-
20 & Over..............	1	5.55%
Not stated.............	10	....55.55%
Total	18	99.98%

    c) Teacher evaluation of cause of failure

CHILD NO.

	1	2	3	4	5	6	7	8	9	10	11	12	13	14	15	16	17	18
i) Auditory visual problems									X									
ii) Retardation	X	X	X					X	X									
iii) Degree of involvement										X						X		
iv) Learning problems	X	X	X				X				X						X	
v) Behavior/emotional				X													X	X
vi) Too young	X	X	X	X														
vii) Not stated					X	X						X	X	X	X			

DISCUSSION OF FINDINGS

From the 66% response of the questionnaire, information is given for 150 children. Of this number, 55% are between ages 6 and 12; 27% are in their teens. The use of symbols with the kindergarten and prekindergarten child and with adults is minimal and remains an important area for future exploration.

The population of reported symbol users is still a very new one with 75% of the children having spent less than 1 year with symbols. Few mildly disabled children are receiving instruction. At the present time, 27% are moderately involved children; 36% are described as severely involved but able to indicate symbols without using an electronic display. Thirty-one per cent of the total population require electronic equipment; this points out the need for attention continuing to be directed toward setting up the means of production of communication technical aids and for further research into interface alternatives.

Information regarding advanced symbol usage remains to be discovered. At the present time, the majority of children,67%,are using under 200 symbols with the maximum utterance length reported as 3 symbols or more for 59% of the children.

It may prove helpful to summarize the remainder of the results by giving a general description of the symbol-using population. Seventy-eight per cent of the children use symbols as a substitute for speech rather than as a compliment to speech. In over half the cases (63%) no change is apparent in their vocalization, but improvement has been noticed for 30% of the children. (It is reassuring to note that a decrease in vocalization was reported for only 2 children.) The teachers' ratings of children's communication ability follows a normal distribution, with most of the children (68%) being rated as good or fair, and small numbers rated as excellent or poor. Parents generally support the programme. Only 13% give no support and only 1 parent is reported as opposing the use of symbols. Regarding academic placement, the larger number of children are reported in either settings for retarded (39%) or in academic programs (53%). It is particularly interesting to note that within the population of symbol-using children located in institutions for retarded, (43% of total symbol-using population), 44% of these children are reported by their instructors as learning symbols quickly - a characteristic not usually ascribed to the "retarded" child! With regard to use of the alphabet, a sufficient number of symbol-using children are reported as using the alphabet (43%) to indicate that instructors are finding ways of continuing reading instruction and/or utilizing the alphabet to refine communication. This is an interesting area for further investigation and development.

Little information is available regarding children with whom symbols have been ineffective. Of the 18 children reported as failing to learn the symbols, reasons were not stated for 6 of the children. When reasons were stated, several factors usually were given as contributing to the failure, among them - retardation, learning-problems, age (see Item 14). More detailed information should be sought regarding reasons for failure in the future.

Although this first survey is limited in the amount of information it has been able to collect and organize, it has been valuable in defining the extent of symbol usage, in providing preliminary information regarding the effect of symbol usage, and in indicating areas for further development and exploration. A two-year Formative Evaluation funded by the Ontario Ministry of Education and undertaken by the O.C.C.C. Symbol Communication Programme, September 1974 to August 1976, will continue studying symbol communication in many settings. One of its objectives will be the production of a Hand-book for teachers, parents and administrators. Through the collective experience of many instructors, it is hoped that a body of knowledge re Symbol Communication can be made available to all potential symbol users.

Shirley McNaughton, Director
Ontario Crippled Children's Centre.
Symbol Communication Research Project

RESPONSE TO

COMMON MISCONCEPTIONS REGARDING

BLISSYMBOLICS

AS A COMMUNICATION MEDIUM FOR

NON-SPEAKING PHYSICALLY-HANDICAPPED CHILDREN

BY: SHIRLEY McNAUGHTON, DIRECTOR
      SYMBOL COMMUNICATION PROGRAMME
      ONTARIO CRIPPLED CHILDREN'S CENTRE

STATEMENT ONE:

"Why not teach him to read instead?" If a child is
bright enough to learn symbols, it would be better to
devote attention to teaching him words which everyone
else uses and thus spare the child the time and
effort involved in learning two different systems.

RESPONSE ONE:

This argument is based on the following premises:

1. words and symbols are organized in the same way;
2. words and symbols require the same learning
    abilities;
3. communication facility utilizing each system can
    be acquired with an equal amount of effort and
    time;
4. words and symbols fulfill the same function.

However:

1. Written words are composed of visual elements
    (letters and groups of letters) which are
    related to sound. Blissymbols are composed of
    visual elements which are related to meaning --
    sometimes directly through pictorial representa-
    tion; sometimes indirectly through representing
    an idea related to the meaning; sometimes
    arbitrarily.

2. When the young child first learns words, he must remember an abstract visual configuration; any clues relating this configuration to other parts of the system are based on sound-shape relation-ships. When the young child first learns Blissymbols he must remember a pictorial represen-tation which refers by its outline directly to the object it portrays.

3. Communication facility utilizing the word system is dependent upon skill in spelling - for which training and practice is required. Facility utilizing the Blissymbol system is dependent upon the ability to select the meaning elements (essen-tial characteristics) required to transmit meaning - for which the abilities to classify and describe are required.

4. Both systems do indeed share the common function of providing a vehicle for communication; however, the degree of communication comprehensiveness of each system which can be acquired by the young child and the additional functions served by each system are different and should be recognized.

   a. Words prepare the child for reading and typing (the physically-handicapped child's potential written output medium). Words also provide the child with a communication medium which can gradually expand as he masters a growing vocabulary.

   b. Blissymbols equip the child with a complete communication system (accessible to the bright child within a four to fifteen month period). Blissymbols also provide the child with a medium which facilitates creative thinking, inductive processing and concept clarification. Utilization of the medium involves a conceptual framework which gives the child another perspective in viewing and relating to his world. Blissymbols provide experience in the processing of visual information and thus contribute to learning to read. Incidental experience with words is provided through the child's constant access to the words which appear under each symbol on his display.

In Summary:

Words provide early limited communication which gradually expands; they prepare for reading and typing. Blissymbols provide earlier comprehensive communication and contribute to creativity and cognitive development; they prepare for reading through experience with the process but not directly with the content of the written English system.

- - - - - - - - - - - - - - - - -

STATEMENT TWO:

"Words can do as much as symbols can do." If a child has 100 spaces which can be clearly indicated by him, he will be able to communicate as fully with 100 words in the spaces as he would do with 100 symbols occupying the spaces.

RESPONSE TWO:

This statement fails to recognize the communication potential arising from the structure of the Blissymbol System. Each symbol, whether it be a simple or compound symbol, represents a concept which can encompass a range of meanings and be translated by many words. e.g. The symbol for "building" can be interpreted as house, home, structure, hotel, garage, shack, palace, office, tent, etc., through utilizing information from the situational context or by responding to additional symbol clues.

Secondly, each symbol element can be combined and recombined with other elements to form new concepts.

One hundred symbols can lead to an infinite number of words - as many as the child's creative ability will allow. Only through the ability to spell could the word system provide the same communication potential. It can be argued that a broad meaning can also be taken from individual words and that symbols are not necessary. This can certainly be done by those skilled in relating with the children but it involves mis-using a system which is based upon precision and accuracy of word meaning. One feels that the child is using a rudimentary form of the word system (e.g. pidgin English); whereas with symbols, the child is creatively using a device which is an integral part of the system. The child is indicating a mastery of the symbol system which gains him recognition rather than utilizing an inferior form of the word system which tends to minimize his capabilities as perceived by others.

- - - - - - - - - - - - - - - -

STATEMENT THREE:

"Symbols emphasize that the child is different and present a negative image to others."

RESPONSE THREE:

Our experience has been just the opposite. When open-minded newcomers meet symbol-using children for the first time, they are intrigued by the uniqueness of the children's communication mode. They are impressed with the children's ability to relate with others and to communicate unanticipated information. As they become aware of the children's ability to create new symbols and the manner in which the symbol output is integrated with gesture, early alphabet skills and vocalization, most persons become highly motivated to interact with the children and to learn enough about the symbols to communicate at a level which utilizes the many strategies inherent in the structure of the system.

- - - - - - - - - - - - - - - -

STATEMENT FOUR:

"Symbols restrict the number of persons with whom the children can communicate, for one must know the symbol system before one can understand the children's output."

RESPONSE FOUR:

Not true! One does not have to learn the symbol system in order to communicate with a symbol-using child. A WORD APPEARS UNDER EVERY SYMBOL on the child's display. Those persons who do not have the time or the desire to learn the symbols can communicate at the word level with every symbol-using child. Basic communication is possible with everyone.

STATEMENT FIVE:

"Blissymbols are best suited to serve as a communication medium for the mentally retarded child. The bright child should learn words." OR CONVERSELY "Blissymbols are too difficult for the mentally retarded child; only the child with average or above average intellectual ability should be introduced to the symbols."

RESPONSE FIVE:

There is need for exploration of symbol use by children at differing intellectual levels. The child's intellectual ability will determine the use he makes of the symbols. The child with limited mental ability will require a teaching approach suited to his needs and will limit his communication to basic needs and immediate situations. The brighter child can become involved with the organization and strategies of the system and can become proficient at communicating at various levels, dependent upon the symbol expertise of the person with whom he is communicating. Inherent in the Blissymbol system is a complex, comprehensive, creative communication potential, (the details of which are outlined in C.K. Bliss' text Semantography - Blissymbolics, Semantography-Blissymbolics Publications) which can serve the symbol-user into adulthood, should he wish to continue an involvement with the system!

- - - - - - - - - - - - - - - - -

STATEMENT SIX:

"Blissymbols are only useful as a bridge to reading."

RESPONSE SIX:

Blissymbols do provide an excellent preparation for learning to read (see response number 1). They are, however, components of an independent communication medium and deserve recognition in this capacity. The symbol system, Blissymbolics, contains an organization and structure which makes it a valuable communication medium with potential application to a wide range of children and adults with communication difficulties.

FOR MORE INFORMATION

ON THE BLISS SYMBOLS

The following are available:

Blissymbols Teaching Guideline: Dictionary

30 symbol Introductory Set
100 symbol Display
200 symbol Display
400 symbol Display

MR. SYMBOL MAN

-50-minute film on Charles Bliss and Blissymbols

SYMBOL BOY

-short instructional cartoon film

Semantography (Blissymbolics) by Charles K. Bliss

Reports and Papers on the OCCC Symbol Research Program

For information, write:

      Blissymbolics Communication Foundation
      862 Eglinton Avenue E
      Eglinton
      Toronto, Ontario, Canada M4G 2L1

1974

MASTERCHART OF COMMUNICATION AIDS

Compiled by:

Craig S. Holt

Gregg C. Vanderheiden

Published by the Trace Research and Development Center For the Severely Communicatively Handicapped, 922 ERB, 1500 Johnson Drive, University of Wisconsin-Madison, Wisconsin 53706. Preparation of this document was supported in part by the Bureau for the Education of the Handicapped (BEH) Grant #OEG-0-7461, and the National Science Foundation, Grant #EC-40316.

CONTENTS

ABBREVIATIONS AND DEFINITIONS FOR
THE MASTER CHART OF COMMUNICATION AIDS

TYPE OF IMPLEMENTATION

FUNDAMENTAL
Fundamental aids are aids which have no electronic or moving parts. (Most of the aids in this
category can be easily fabricated in the classroom
or by a handyman with simple tools.) With these
aids a second person is required to determine which
character the user is trying to indicate, to write
down or remember each character as it is chosen,
and finally to assemble the complete message.

SIMPLE ELECTRONIC AND MECHANICAL AIDS
Aids in this category are mechanical and/or
electronic devices which must be used with the
help of a second person. The user chooses characters without assistance, but a second person is
required to record the chosen characters and
assemble the message.

NON-PORTABLE INDEPENDENT AIDS
An "Independent Aid" allows the user to produce entire messages in an assembled form without
assistance. A second person need only read or
listen to the message. Most independent aids
either produce a printed copy of a message or are
able to store and display (or play back) a completed message. An aid is classified as non-
portable if it requires an external power source
for operation, or weighs more than 20 lbs.

FULLY PORTABLE INDEPENDENT AIDS
A "Fully Portable Independent Aid" is an
"Independent Aid" which requires no external
power source for operation and weighs less than
20 lbs. In addition to providing an independent
means of writing, a "Fully Portable Independent
Aid" can also serve as a mobile "voice" to fulfill
communication needs in everyday living situations.

THREE BASIC APPROACHES

SCANNING

In a scanning device, selections are offered to the user by a display, and the user selects characters[1] by responding to the display. Depending on the device, the user may respond by simply signaling when he sees the right choice presented, or by actively directing an indicator (e.g. light or arrow) towards the desired choice.

Rectangular Scanning: A row-column scan uses a rectangular matrix of character squares. The scan begins with an indicator (light) moving vertically on the display panel, indicating successive character rows. When the row containing the desired character is reached, a signal from the user causes the indicator to scan horizontally across the chosen row. Another signal then stops the scan when it reaches the desired character within the row. If the scheme calls for choosing a column first, then choosing a character within the column, it is called a column-row scan.

Directed Scanning: In a directed scan, the user has control over the direction of motion of the scanning indicator. Instead of waiting for it to reach a character by some prescribed pattern, the user can cause the indicator to proceed in the direction which will bring it to the next character in the fewest number of steps. This type of scanning is therefore faster than a normal row-column scan, but it requires the user to operate more input switches.[2]

The position of the scanning indicator may be displayed by small lights within each square, by back-lighting the entire square, or by "cursor" lights along the edges indicating the row and column.

ENCODING

Any technique or aid in which the desired character is indicated by a pattern or code of input signals. The character codes may be memorized or referred to on a chart.

Most codes involve from one to ten input switches. The switch(es) may be actuated sequentially, simultaneously, or in a specific time pattern.

---

[1]In these definitions "character" is a general term, encompassing any kind of output selection: letters, numbers, symbols, pictures, words, phrases, or even sentences.

[2]"Input switches" include any of the types of input interfaces in the Glossary of Input Interfaces.

178

DIRECT SELECTION
Any technique (or aid) in which the desired output is directly indicated by the user. In direct selection aids there is a key or sensor for each possible output selection. (Note: Do not confuse the term "Direct Selection" with "Directed Scanning", defined above.)

COMBINATION TECHNIQUES
It is possible for an aid to use a combination of the above selection techniques. For example, a scanning scheme could be used to select numbers which in turn form codes for words. The resulting device would be a scanning-encoding hybrid.

LEVELS

The term "levels" is used in the descriptive columns, and may require some clarification.

In some devices a given selection can produce several different characters at the output, depending on which state or "level" the device is in. The typewriter, for instance, is a two level device. A single typewriter key can produce a 3 or a #, depending on the state of the "shift". Notice that the total number of characters available to the typist is the number of selections on the keyboard, multiplied by the number of levels.

In most of these aids, once a level is chosen, the device stays in that level until switched to some other level. (In the typewriter, changing to "upper case level" would mean striking the "hold shift" key. The typewriter would then remain in the "upper level" until the shift was released.)

ABBREVIATIONS

PORTABILITY

N - Stationary: (Non-portable) systems which are not
    designed to be moved regularly, except perhaps on
    a wheeled cart.

M - Movable: Not meant to be moved regularly, but can
    be transported without major difficulty. No one
    piece of equipment weighing more than 30 lbs.

S - Semi Portable: Under 25 lbs and needs external
    power (i.e., from wall outlet).

P - Fully Portable: Under 25 lbs and needs no external
    power (i.e., need not be plugged into wall except
    for recharging batteries).

POWER

BAT - Battery operated
AC - Operates on standard U.S. wall plug (approximately
      117 volts a.c.)

ARROWS

- A back arrow means "see the General Description
  column" to the left.
- A forward arrow means "see the Features-Comments
  column" to the right.

NAME OF AID
AND MANUFACTURER
(OR DEVELOPER, IF THERE IS NO MANUFACTURER)

NAME OF AID - Capital letters denote the name used by the manufacturer or developer of the aid. The non-capitalized titles are purely descriptive.

GENERAL DESCRIPTION

TIME ADJUSTMENTS - Virtually all time-dependent aids (aids which require the user to do something within a certain time limit, to activate something for a certain time, or which have any kind of time delay action) have time adjustment controls to accommodate users with different levels of proficiency and body control. Generally these controls are not designed to be adjusted by a disabled person. (Exceptions are noted.)

"SWITCHES" - Refers to any of the types of input interfaces in the Glossary of Input Interfaces.

SYMBOL SELECTION PROCESS
TYPE OF INPUT INTERFACE - See the Glossary of Input Interfaces.

NUMBER OF ACTIONS REQUIRED PER SELECTION - This is the maximum number of actions required to designate a character. In some devices certain selections require more actions than others. For instance, in Morse code, the maximum number of actions required to select a letter is 5, but the more common letters have shorter codes, so the average number of actions per selection is much smaller.
The actions required to change to a different level are not counted here, since level changing is not usually required as part of every character selection.

CHANGEABLE CHARACTER SET
Any aid which controls an IBM Selectric Typewriter with the "golf ball" printing head can print different sets of characters by using different type balls. However, such aids were not considered to have a changeable character set unless the manufacturer offered special printing heads (not just different type styles) for use with the aid, and unless the selection display on the aid could be easily changed by the user to accommodate the different character sets.

OUTPUT DEVICES

If no output device is checked, a human receiver is always required. (Simple aids)

TELETYPE An aid which will operate a teletype has the capability of operating any computer attached to the teletype. Thus the teletype provides access to all computer capabilities, including output forms such as line printers, cathode ray tubes, and chart recorders. Some teletypes also have a paper tape punch attached, which allows messages to be stored on tape and re-typed at any time. (The on-off controls on the paper tape punch, however, are not designed for use by handicapped persons.)

Correctability of output devices:
TV and alphanumeric readouts are generally completely correctable.
Teletypes and strip printers are not correctable.
Typewriters are not correctable, except for special cases:
1) If the aid provides ribbon control, and a black and white correcting ribbon is used, correctability is obtained on the current line.
2) The IBM Correcting "Selectric" Typewriter also provides correctability on the current line of type for any aid that can operate the "correct" key.
(These corrections can only be made on the current line since there is no provision for rolling the platen back to a previous line.)

ENVIRONMENTAL CONTROL

Environmental control capability means that by operating the aid, the user can control one or more power sockets and thus switch other electric devices (lights, radios, electric locks, etc.) off and on.

PORTABILITY (See "Abbreviations")

Independent aids are rated including their most portable output form. Thus an aid which requires a standard electric typewriter for output is rated movable, because the entire system weighs more than 25 lbs, no matter how portable the rest of the aid is. If, however, the aid can also be operated with a lighweight alphanumeric readout, then it would be rated fully portable or semi-portable.

PRICE

Prices are approximate and subject to change. They generally do not include shipping costs.

182

SPECIAL NOTES REFERENCED IN MASTERCHART

*Not including electric typewriter and solenoid control for
typewriter. Typical specifications:

```
    Typewriter
        size:   9"x20"x16"
        weight: 30 lbs
        price:  Used IBM Selectric (not the new
                correctable models) $150-$300
                (for handicapped only)
                New correctable Selectric $600

    Solenoid unit (attaches over typewriter keys)
        price:  about $1000
```

*1 Duplicate feedback displays can be generated from the
    main unit.

*2 Free construction plans available from person or
    organization listed in the "NAME OF AID" column.

*3 Slide projector.

*4 A strip printer is being developed as an option,
    which would make this a Portable INDEPENDENT aid,
    instead of a Simple ELECTRO-MECHANICAL aid.

*5 Semi-portable without typewriter.

*6 The user can activate a buzz or tone.

*7 Remote light unit: a buzzer and eight lights with
    associated messages.

*8 The user can ring a bell.

*9 Recording module

*10 Punched-tape cassettes

*11 Punctiform typewriter

*12 Printer

*13 Control module only. Input and output devices not included.

*14 Tape recorder control

*15 Designed for 220 V but will operate on 117 V with a transformer.

*16 Not including typewriter.

*17 Not including battery pack.

*18 Votrax voice synthesizer (Federal Screw Works)

*19 PLATO student terminal

MASTERCHART OF COMMUNICATION AIDS

Every effort has been made to present this information as clearly and accurately as possible. However, the Trace Center welcomes any corrections of inaccurate, incomplete, or outdated information.

These descriptions are necessarily brief and we, therefore, recommend that interested persons send for information from the developers or manufacturers.

		NAME OF AID & MANUFACTURER (OR DEVELOPER IF THERE IS NO MANUFACTURER)	GENERAL DESCRIPTION	SYMBOL SELECTION PROCESS			
				TYPE OF INPUT INTERFACE (SEE "KEY")	NUMBER OF ACTIONS REQUIRED PER SELECTION (MAXIMUM)	CHANGEABLE CHARACTER SET	FEEDBACK DISPLAY (INDICATES THE LAST SELECTED CHARACTER)
VERY SIMPLE AIDS	SCANNING	(communication card system) Kathleen Birkel Huron Road Hospital	A set of plastic-coated cards asking common questions about a hospital patient's condition. The patient must signal his answer (yes or no) to the person holding the cards.	←	1		●
	ENCODING	ETRAN Cerebral Palsy Communication Group	Eye position encoding. Sender looks at character groups on a standing, clear plastic panel. Receiver watches the sender's eyes. 36 characters (alphabet, numbers, and period), in 8 groups.	←	2		
	DIRECT SELECTION	Conversation Board (F. Hall Roe board) Ghora Khan Grotto	A conventional masonite letterboard. The user points at the letters and/or words in sequence.	←	1		
SIMPLE ELECTRONIC AIDS	SCANNING	(radial pointer) Ontario Crippled Children's Center	User selects from 100 Bliss symbols with an electronically controlled radial pointer (240° arc). Symbols are in 2 rows of 50.	2 N	1		●
		(rotating arrow scanner) Miller & Carpenter Crotched Mountain Foundation	Motor driven rotating arrow scanner. Clockwise only. 2 concentric levels (rings). A switch operates the level indicator light.	2 Bf	2	●	●
		Roto-Com Cerebral Palsy Communication Group	Motor driven rotating arrow scanner. Arrow rotates one direction (clockwise mode) or both directions (alternating mode).	] Bh,C H,M	1 OR 2	●	●
		Speakeasy Veteran's Administration	Motor driven rotating arrow scanner. Both directions (alternating). 3 concentric color coded levels (rings).	] A,Ke	2	●	●

| OUTPUT DEVICES | | | | | | ENVIRONMENTAL CONTROL (NUMBER OF SOCKETS CONTROLLED) | PORTABILITY (SEE "KEY") | SIZE (INCHES) | WEIGHT (LBS.) | POWER REQUIREMENTS | PRICE (APPROX.) | FEATURES--COMMENTS |
DYNAMIC ALPHANUMERIC CHARACTER DISPLAY	TELEVISION	STRIP PRINTER (TICKER TAPE)	TELETYPE	TYPEWRITER	OTHER							
							P			NONE		7 languages
							P	$24 \times 20\frac{1}{2} \times 10$	$4\frac{1}{2}$	NONE	NOT COMM. AVAIL.*2	A unique feature of ETRAN is the frequent eye contact experienced between the sender and receiver.
							P	$19 \times 14 \times \frac{1}{8}$	14	NONE		Words are organized alphabetically by function. Board is made to hang on the push handles of a wheelchair.
											NOT COMM. AVAIL.	Display is color coded by word function.
											NOT COMM. AVAIL.	
							P	$14\frac{1}{2} \times 7\frac{3}{4} \times 13\frac{1}{2}$	12	BAT	UNDER DEVELOPMENT	
							M	$48 \times 60 \times 20$			NOT COMM. AVAIL.*2	The level is indicated by selecting a color dot. The outer level (ring) is letters and symbols, and the two inner rings are "blackboard paint", (changeable).

SIMPLE ELECTRONIC AIDS

SCANNING (CONT.)

NAME OF AID & MANUFACTURER (OR DEVELOPER IF THERE IS NO MANUFACTURER)	GENERAL DESCRIPTION	TYPE OF INPUT INTERFACE (SEE "KEY")	NUMBER OF ACTIONS REQUIRED PER SELECTION (MAXIMUM)	CHANGEABLE CHARACTER SET	FEEDBACK DISPLAY (INDICATES THE LAST SELECTED CHARACTER)
Cyber-Go-Round Cybernetics Research Institute	Control of carrousel slide projector. Slides can be accessed sequentially in either direction.	3 A			●
Parallel Wheel Spelling Machine National Institute for Rehabilitation Engineering	Control of mechanical wheel display (similar to the mileage indicator of a car). 8-12 wheels with alphanumeric characters and words.	1	1		
(roller scanner) Rancho Los Amigos Hospital	Motor driven roller (drum) with messages printed on it.	1 N		●	●
VAPC communicator Veteran's Administration	Linear illuminated scan of ten changeable messages. In addition to the message, each message square contains the word "yes" or "no" (alternating).	1		●	●
(scanner) model "144" Ontario Crippled Children's Center	Illuminated rectangular scan of 144 Bliss symbols. 2 switches for "down" and "across".	2	2		●
SCRP "100 + 100" MK II Ontario Crippled Children's Center	Directed scan of 2 (10 x 10) matrices of lights and associated Bliss Symbols (200 symbols total).	2 Bh,N 4 E	3		●
Alphabet Message Scanner Prentke-Romich Co.	Column-row scan of 6 x 7 light array.	1 B,L, Kt	2	●	●
MC-2 Matrix Communicator DUFCO	Backlit directed scan of a 10 x 10 matrix. Changeable symbol overlays.	4 E,A	2	●	●
Viewcom Fairchild Hiller Corporation	Directed scan of illuminated squares (6 x 6).	2 C,E,M 4 Ah,C, E,Kv, M		●	● *1
ENCODING CP Light/Sound Communicator Rancho Los Amigos Hospital	When a lever is actuated, the device produces a clear (adjustable pitch) tone and/or flashes a small light. A code can be devised for communication.	1 Bh			
Myocom Robert G. Combs U. of Missouri	Myoelectrically controlled beeper. Two tones can be generated, corresponding to strong and weak muscle contractions.	1 Y	1		

DYNAMIC ALPHANUMERIC CHARACTER DISPLAY	TELEVISION	STRIP PRINTER (TICKER TAPE)	TELETYPE	TYPEWRITER	OTHER	ENVIRONMENTAL CONTROL (NUMBER OF SOCKETS CONTROLLED)	PORTABILITY (SEE "KEY")	SIZE (INCHES)	WEIGHT (LBS.)	POWER REQUIREMENTS	PRICE (APPROX.)	FEATURES--COMMENTS
					*3		M			AC		Option - a prerecorded message can accompany each slide.
						←						
						←					NOT COMM. AVAIL.	
							S				NOT COMM. AVAIL.	
											NOT COMM. AVAIL.	Display color coded by word function.
							P	23x12x1		BAT	$500 →	Price includes one input interface. Additional interfaces $50 each.
	*4				*6			5x8x6	5	BAT or AC	$300	Built in battery recharger. Options: special package configurations, environmental control interface.
							P	13x17x2 (OR 13x 31x2 WITH INPUT SWITCHES)	$7\frac{3}{4}$	BAT or AC	$855 WITHOUT INPUT SWITCHES →	Input switches: Hand or elbow buttons --$120. Joy-stick--$95. Options: Audible alarm--$25. Bliss symbol and alphanumeric overlays--$20 ea
					*6		P	$19\frac{7}{8}$x$6\frac{3}{4}$ x$14\frac{3}{4}$	16	BAT or AC	$250	Display squares can be rearranged individually. Characters, words, phrases, pictures and blanks are available.
						←	P	3x6x2	2	BAT	$10 FOR OSCILLATOR ONLY (NO SWITCH)	
						←	P			BAT	NOT COMM. AVAIL.	The Myocom can be used for yes-no signalling or some code can be devised for communication.

		NAME OF AID & MANUFACTURER (OR DEVELOPER IF THERE IS NO MANUFACTURER)	GENERAL DESCRIPTION	TYPE OF INPUT INTERFACE (SEE "KEY")	NUMBER OF ACTIONS REQUIRED PER SELECTION (MAXIMUM)	CHANGEABLE CHARACTER SET	FEEDBACK DISPLAY (INDICATES THE LAST SELECTED CHARACTER)
SIMPLE ELECTRONIC AIDS	DIRECT SELECTION	(mechanical pointer) Institute of Physical Medicine and Rehabilitation	A sliding block is mechanically coupled to a radial pointer (180° arc), which indicates letters or numbers.	←	1	⊙	⊙
		Slip 'N Slide Michael Flahive	1.5" blocks with pictures, words, or symbols on them are mounted in grooves on a wooden board. The operator selects blocks from the perimeter oval and assembles them in the center groove.	←		⊙	⊙
NON-PORTABLE INDEPENDENT AIDS	SCANNING	Clock Face Selector Centre Industries	Illuminated scan of dots in a circular pattern. Each dot is associated with a typewriter key.	1	1		⊙ *1
		Comhandi (scanner) Physico-Medical Systems Co.	Backlit column-row scan (8 x 8) using a single switch, or directed scan.	1 A,B 5 A,B,U 7 B,E,U 10 A,B	3		⊙
		MAID (Multi-Access Interface for the Disabled) Agzarian & Read	Illuminated row-column scan (9 x 9).	1	4		⊙
		Possum (scanner) Possum Controls Ltd.	Row-column scan or directed scan (6 x 8) using "cursor" lights along 2 edges of the matrix to indicate squares.	1 L 2 L,E, Kc,Kn 4 E,Kc, Kn	3		⊙
		(scanner) Holmund & Kavanagh University of Saskatchewan	Illuminated row-column scan (7 x 7). Each square contains a character and 3 color coded words (4 levels total). A 2-letter code is typed for each word selected.	4 Ke 4 BFf	3		⊙
		System 8 Zambette Electronics	Backlit row-column scan (4 x 10).	1 R		⊙	⊙
		TIC (Tufts Interactive Communicator) Richard Foulds Tufts New England Medical Center	Backlit row-column scan (8 x 7). 8 of the selections are entire words.	1 R,Ka, Kc, Kn,Kw	2		⊙
		Vista Bush Electronics Co.	Backlit row-column scan (5 x 10).	1 Af,Kn	2		⊙

DYNAMIC ALPHANUMERIC CHARACTER DISPLAY	TELEVISION	STRIP PRINTER (TICKER TAPE)	TELETYPE	TYPEWRITER	OTHER	ENVIRONMENTAL CONTROL (NUMBER OF SOCKETS CONTROLLED)	PORTABILITY (SEE "KEY")	SIZE (INCHES)	WEIGHT (LBS.)	POWER REQUIREMENTS	PRICE (APPROX.)	FEATURES--COMMENTS
							P			NONE	NOT COMM. AVAIL.	The numbers can be used to indicate common words, sentences or phrases.
					←		P	18x24x3$\frac{1}{4}$	16	NONE	NOT COMM. AVAIL. AT THIS TIME	Up to 30 "information blocks" can be used. The symbols on these blocks are easily changed.
				●			M *5 *	16x10x8		AC		Characters are arranged according frequency of usage.
			●			4	N	22x20x44	100	AC	$3400	The scan can be restricted to the alphabet only or to numbers and symbols only. Entire system mounts on a teletype stand. Feedback display panel is detachable for more convenient placement.
			●	● *7		4				AC		Assembles on a bed trolley. Selection display can be positioned to suit the operator. 11 of the selections are entire words of the user's choice.
				●			M			AC	PRICES BY QUOTATION ONLY	Characters are arranged according to frequency of usage.
				●						AC	NOT COMM. AVAIL.	To change levels, select the "change frame" square. This results in a scan of 4 colored lights representing the levels; Trigger at the desired level. Characters are arranged according to frequency of usage.
				●			M	18x11$\frac{1}{2}$ x7$\frac{1}{2}$ *	72 *	AC		Special motion-sensing input switch detects movements as small as 1/4".
●		●					S	16x12x6$\frac{3}{4}$	20	AC		In case of a selection error, print can be cancelled by triggering the input switch a third time during the delay between selection and printing.
				● *8			M			AC	$995 *16 PRODUCTION TEMPORARILY DISCONTINUED	

NON-PORTABLE INDEPENDENT AIDS — ENCODING

NAME OF AID & MANUFACTURER (OR DEVELOPER IF THERE IS NO MANUFACTURER)	GENERAL DESCRIPTION	TYPE OF INPUT INTERFACE (SEE "KEY")	NUMBER OF ACTIONS REQUIRED PER SELECTION (MAXIMUM)	CHANGEABLE CHARACTER SET	FEEDBACK DISPLAY (INDICATES THE LAST SELECTED CHARACTER)
Communication Terminal for the Loss of Speech Handicapped Logan & Fieg	The characters which can be selected are displayed in 2 rows at the bottom of a TV screen. A curser bar (underline) moves along these rows in response to joystick control. Selected characters are assembled at the top of the screen.	4 Eh PLUS 2 A	2 OR 3		◉
Comhandi (binary) National Research Council of Canada	Six frames are illuminated sequentially. The user turns on certain frames as the scan comes over them, forming a binary code for the desired character.	1	6 OR LESS		◉
Code Operated Selector Centre Industries	Morse code decoder. Operator uses 2 buttons (dot and dash). The more common characters have shorter codes.	2	5 OR LESS		◉
MC 6400 Medicel, Inc.	Morse code decoder. Operator uses 2 buttons (dot and dash). The more common characters have shorter codes.	2 Bh	5 OR LESS		
Hengrove Possum Controls Ltd.	Suck and puff coding in coordination with beeper for timing. Also 4 switch input (select 2 sequentially), again with beeps for timing.	4 Ah,L	2		
ANROWD (Pneumatic) PHAPCO Society	Suck and puff coding.	L			
ANROWD (octal binary) PHAPCO Society	A character is selected by activating 2 of 8 switches simultaneously.	A	2		
Tongue-Controlled Typewriter Technical Aids To Independence	To type a character, 2 of 8 touch switches are activated in sequence by the tongue.	8 N	2		
(encoder) Loren Wymore	Keyboard of 4 color coded, widely spaced 3" disks. User passes hand over 3 disks in sequence to select a character.	4 Ar	3		
Possum (encoders) Possum Controls Ltd.	A wide variety of inputs and codes for typewriter control, including suck and puff. Some configurations require timing coordination with a beeper or light.	1 L,D, Kc,Kn 2 L,Af 4 Ks,L 7 8 E,Ef			
Cybertype Cybernetics Research	User selects a character by activating 2 switches sequentially from a set of 7 switches, or by choosing 2 simultaneously from 2 sets of 7 switches (one from each set).	7 A,Ar 8 A,Ar, E,P, Kt 11 B 14 A,B	2		◉

DYNAMIC ALPHANUMERIC CHARACTER DISPLAY	TELEVISION	STRIP PRINTER (TICKER TAPE)	TELETYPE	TYPEWRITER	OTHER	ENVIRONMENTAL CONTROL (NUMBER OF SOCKETS CONTROLLED)	PORTABILITY (SEE "KEY")	SIZE (INCHES)	WEIGHT (LBS.)	POWER REQUIREMENTS	PRICE (APPROX.)	FEATURES--COMMENTS
	●						M			AC	NOT COMM. AVAIL.	8 rows of text, 48 characters each, can be assembled. Characters are selected and printed using the joystick. Two buttons provide "clear screen" and "space" functions.
			●									Error correct: If the sixth frame is not lit, the print will be cancelled.
				●		13	M					The chosen character lights up on a selection display before printing. In case of error, print can be cancelled by hitting both switches at once.
	●			●	*12		M	6x18x6 *13	9 *13	AC		With the appropriate options, can be connected to a computer via telephone.
				●			M	20x18½x8 *		AC	PRICES BY QUOTATION ONLY	Two degrees of suck and puff (strong and weak) are required. Feature: Automatic character repeat (for underlining, etc.)
●	●			●	*9						UNDER DEVELOPMENT	All ANROWD input and output modules will be compatible.
●	●			●	*9						UNDER DEVELOPMENT	All ANROWD input and output modules will be compatible.
				●		15	M	12½x7¼ x7¾ *	18 *	AC	$1500 *	Special functions include: index, automatic character repeat, and continuous paper feed. An environmental control option is under development.
			●				N			AC	NOT COMM. AVAIL.	
				●	*14		M			AC	PRICES BY QUOTATION ONLY	Option: Wordstore of 400 words. Entire words or phrases can be selected by code.
				●	*10 *11		M			AC		Very large variety of input interfaces.

	NAME OF AID & MANUFACTURER (OR DEVELOPER IF THERE IS NO MANUFACTURER)	GENERAL DESCRIPTION	TYPE OF INPUT INTERFACE (SEE "KEY")	NUMBER OF ACTIONS REQUIRED PER SELECTION (MAXIMUM)	CHANGEABLE CHARACTER SET	FEEDBACK DISPLAY (INDICATES THE LAST SELECTED CHARACTER)
DIRECT SELECTION	ANROWD: (keyboard) PHAPCO Society	Keyboard control of Anrowd output devices.	50 Ak	1		
	(enlarged keyboard) Suzanne D. Hill	Enlarged keyboard--one inch square plexiglass keys in 4 semi-circular rows on a sloping table.	51 A	1		
	(foot operated keyboard) MEFA	Enlarged keyboard for feet. Four sloping semi-circular rows of keys.	50 Af	1		
	Minimum (keyboard) PMV	Select characters on a small square keyboard by inserting a special pointer in the appropriate hole.	57 G	1		
	Medium (keyboard) PMV	Enlarged keyboard with large, round, shielded buttons in a rectangular pattern.	57 Ar	1		
	Maximum (keyboard) PMV	Very large keyboard, with large, round, shielded keys, in a curved pattern.	58 Ar	1		
	Combination (keyboard) PMC	4 small keyboards to be arranged in the most convenient positions. Each keyboard has 15 shielded buttons.	60 Ar	1		
	Possum Expanded Keyboard Possum Controls Ltd.	Enlarged keyboard with recessed buttons. (button diam. 7/8", spacing 1 1/2", recessed 1/4")	49 Ar	1		
	(magnet controlled typewriter) Reva-Aids	Enlarged keyboard with magnetic sensing keys. 4 tiered rows of 12 characters each.	48 S	1		
	(electric typewriter with keyboard shield) NIRE (National Institute for Rehabilitation Engineering)	An electric typewriter with keys shielded (recessed in a template) to prevent accidental triggering. Pushbutton correctable. No electric carriage return. Portable carrying case.	50 Ak	1		
	(reconditioned IBM Selectric Typewriter with Keyguard) Spastics Society	Reconditioned typewriters in perfect working order. The Keyguard shield helps to prevent the user from striking unwanted keys.	60 Ak	1		

Output Devices: Dynamic Alphanumeric Character Display	Television	Strip Printer (Ticker Tape)	Teletype	Typewriter	Other	Environmental Control (Number of Sockets Controlled)	Portability (See "Key")	Size (Inches)	Weight (Lbs.)	Power Requirements	Price (Approx.)	Features—Comments
●	●			●	*9						UNDER DEVELOPMENT	All ANROWD input and output modules will be compatible.
				●			N	48x30x32		AC	NOT COMM. AVAIL.	
				●			N			AC		Continuous paper feed.
				●			M	$4\frac{3}{4}$x$3\frac{3}{4}$ * KEYBOARD	$1\frac{1}{2}$ *	AC	$754 *	For weak but precise motion, limited reach.
				●			M	$24\frac{1}{2}$x$9\frac{3}{4}$ * KEYBOARD	14 *	AC	$1042 *	For moderate uncoordinated motion, headstick, arm, or foot control.
				●			M	30x$19\frac{1}{2}$ * KEYBOARD	28 *	AC	$1090 *	For large uncoordinated movements, arm or foot control.
				●			M	4 KEY-BOARDS * $2\frac{3}{8}$x$4\frac{1}{2}$	1.1 *	AC	$906 *	For very limited motion, short extremities, bedridden patients.
				●			M	$22\frac{1}{2}$x11 x$2\frac{5}{8}$ *	14 *	AC	PRICES BY QUOTATION ONLY	
				●			M			AC		
				●			S		142	AC	$269.50	Options at extra cost: electric carriage return, automatic paper feed, wrist support, adjustable height and tilt table, special keys.
				●			M			AC		A Variable Height Typing Table designed for wheelchair users is also available.

	NAME OF AID & MANUFACTURER (OR DEVELOPER IF THERE IS NO MANUFACTURER)	GENERAL DESCRIPTION	SYMBOL SELECTION PROCESS			
			TYPE OF INPUT INTERFACE (SEE "KEY")	NUMBER OF ACTIONS REQUIRED PER SELECTION (MAXIMUM)	CHANGEABLE CHARACTER SET	FEEDBACK DISPLAY (INDICATES THE LAST SELECTED CHARACTER)
NON-PORTABLE INDEPENDENT AIDS (CONT.) — DIRECT SELECTION	LOT (Lightspot Operated Typewriter) Soede & Stassen	A head-mounted spotlight is used to select characters from a 6 x 9 array. Nothing is typed until the light has stayed on a character for a certain pre-selected time.	54 T	1		
	PILOT (Patient Initiated, Lightspot Controlled Telecontrol) Hugh Steeper Ltd.	A spotlight is used to select characters from a 5 x 11 array. Nothing is typed until the light has stayed on a character for a certain pre-selected time.	53 T	1		
	OCCUR (Optical Controlled Communication Unit for Rehabilitation) ROY & CHARBONNEAU	A spotlight is used to select characters from a 8 x 8 array. Nothing is typed until the light has stayed on a character for a certain pre-selected time.	64 T	1		
	(speech synthesizer) Prof. Yasuo Ogawa Assist. Prof. Takashi	Speech synthesizer. Messages are spelled out phonetically on a keyboard. When the desired words have been entered, the synthesized voice speaks them.	26 Ak	1		
	Votrax Federal Screw Works	Speech synthesizer. Messages are spelled out phonetically on a keyboard. When the desired words (up to 80 characters) have been entered, the synthesized voice speaks them.	73 Ah	1		
FULLY PORTABLE INDEPENDENT AIDS — SCANNING	Porta-Printer Vendacom Inc.	Illuminated row-column scan (7 x 8). Unit is self-contained in an attache case. The character arrangement is designed to minimize selection time.	1	2		●
FULLY PORTABLE INDEPENDENT AIDS — DIRECT SELECTION	Talking Brooch Newell & Brumfitt	Portable alphanumeric display controlled by hand-held conventional-style keyboard. The 5 character panel features "times square" display: New characters move in smoothly from the right as the displaced ones roll off to the left.	32 Ak	1		
	Lightwriter Toby Churchill Ltd.	Portable typewriter keyboard with a dynamic alphanumeric 32 character display. The display faces away from the keyboard, so that it can be read by someone facing the user. Powered by a separate battery pack.	Ak	1		
	Portable Auto-Com Cerebral Palsy Communication Group	A pointer or slider with a magnet on it is used to indicate the desired symbol on a 7 x 12 array. Delay action proximity switch system is designed to work even with sporadic pointing of cerebral palsied individuals.	84 S	1	●	

Dynamic Alphanumeric Character Display	Television	Strip Printer (Ticker Tape)	Teletype	Typewriter	Other	Environmental Control (Number of Sockets Controlled)	Portability (see "KEY")	Size (Inches)	Weight (Lbs.)	Power Requirements	Price (Approx.)	Features--Comments
					●		N			AC *15	NOT COMM. AVAIL. AT THIS TIME	The time delay can be adjusted by the operator, using the light beam. The light source can be attached to any body part having the necessary range of motion.
					●	2		33x29x21 *16		AC *15	$1550 *16	Alternative operation mode: Use switch to activate typewriter when the lightspot is on the desired character.
			●				N	8x12x2 (NOT INCL TELETYPE)		AC	UNDER DEVELOPMENT	
				←			N	30x18½ x40	142		NOT COMM. AVAIL.	The keyboard contains 21 phonemes, 2 inflections.
				←			S	10x4x11	15	AC	$4200	Messages can be repeated, and individual phonemes edited. Variable speech rate. 63 phonemes, 4 inflections.
		●		*8		2	P	11½x11½ x4½	12	BAT AC	$1500	Can be operated from the cigarette lighter of a car. After a letter selection, the row scan resumes at the current row, instead of jumping to a standard starting point.
●							P			BAT	UNDER DEVELOPMENT	The display can be fitted to the user's shirt pocket, enabling natural face-to-face conversation. The keyboard size has been reduced by elimination of the numbers keys. (Numbers are available in upper case.)
●							P	12x9x3 *17	5½ *17	AC BAT	$1700	Two Lightwriters can be connected to the same display, or linked so that entries from either keyboard appear on both displays. With telephone modems, communication over phone lines is possible.
	●	●	●	●	● *6 *18 *19		P	24x20x2½	14.2	BAT	UNDER DEVELOPMENT ESTIMATED- $2000	The basic unit prints 63 characters and 62 entire words. The wordmaster option provides access to additional custom sets of words, phrases, or sentences, on a plug-in memory cartridge.

GLOSSARY OF INPUT INTERFACES

<u>MECHANICAL SWITCHES FOR THE EXTREMITIES</u> - fingers, hands, elbows,
feet (Many can also be used with a headstick

Sub-types: h - intended for fingers or hands
            f - intended for feet
            t - intended for tongue

A. PUSH BUTTONS There is a very wide variety of shapes and
        sizes. Two special types are noted:

Ak - Keyboard-style buttons, similar to those found on an
     ordinary electric typewriter.

Ar - Recessed (shielded, guarde) buttons. The "shield" helps
     prevent accidental activation of buttons.

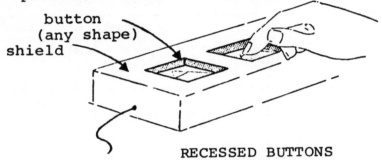

button
(any shape)
shield

RECESSED BUTTONS

B. PADDLES AND LEVERS - There are many shapes and sizes.
        For example:

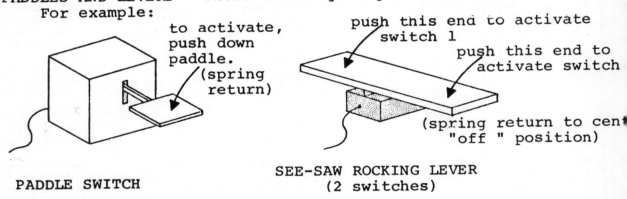

to activate,
push down
paddle.
(spring
return)

push this end to activate
switch 1

push this end to
activate switch

(spring return to cen
"off " position)

PADDLE SWITCH

SEE-SAW ROCKING LEVER
(2 switches)

C. PILLOW SWITCH - Punch a "pillow" or pad to activate the switch.

MECHANICAL SWITCHES FOR THE EXTREMITIES (cont.)

D.   WOBBLESTICK - (Possum Controls Ltd.)

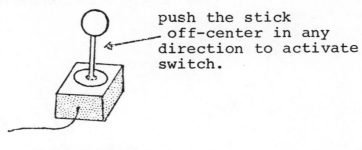

push the stick off-center in any direction to activate switch.

WOBBLESTICK

E.   JOYSTICK - Multiple switches are operated by one control
     stick.   In general, 2 to 8 switches are incorporated.

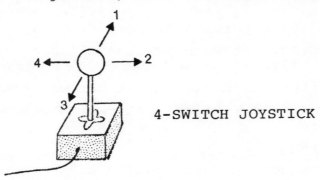

4-SWITCH JOYSTICK

F.   SLIDING OR TROLLEY SWITCHES - Switching is accomplished by
     motion along a slide, groove, or track, These switches
     usually have 2 positions ("on" at one end, "off" at the
     other) or three positions (one switch at each end, "off"
     in the middle).

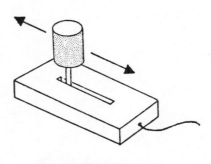

SLIDE SWITCH

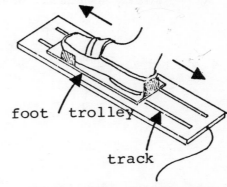

foot trolley

track

FOOT-TROLLEY SWITCH

G.   POKE SWITCHES - Activate by poking a pointer in a hole or
     indentation (PMV "Minimum").

MECHANICAL SWITCHES FOR THE EXTREMITIES (cont.)

H. TIP OR TILT SWITCHES - Tilted one way the switch is "off",
    tilted the other way it is "on." The switch would be
    strapped to the arm or any other body part which can
    be tilted.

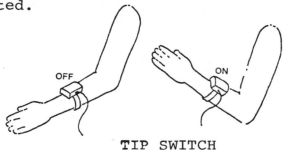

TIP SWITCH

MECHANICAL SWITCHES FOR A SPECIFIC BODY PART

K. These switches are fitted to a specific body part and are
    activated by a particular motion.

  Ka - Head switch. Activate by lateral (side to side) head
       motion. ("Tic"- Tuft's Interactive Communicator)

  Kc - Chin switch. Squeeze switch between chin and chest.

  Ke - Eyebrow switch. Raise eyebrows. (Veteran's Administration,
       "speakeasy")

  Kn - Knee switch.

  Kp - Palate switch. Press toungue up against switch molded
       to fit in the palate.

  Ks - Splint switches. Amolded hand splint with miniature
       paddle switches mounted above or below the fingers.
       (Possum Controls Ltd.)

  Kt - Tongue switch-lever operated by the tongue.

  Kv - Thumb switch. (Fairchild-Hiller, "Viewcom")

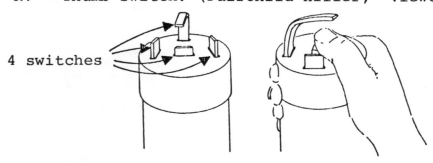

4 switches

THUMB SWITCH

  Kw - Wrist switch, Rotate wrist. ("Tic": Tuft's Interactive
       Communicator)

PNEUMATIC SWITCHES

L.   SUCK AND PUFF - The switch is operated by very small pressure
     changes in the tube. Mouth control rather than respiratory
     control, is usually sufficient to operate this switch.

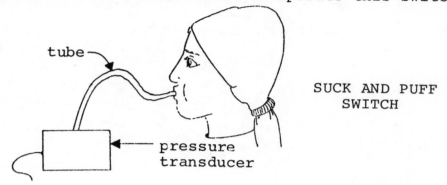

tube

pressure
transducer

SUCK AND PUFF
SWITCH

M.   AIR PADDLES - Activated by blowing at a sensitive paddle
     switch.

AIR PADDLE

sensitive
paddle
switch

TOUCH SWITCHES - These require contact, but no physical pressure.

N.   TOUCH-PLATE - Activated by touching a prescribed sensor area
     with any skin surface.

     Nt - Designed for use with the tongue.

TOUCH SWITCHES (cont.)

P. CYBERGLOVE AND CYBERPLATE - (Cybernetics Research Institute)
    Gloves with contacts on the fingers are touched to a
    metal contact plate.

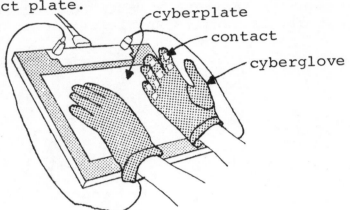

CYBERGLOVE AND CYBERPLATE

MOISTURE SENSITIVE SWITCHES

Q. MOISTURE SWITCH - Activated by contact with the tongue.
    A moisture sensitive switch will not be activated by
    contact with dry skin.

PROXIMITY SWITCHES

R. PROXIMITY SWITCH SENSITIVE TO BODY - Activated when a body
    part is brought within a certain range of the switch.

S. PROXIMITY SWITCH SENSITIVE TO A SPECIAL TRIGGER ELEMENT -
    Activated when a special object (metal, magnet, circuit,
    etc.) is brought within a certain range of the switch.

OPTICAL SWITCHES

T. LIGHTSPOT - The beam from a light source (attached to the
    head or some other body part) is used to operate
    photosensitive switches on a panel in front of the user.
    The user can see the lightspot on the panel and maneuver
    it to the desired photosensor.

OPTICAL SWITCHES (cont.)

U.   INTERRUPTED-BEAM SWITCH - Activated whenever a beam of light
       is interrupted (by a finger or some other body part).

here a beam is broken
when a finger is placed
in the hole.

INTERRUPTED-BEAM SWITCH

SONIC SWITCHES - Activated by sound

X.   WHISTLE SWITCH - The switch is activated by the sound of an
       ultrasonic dog whistle. The whistle can be blown by
       punching a rubber bulb connected to its mouthpiece.
       With this type of switch, no physical connection is
       needed between the user and the communication aid.
       ("Tic": Tufts Interactive Communicator)

BIOELECTRIC SWITCHES - Activated by the electrical impulses
    generated in nerves and muscles of the body.

Y.   MYOELECTRIC SWITCH - Electrodes are applied to the skin
       near a controllable muscle group. Contraction of the
       produces electrical signals whech are detected by the
       electrodes and used to activate the switch.

APPENDIX C ────────────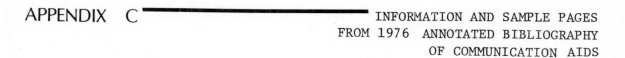 INFORMATION AND SAMPLE PAGES
FROM 1976 ANNOTATED BIBLIOGRAPHY
OF COMMUNICATION AIDS

THE 1976 ANNOTATED BIBLIOGRAPHY

The 1976 Annotated Bibliography of Communication Techniques and Aids is being compiled in an effort to provide summary information to professionals working with non-vocal severely physically handicapped, concerned individuals, researchers, and handicapped individuals themselves. The content of the bibliography describes some of the communication techniques and aids currently being designed, developed or manufactured in the United States, Canada and abroad. The information within each entry is based upon information submitted by the developers, manufacturers, and/or distributors, and all entries are reviewed by the developers etc. prior to inclusion.

Although an effort was made to include descriptions of all known communication aids, entries have not yet been submitted by all researchers and distributors. Contact with the researchers, institutions and distributors working in the field is continuing. In conjunction with this effort, the Trace Center welcomes information related to any communication aid not described in the bibliography. New entries will be made available through periodic updates.

The following pages are sample entries from the 1976 Annotated Bibliography of Communication Aids being compiled by the Trace Center, University of Wisconsin. The bibliography is being prepared in loose-leaf form to facilitate updating and will be available from the Trace Center in the summer or fall of 1976.

Following the sample pages is a listing of aids which will be part of the Annotated Bibliography or its updates.

CRITERIA USED TO DETERMINE PORTABILITY RATINGS

Fully Portable: Under 25 lbs (including battery) - needs no external power (i.e., need not be plugged into wall)

Semi Portable: Under 25 lbs - needs external power (i.e., from wall outlet)

Movable: Not meant to be portable but can be transported without major difficulty. No one piece of equipment weighing more than 30 lbs.

Stationary: Systems which are not designed to be taken apart regularly or moved except perhaps on a wheeled cart.

BIRGITTARULLEN

TYPE OF AID: *Scanning*   SIZE: *4"D and 5"L*

PORTABILITY: *Fully Portable*   WEIGHT: *1 lb.*

AVAILABILITY: POWER: *None*

BRIEF DESCRIPTION OF AID

    Birgittarullen is a transparent plastic cylinder in which there is a paper roll. The paper roll, which contains 20-30 short phrases, can be turned with a wheel outside the cylinder. The cylinder is covered with self-adhesive plastic except for two small windows. (The windows are provided so that the aid may be operated by either the right or left hand of the user.) In order to remove or insert the paper roll, the plastic cylinder is removed from the base.

206

BRIEF DESCRIPTION OF OPERATION

When the wheel outside the plastic cylinder is turned, the paper roll also moves. As the paper roll moves, priorly typed or written symbols, pictures or phrases appear in the window. Using the wheel, the user manipulates the position of the priorly typed or written symbols, words, phrases or pictures until the desired symbol(s) are displayed in the window.

OTHER INFORMATION

A brochure which is written by Kerstin Brieditis provides directions for use of Birgittarullen as an aid for education. Further information may be secured from Kerstin Brieditis, Teacher of Severely Disabled Children, Bernadottehemmett, Uppsala, Sweden. This brochure is available in Swedish.

COST

Price listing is available from Gunnar Kahlstrom. The cost of ten aids is $10.00 each plus freight costs (minimum order for U.S. residents).

ESTIMATED DELIVERY TIME

One month

PERSON/INSTITUTION WHO DEVELOPED

Gunnar Kahlstrom

FOR MORE INFO WRITE

Gunnar Kahlstrom
Barkspadevagen
S-752 47 Uppsala
Sweden

Photograph courtesy of Gunnar Kahlstrom, Uppsala, Sweden, 1975.

207

COMHANDI

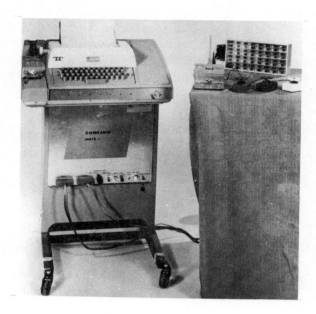

TYPE OF AID:	Scanning	SIZE:	Teletype stand 22" x 20" x 44"
PORTABILITY:	Stationary	WEIGHT:	100 lbs.
AVAILABILITY:	Commerc. Avail.	POWER:	110v, 60 hertz, 300 watts

BRIEF DESCRIPTION OF AID

The Comhandi consists of input transducers, a mode selector, a visual display and a teletypewriter. The entire system is contained in the base of a teletypewriter stand. A total of 64 squares are arranged in alternating rows of letters and symbols, forming an 8 x 8 matrix. All the squares can be made available to the child, or half the display can be used giving the child access to only the 32 (8 x 4 matrix) containing the alphabet or only the 32 containing the symbols. A color distrinction between the alphabet and the symbols is made for the sake of clarity.

The output of the device is in the form of printed letters or numbers which are produced by a standard teletypewriter. The display board, which is portable and detachable, can be placed next to the child for easy viewing. Audio and visual feedback is provided to the child by illuminating each square as it is turned on and simultaneously generating the audio tone.

BRIEF DESCRIPTION OF OPERATION

To select a character in the scanning mode, the operator activates a switch for a scan of the top row, releasing the switch when the correct column is reached. Activating a second time causes the light to scan down the selected column until the operator releases at the desired square. The chosen character is then printed out on the teletype. The operator must trigger once more to reset to the starting point.

In the joystick mode the operator directs the roving light horizontally, vertically, or diagonally using multiple switch arrangements, such as a joystick.

OPTIONS

Several alternative input switches are provided:

1) Optical switches operated by breaking a light beam with a finger. These require no force and can be used by those with a very weak motion.

2) Mechanical joysticks

3) Mechanical paddle switches

COST

The estimated cost of manufacture is $3500

ESTIMATED DELIVERY TIME

6 months

PERSON/INSTITUTION WHO DEVELOPED

*O. Z. Roy and J. R. Charbonneau
National Research Council*

FOR MORE INFO WRITE

*George Bata
Physico-Medical Systems Co.
9250 Park Avenue, Suite M-101
Montreal 354, Quebec
Canada*

Photograph courtesy of Radio and E. E. Division, National Research Council, Ottawa, Canada, 1974.

LIGHTWRITER

TYPE OF AID: *Direct Selection*   SIZE: *12" x 9" x 3"*

PORTABILITY: *Fully Portable*   WEIGHT: *5-1/2 lbs.*

AVAILABILITY: *Commerc. Avail.*   POWER: *Separate battery pack,*
                                           12 v. 1.7 amp.

BRIEF DESCRIPTION OF AID

   *The Lightwriter is a unit which contains a waterproof keyboard with the layout of a typewriter, an integral keyguard, and a gas-discharge type 32 character display. The height of each character is 0.2 inches (5mm). The repertoire of characters on the keyboard include: A B C D E F G H I J K L M N O P Q R S T U V W X Y Z 1 2 3 4 5 6 7 8 9 0 ! * / @ $ & ? ( ) + - " ' : ; , . .*

BRIEF DESCRIPTION OF OPERATION

In order to operate the Lightwriter, the user depresses a key. As each key is pressed, the character appears at the right-hand end of the luminous display, displacing previously keyed characters to the left. Messages move leftward like a news-strip, and disappear eventually as they reach the left-hand end. The display is orientated away from the user and toward the reader.

OPTIONS

The Lightwriter may be adapted to be used with a telephone.

OTHER INFORMATION

When the Lightwriter is produced, a variety of keyboard types (to suit different physical abilities) and a variety of keyboard layouts (to suit the national typewriter layout of the particular country) will be offered. Also being developed is a detachable display mechanism. For flexibility of use, the display will be able to sit in the Lightwriter either way up, depending on the location of the reader or it will be removable in order to be placed on a table.

COST

Approximately £500 ($1250.00 United States Currency)

PERSON/INSTITUTION WHO DEVELOPED

Toby Churchill, D. F. Battison, H. L. Love, T. H. Gossling. Four individuals (one unable to speak) who met through the Engineering Department of Cambridge University, Cambridge, England.

FOR MORE INFO WRITE

*Mr. Toby Churchill
Toby Churchill Limited
Designers of Equipment for the Disabled
20 Panton Street
Cambridge CB2 1HP
England*

Photograph courtesy of Toby Churchill Limited, Cambridge, England, 1974.

PICTURE COMMUNICATION BOARD

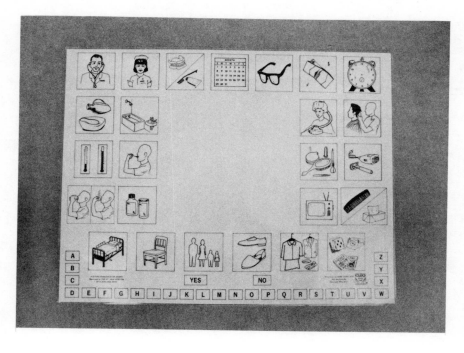

TYPE OF AID: *Direct Selection*

PORTABILITY: *Fully Portable*

AVAILABILITY: *Commerc. Avail.*

SIZE: *22-1/2" x 17-1/2"*

WEIGHT: *less than 5 lbs.*

POWER: *None required*

BRIEF DESCRIPTION OF AID

The Picture Communication Board is a communication aid designed for hospital use. Made of flexible plastic, the board consists of black and white line drawings, a calendar, letters of the alphabet, the words "yes" and "no", and blank space in the center for additional entries. On the back of the board are line drawings depicting front, back and side views of a human being. Beneath the drawings is the statement: "Do you have pain?" Additional space is also provided for pictures, words, phrases, etc. which the user may want displayed on the board.

212

DESCRIPTION OF OPERATION

The user indicates his/her need by pointing to the desired drawing on the board. The "listener" verbalizes the need and watches the user of the board for confirmation.

PERSON/INSTITUTION WHO DEVELOPED

*The Mt. Sinai Hospital
of Cleveland, Ohio*

FOR MORE INFO WRITE

*Cleo Living Aids
3957 Mayfield Road
Cleveland, Ohio 44121*

COMMUNICATION AID REFERENCE LISTING

ALPHABET-MESSAGE SCANNER
STRIP PRINTER
  Prenke-Romick Co.
  Barry Romich
  R.D. 2, Box 191
  Shrever, Ohio 44676
  216/567-2906

ANROWD (ALPHA NUMERIC
  WORD DISPLAY)
SUCK & PUFF
OCTAL BINARY
KEYBOARD
  PHAPCO Society
  49 Commerce Building
  University of
    Saskatchewan
  Saskatoon, Saskatchewan,
  Canada S7N0W0

AUTO-COM
VERSICOM
ROTO-COM
  Trace Research and Devel-
  opment Center for the
  Severely Communicatively
  Handicapped
  University of Wisconsin-
    Madison
  922ERB
  1500 Johnson Drive
  Madison, Wisconsin 53706

BALDER-BOARD-JOYSTICK
  SCANNING BOARD
  Judith Anne Balder
  19 Larissa Lane
  Wappingas Falls,
    New York 12590

BIRGITTARULLEN
  Gunnar Kahlström
  Barkspadevagan 1
  S-752 47
  Uppsala, Sweden

BLISS SYMBOL BOARD
  Spastic Children's Society
  of Victoria
  P. O. Box 108
  Toorak 3142, Victoria, Australia

BLISSYMBOLS
BLISSYMBOLICS COMMUNICATION
  FOUNDATION
  Dr. Harry Silverman, Director
  Shirley McNaughton,
    Program Director
  862 Eglinton Avenue E
  Toronto, Ontario M4G 2L1, Canada
  416/425-7835

CAC (COMPUTER ASSISTED COMMUNI-
  CATION
CLB (COMPUTERIZED LANGUAGE BOARD)
  Travis M. Tallman, Speech
    Pathologist
  Winifred Parker, Occupational
    Therapist
  United Cerebral Palsy of
    Middlesex Co.
  Roosevelt Park
  Edison, New Jersey

CANON COMMUNICATOR
  Canon Inc.
  Mr. Saburo Nagata, Director
  Audio Visual Aids Department
  Canon Inc.
  P. O. Box 50
  Tokyo Airport, Japan

CLOCK FACE SELECTOR (CFS)
CODE OPERATED SELECTOR (COS)
  Centre Industries
  Allambie Road
  Allambie Heights
  New South Wales, Australia

CLOCK HAND SCANNING AIDS
T4 (ELECTRONIC APPARATUS
   WITH 4 CHARACTERS DISPLAYED
PISA (PROGRAMMED ELECTRONIC
   APPARATUS FOR LEARNING
   AND COMMUNICATION)
AND OTHERS
   Rikscentralen
   Ulf Lekemo, Director
   Bracke Ostergard
   S-417 22
   Goteborg, Sweden

COCOM CENTER, MODEL 25
MANUAL COMMUNICATION BOARD
   David A. Kucherawy
   Department of Speech &
      Hearing Services
   Pennhurst State School
      and Hospital
   Spring City, Pennsylvania
      19475

COMHANDI
OCCUR
   National Research Council
      of Canada
   O.Z. Roy, J.R. Charbonneau
   Medical Engineering Section
   Division of Electrical
      Engineering
   Ottawa, Ontario, Canada
   K1A OR8
   202/389-6345

A COMMUNICATION AID WITH
   SPEECH OUTPUT AND BUILT-IN
   GRAMMAR
   G. Jismalm
   Department of Speech
      Communication
   Royal Institute of
      Technology
   S-100 44
   Stockholm 70, Sweden

COMMUNICATION AIDS I AND II
EMECCA (EYE MOVEMENT CONTROLLED
   COMMUNICATION AID)
   D. W. Lywood, J. J. Vasa
   Queen's University
   Biomedical Engineering Unit
   Kingston, Ontario, Canada

COMMUNICATION BOARD (ENCODING)
   Victor Almonte
   276 Red Chimney Drive
   Warwick, Rhode Island   02886

COMMUNICATION BOARDS
   Home of the Merciful Savior for
      Crippled Children
   4400 Baltimore Avenue
   Philadelphia, Pennsylvania
      19104
   215/222-2566

COMMUNICATION BOARDS
GRID LANGUAGE BOARDS
MATRIX LANGUAGE BOARD
   Mrs. Randy Tauber CCC-SP
   The Matheny School
   Peapack, New Jersey   97977

COMMUNICATION BOOK FOR THE
   AMBULATORY CEREBRAL PALSIED
   Barbara A. Nelson
   Department of Speech-Hearing
      Services
   Pennhurst State School and
      Hospital
   Spring City, Pennsylvania   19475

COMMUNICATION DISPLAY/PRINTOUT
   AID WITH A MEMORY
   Georg Bruun, Björn Jarkle,
      Peter Speldt
   Electronics Laboratory
   Technical University of Denmark
   Lyngby, Denmark

COMMUNICATION PROTHESIS FOR
THE CEREBRAL PALSIED
(ENCODING AID)
Loren Wymore
3 Gregory Court
Barrington, Rhode Island
02806

COMMUNICATION TERMINAL FOR
THE LOSS OF SPEECH
HANDICAPPED
H.C. Logan, R.J. Fieg
1232 Laurel Lane
Naperville, Illinois 60540

THE COMMUNICATOR
Adaptive Therapeutics
Systems, Inc.
162 Ridge Road
Madison, Connecticut 06443

CONVERSATION BOARD - F. HALL
ROE BOARD
Ghora Khan Grotto
Fremon Metcalf
2245 Freemont Avenue
St. Paul, Minnesota 55119

CORSEFORD SELECTOR
Ellis Cohen
Medical Aids Electronic
Development Co., Ltd.
19 Cochrane Street
Glasgow, C.I., Scotland

CP LIGHT/SOUND COMMUNICATOR
SCANNER
Rancho Los Amigos Hospital
Chris Hagan, Ph.D.
Chief,Communication
Disorders Section
7601 East Imperial Highway
Downey, California 90242

CULHANE BLISS SYMBOL COMMUNI-
CATION BOARDS
Karen Culhane, Speech and
Language Clinician
9248 Stokes Avenue
Downey, California 90240

CYBERCOM FAMILY OF AIDS
CYBERTYPE
CYBER-GO-ROUND
CYBER PHONE
WHISPER TYPE
AND OTHERS
Cybernetics Research Institute
Inc. (C/R/I)
Haig Kafafian, President
2233 Wisconsin Avenue, N.W.
Washington, D.C. 20007
202/333-4112

DIY SPELLING BOARD
British Red Cross Society
Home Made Aids for the Disabled
9 Grosvenor Crescent
London SW1, England

ECP ELECTRONIC CHOICE PEEPER -
DOMINOLAN COMMUNICATOR
Dr. J.M.A. van Mierlo
Miss J.A.C.B. van Doremaele
Huize "Zonhove"
Nieuwstraat 70, SON (N.B.)
Netherlands

ELECTRAID
J.W.F. Electraid Ltd.
8 Bramcote Close
Aylesbury, Bucks., England

ELECTRO-COM
Mrs. Joie Tenebaum
5720 Reinhardt Drive
Mission, Kansas 66205

ELECTRONIC LETTERBOARDS
MODIFIED TYPEWRITERS
AND OTHERS
NIRE (National Institute for
Rehabilitation Engineering)
Donald Selwyn, Director
Pompton Lakes, New Jersey 97442

ELECTRONIC TYPEWRITER CON-
TROLLER
Kingma-Harding Associates,
Ltd.
9639 - 62nd Avenue
Edmonton, Alberta T6E OE1
Canada

ELECTRONIC VISUAL COMMUNI-
CATOR HOSPITAL COMMUNI-
CATION AID
Cheryl A. Rodgers/
Joseph Bruder
Senior Speech Pathologist
United Cerebral Palsy
Association of Western
New York
100 Leroy Avenue
Buffalo, New York 14214

ENLARGED KEYBOARD
Suzanne D. Hill
Department of Psychology
University of New Orleans
Lakefront
New Orleans, Louisiana
70122

ETRAN CHART
Jack H. Eichler
P. O. Box 685
Westport, Connecticut
06880
or
Trace Center
University of Wisconsin-
Madison

EYE-CONTROLLED "TYPEWRITER"
National Aeronautics and
Space Administration
John Samos
Technology Utilization
and Application Programs
Officers
Langley Research Center
Hampton, Virginia 23665

FOOT OPERATED KEYBOARD
MEFA GmbH Bonn
518 Eschweiler
Postfach 466
Germany

4 GEORGE
Idaho State School Hospital
Speech and Hearing Department
Box 47
Nampa, Idaho 83651

GMMI (GENERAL MAN-MACHINE
INTERFACE)
Zolan Torok
Warren Springs Laboratory
P. O. Box 20
Gunnels Wood Road
Stevenage, Herts. SG1 2BX,
England

HELP ME TO HELP MYSELF
(Communication flipcards)
Carol N. Green
R. 1, Box 316D
324 Acre Avenue
Brownbury, Indiana 46112

HERALD I
HERALD II
The Herald Co.
R. Lee Wilkins, President
3840 Railroad Avenue
Pittsburg, California 94565
415/439-5300

JEFFREY COMMUNICATOR
Chas. F. Thackray, Ltd.
P. O. Box 171
Park Str-et
Leeds LS1 1RQ, England

LIGHTWRITER
    Toby Churchill Ltd.
    20 Panten Street
    Cambridge CB2 1HP, England

LINGUADUC
    Jean-Claude Gabus
    Technuscher Berater
    3097 Liebefeld-Bern
    Switzerland

LOT (LIGHTSPOT OPERATED
    TYPEWRITER)
    Dr. H. G. Stassen
    Associate Professor of
        Control Engineering
    Laboratory for Measure-
        ment & Control
    C. Drebbelweg 1
    Delft University of
        Technology
    Delft, The Netherlands

LINGUISTIC COMMUNICATION
    BOARDS
    University of Iowa
        Hospital School
    Mary Ellen Brissey/
        Susan Shieders
    Speech Pathologists
    Iowa City, Iowa   52242

MAGNET-CONTROLLED TYPEWRITER
    Reva-Aids
    Solvgade 32
    Copenhagen K, Denmark

MAID (MULTI-ACCESS INTERFACE
    FOR THE DISABLED)
    Mr. J. Agzarian
    Department of Medical
        Physics
    Prince Henry Hospital
    P. O. Box 233
    Matraville, New South
        Wales 2036, Australia

MC-2 MATRIX COMMUNICATOR
    DUFCO
    901 Iva Court
    Cambria, California 93428
    805/927-4392

MCM COMMUNICATIONS SYSTEM
    Micon Industries
    252 Oak Street
    Oakland, California 94607

MC 6400
    Medical, Inc.
    Medical Electronics Laboratory
    222 Foxhill Road
    Burlington, Maryland
    617/273-1909

MYOCOM
    Robert G. Combs, PE, Ph.D.,
        Associate Professor
    Department of Electrical
        Engineering
    College of Engineering
    239 EE Building
    University of Missouri
    Columbia, Missouri 65201

ONE HAND TYPEWRITERS
    Dvorak
    A. A. Jaffe, Business Manager
    3109 West Augusta Avenue
    Phoenix, Arizona   85021

PICTURE COMMUNICATION BOARDS
    Cleo Living Aids
    3957 Mayfield Road
    Cleveland, Ohio   44121

PICTURE-SYMBOL WHEEL
    Susan Webb, OTR,
        Janet Jensen, M.A., C.C.C.
    Augustana Nursery
    400 West Dickens
    Chicago, Illinois   60614

PILOT (PATENT INITIATED
LIGHTSPOT OPERATED TELE-
CONTROL)
Hugh Steeper, Ltd.
Queen Mary's Hospital
Rochampton Lane
London, SW 15 5PL, England

PMV KEYBOARDS (MINIMUM, MAXIMUM,
MEDIUM, COMBINATION)
AA-MED, Incorporated
1215 S. Harlem Avenue
Forest Park, Illinois 60130
312/626-1500

PORTABLE COMMUNICATION AID FOR
THE DEAF
Anders Torberger
Research Engineer
The Royal Institute of
Technology
Department of Telecommuni-
cations, Networks & Systems
S-10044 Stockholm 70, Sweden

PORTAPRINTER
Portacom Co.
Vernon Cooper,
Eliot Tropiansky
164 Dwane Street
New York, New York 10013
212/925-0909

POSSUM AIDS
PSU3
HENGROVE TYPEWRITER CONTROL
Possum Controls, Ltd.
P. D. Waters
63 Mandeville Road
Aylesbury, Bucks.,
England HP21 8AE

PROGRAMMED COMMUNICATION AID
Arne Nybroe Sorensen, MScEE
Rigshospitalet
Engineering Department
21 00 Copenhagen, Denmark

RECONDITIONED IBM TYPEWRITERS
Spastics Society
Supplies Officer
12 Park Crescent
London Win4EQ, England

RUMBLE COMMUNICATOR MK1
L. A. Rumble
30 Benton Road
Ilford, Essex 1G1 4AT, England

S.C.R.P. 100 & 100 MK II DISPLAY
512 BLISSYMBOL DISPLAY
AND OTHERS
Ontario Crippled Children's
Centre
Dr. G. H. Isles
Rehabilitation Engineering
Department
350 Rumsey Road
Toronto, M46 1R8, Ontario,
Canada

SCANNER
Holmland, B.A. and Kavanagh R.N.
University of Saskatchewan
Saskatoon, Saskatchewan
Canada

SCANNER, ROTATING
Miller-Carpenter
Crotched Mountain Foundation
Greenfield, New Hampshire

SIMPLIFIED COMMUNICATION SYSTEM
FOR THE AGED INFIRM
Keith Copeland, Biophysics
Department
Faculty of Medical Sciences
University College
London, England

SIX BANK SCANNER
Ellen S. Adler
Easter Seal School & Treatment
Center
3575 Donald Street
Eugene, Oregon 97405

SLIP N' SLIDE
  Michael Flahive
  Director of Speech and
    Hearing Services
  Marywood College
  Scranton, Pennsylvania
    18509

SYSTEM 7
SYSTEM 8
  Zambette Electronics, Ltd.
  Douglas Steele
  17 High Street
  Southend-on-Sea, Essex,
    England

TALKING BROOCH
VOTEM
  Dr. Alan F. Newell,
    Johnathan P. Bromfitt
  Department of Electronics
  University of Southampton
  Southampton, England S09 5NH

TARC (TYPING AID REMOTE
  CONTROLLED)
  O. I. Butler
  University of Sheffield
  Mappin Street
  Sheffield S1 3JD, England

TIC
  Richard A. Foulds
  Box 372
  New England Medical Center
    Hospital
  185 Harrison Avenue
  Boston, Massachusetts 02111

TONGUE CONTROLLED TYPEWRITER
  Technical Aids to Inde-
    pendence, Inc.
  John F. Fenton
  12 Hyde Road
  Bloomfield, New Jersey 07003

TVPHONE
  Phonics Corp.
  Molly H. Poole
  814 Thayer Avenue
  Silver Springs, Maryland 20901
  301/588-8222

TYPEWRITER CONTROL AIDS
  Maling Rehabilitation Ltd.
  Bicester Road
  Aylesbury, Bucks., England

TYPEWRITER CONTROL BY DENTAL
  PALATE KEY
  Ilkka Saarnia
  Research Institute for
    Bioengineering
  Tampere, Finland

VAPC COMMUNICATOR
  Veteran's Administration
    Prosthetics Center (VAPC)
  Edward Peizer, Ph.D.
  Assistant Director
  Veteran's Administration
    Prosthetics Center
  252 Seventh Avenue
  New York, New York 10001
  212/620-6511

VIDIALOG
  M. Tolstrup, Electronics
    Laboratory, Building 344
  Technical University of Denmark
  2800
  Lyngby, Denmark

VIEW COM
  Fairchild Hiller Corp.
  G. P. Sommers
  Medical Products Division
  Germantown, Maryland 29767

VISTA (VISUAL INSTANT SCANNING
  TYPEWRITER ADAPTOR)
  Bush Electronics Co.
  1245 Folsam Street
  San Francisco, California 94103

VOTECS (VOICE OPERATED TYPE-
    WRITER AND ENVIRONMENTAL
    CONTROL SYSTEM
VDETS (VOICE DATA ENTRY
    TERMINAL SYSTEM)
    SCOPE Electronics Inc.
    1860 Michael Faraday Drive
    Reston, Virginia 22090
    703/471-5600

VOTRAX
    Federal Screw Works
    Vocal Interface Division
    500 Stephenson Highway
    Troy, Michigan 48084

ZYGO COMMUNICATOR
    ZYGO Industries, Inc.
    Box 1008
    Portland, Oregon 97207
    503/292-4695

This bibliography has been arranged in a categorical manner to aid in further research on particular topic areas. References from the chapter as well as additional references are cited.

Summary Information

Copeland, K., Aids for the Severely Handicapped, Spector Publishing Co., Ltd., London, England, 1974.

Kafafian, H., A Study of Man-Machine Communication Systems for the Handicapped, 3 volumes (1970-73), Cybernetics Research Institute, Washington, D.C.

Luster, M.J., Preliminary Selected Bibliography of Articles, Brochures and Books Related to Communication Techniques and Aids for the Severely Handicapped, Trace Center, 922 ERB, University of Wisconsin-Madison, Madison, WI, 53706, 1974.

Luster, M.J. and G.C. Vanderheiden, Preliminary Annotated Bibliography of Communication Aids, Trace Center, 922 ERB, University of Wisconsin-Madison, Madison, WI, 53706, 1974.

Vanderheiden, G.C. and M.J. Luster, "Non-Vocal Communication Techniques and Aids as Aids to the Education of the Severely Physically Handicapped," A State of the Art Review, Cerebral Palsy Communication Group, University of Wisconsin-Madison, Madison, WI, 53706, 1975.

Vicker, B., Nonoral Communication System Project 1964/73, Campus Stores Publishers, 17 West College, University of Iowa, Iowa City, Iowa, 52242, 1974.

Vanderheiden, G., and D. Harris-Vanderheiden, "Communication Techniques and Aids for the Non-Vocal Severely Handicapped," in Lyle Lloyd (ed.) Communication Assessment and Intervention Strategies, University Park Press, Baltimore, Maryland, 1976.

Communication Boards

Davis, G.A., "Linguistics and Language Therapy: The Sentence Construction Board," Journal of Speech and Hearing Disorders, 38, (May 1973): 205-214.

222

Dixon, C.C. and B. Curry, "Some Thoughts on the Communication Board," _Journal of Speech and Hearing Disorders_, 38, (February 1973): 73-88.

Dixon, C., "Some Thoughts on Communication Boards," _Cerebral Palsy Journal_, 26, (April 1965): 12-13.

Feallock, B., "Communication for the Non-Verbal Individual," _American Journal of Occupational Therapy_, 12, (March-April 1958): 60-63.

Goldberg, H.R. and J. Fenton, _Aphonic Communication for Those with Cerebral Palsy: Guide for the Development and Use of a Conversation Board_, New York, United Cerebral Palsy of New York State, 1960.

McDonald, E.T. and A.R. Schultz, "Communication Boards for Cerebral Palsied Children," _Journal of Speech and Hearing Disorders_, 38, (February 1973): 73-88.

Miller, K., "Electronics for Communication," _American Journal of Occupational Therapy_, 18, (January-February 1964): 20-23.

Picken, S.R., "Development, Use and Application of a Communication Board with a Cerebral Palsy Child," 114 East Prospect, Marquette, Michigan, August 1974.

Remis, A., _The Cerebral Palsied Child and the Development of a Conversation Device_, New York State College of Teachers, Buffalo, New York.

Robenault, I.P., _Functional Aids for the Multiply Handicapped_, Evanston, Harper and Row, 1973.

Roe, H., _The Hall Roe Conversation Board_, Ghora Khan Grotto, 2245 Fremont Avenue, St. Paul, Minn. 55119.

Sklar, M. and D.N. Bennett, "Initial Communication Chart for Aphasics," _Journal of the Association of Physical and Mental Rehabilitation_, 10, (March-April 1956): 43-53.

United Cerebral Palsy Association, _Aphonic Communication for Those with Cerebral Palsy_, 220 West 42nd Street, New York, New York.

Communication: Its Function and Dysfunction in the Cerebral Palsied Child

Bosley, E., "Normal Language in its Application to the Cerebral Palsied Child," Cerebral Palsy Review, June/July 1954.

Christman, D., "Problems of Communication of Individuals with Cerebral Palsy," Cerebral Palsy Review, September/October 1956.

Mecham, M., "Complexities in the Communication of the Cerebral Palsied," Cerebral Palsy Review, February 1954.

Nicol, E., "Breakthrough to Communication," Special Education, December 1972.

Scanning Communication Aids

Charbonneau, J.R., C. Cote and O.Z. Roy, "NRC's 'Comhandi" Communication System Technical Description and Application at the Ottawa Crippled Children's Treatment Centre," paper presented at the seminar "Electronic Controls for the Severely Physically Handicapped," Vancouver, British Columbia, 1974.

Foulds, R., G. Balesta and W. Crochetiere, "Effectiveness of Language Redundancy in Non-Vocal Communication," Proceedings from the Conference on Systems and Devices for the Disabled, Krusen Center for Research on Engineering, April 29-30, 1975.

Jenkin, R., Special Education, Volume LVI, No. 1 (March 1967): 9-11, (Great Britain).

"Physically Handicapped Children Learn to Communicate," Science Dimension, April 1973: 8-13.

Sampson, D., "A Communication Device for Patients Unable to Speak," Medical and Biological Engineering, (January 1970): 99-101.

Encoding Communication Aids

"Jack H. Eichler Builds Communication Device," Case Alumnus, Cleveland, Case Institute of Technology Alumni Association, 211 (June 1973): 2.

Hagen, C., W. Porter and J. Brink, "Nonverbal Communication: An Alternate Mode of Communication for the Child with Severe Cerebral Palsy," Journal of Speech and Hearing Disorders, 38, (November 1973): 448-455.

"Handicapped Youth 'Talks' with Eyes," News Journal, Mansfield, Ohio, 22, October 1974.

Direct Selection Communication Aids

Bullock, M., G.F. Dalrymple and J.M. Danca, "The Auto-Com at Kennedy Memorial Hospital: Rapid and Accurate Communication by a Non-Verbal Multi-Handicapped Student," American Journal of Occupational Therapy, (in press), 1975.

Dalrymple, G.F., A. Bullock and J.M. Danca, "The Auto-Com at Kennedy Memorial Hospital: Rapid and Accurate Communication by a Non-Verbal Multi-Handicapped Student," Proceedings of the Conference on Engineering Devices in Rehabilitation, May 2-3, 1974.

"Handicapped Aid (PILOT) is Demonstrated," Winnipeg Free Press, Winnipeg, Canada, 16 February 1972.

Harris-Vanderheiden, D., C.D. Geisler, M. Spielman, V. Valley and R. Schultz, "Evaluating the Auto-Com as an Aid to the Non-Vocal Physically Handicapped Child's Education and Communication Skill," submitted for publication to Exceptional Child.

Harris-Vanderheiden, D. and R. Schultz, "Providing Independence through Communication: A Case Study of the Use of the Auto-Com," submitted for publication to Teaching Exceptional Children.

Hill, S.D., J. Campagna, P. Long, J. Munch and S. Naecher, "An Explanation of the Use of Two Response Keyboard as a Means of Communication for the Severely Handicapped Child," Perceptual Motor Skills, 26, (June 1968): 699-704.

Soede, M. and H.G. Stassen, "A Light Spot Operated Typewriter for Severely Disabled Patients," Medical and Biological Engineering, 1973: 641-644.

Stassen, H.G., M.J. Soede and W.J. Luitse, "The Light Spot Operated Typewriter: The Evaluation of a Prototype," 5th International Seminar on Rehabilitation, London, England, 1974: 1-21.

Vanderheiden, G.C., G.A. Raitzer, D.P. Kelso and C.D. Geisler, "An Automated Technique for the Interpretation of Erratic Pointing Motions of Severely Cerebral Palsied Individuals," Cerebral Palsy Communication Group, 922 ERB, University of Wisconsin, Madison, Wisconsin, 1974.

Vanderheiden, G.C., D.F. Lamers, A.M. Volk and C.D. Geisler, "A Portable Non-Vocal Communication Prosthesis for the Severely Physically Handicapped," submitted for publication, Cerebral Palsy Communication Group, 922 ERB, University of Wisconsin, Madison, Wisconsin, 1975.

Vanderheiden, G.C., C.D. Geisler and A. Volk, "The Auto-Monitoring Technique and its Application in the Auto-Monitoring Communication Board: A New Communication Device for the Severely Handicapped," Proceedings of the 1973 Carnahan Conference on Electronic Prosthetics, Lexington, Kentucky, 1973: 47-51.

Wendt, E., "Habilitation: A Team Approach to Communication," Teaching Exceptional Children, (in print), 1975.

Special Language Systems/Techniques

Bliss, C., Semantography, Semantography Publications, 2 Vicar Street, Coogee, Sydney, Australia.

Harris-Vanderheiden, C., W.P. Brown, P. MacKenzie, S. Reinen and C. Scheibel, "Symbol Communication for the Mentally Handicapped: An Application of Bliss Symbols as an Alternate Communication Mode for Non-Vocal Mentally Retarded Children with Motoric Impairment," Mental Retardation, February 1975.

Levett, L.M., "A Method of Communication for Non-Speaking Severely Subnormal Children - Trial Results," British Journal of Disorders of Communication, October, 1972: 125-128.

Lloyd, Lyle (Ed.), Communication Assessment and Intervention Strategies, University Park Press 1976, Baltimore, Maryland.

Lynes, G., Mr. Symbol Man (film of Charles Bliss and the use of Bliss Symbols), National Film Board of Canada, 550 Sherbrooke St., Montreal, Canada.

McNaughton, S. and B. Kates, "Visual Symbols: Communication System for the Pre-Reading Physically Handicapped Child," paper presented at the American Association on Mental Deficiency Annual Meeting, Toronto, Ontario, Canada, June 5, 1974.

Moore, M.V., "Binary Communication for the Severely Handicapped," Archives of Physical Medicine and Rehabilitation, 53, November 1972: 532-533.

Ontario Crippled Children's Centre Bliss Project Team, Ontario Crippled Children's Centre Symbol Communication Research Project 1972-1973, Toronto, Ontario Crippled Children's Centre, 1973.

Symbol Coordination Committee Newsletter, Toronto, Ontario Crippled Children's Centre, 1974.

Other Aids and General Information

Ehrlich, M.D., "The Votrax Voice Synthesizer as an Aid for the Blind," 1974 Proceedings on Engineering Devices in Rehabilitation, Boston, Mass., May 1974.

Goodwin, M., M.D. and T.C. Goodwin, "In a Dark Mirror," Mental Hygiene, October, 1969.

Israel, B.L., "Responsive Environment Program, Brooklyn, New York," United States Department of Commerce, Institute for Applied Technology, Springfield, Virginia, 1969.

Martin, J.H., "Kaleidoscope for Learning," Saturday Review, June 21, 1969.

Rahimi, M.A. and J.B. Eylenberg, "A Computer Terminal with Synthetic Speech Output," paper presented at the National Conference on the Use of On-Line Computers in Psychology, St. Louis, Missouri, 31 October 1973.

Rahimi, M.A. and J.B. Eylenberg, "A Computing Environment for the Blind," AFIPS Conference Proceedings of the 1974 National Computer Conference, Vol. 43, 1974.

"The Responsive Environment Corporation Follow Through Model," Division of Compensatory Education, U.S. Office of Education, Washington, D.C., February 1970.

Rueter, D.B., "Speech Synthesis under APL," Proceedings of the Sixth International APL Users Conference, May 14-17, 1974: 585-596.

Sachs, R.M., "Technology Comes to Telecommunications for the Hearing Impaired," Highlights, The Quarterly Bulletin of the New York League for the Hard of Hearing, 71 West 23rd Street, New York, New York 10010, Fall, 1973, Vol. 52, No. 2.

Smith, N.B. and R. Strickland, "Some Approaches to Reading," Association for Childhood Education International, 3615 Wisconsin Avenue, N.W., Washington, D.C., 1969.

Steg, D. and A. D'Annunzio, "A Learning Print Approach Toward Perceptual Training and Reading in Kindergartens," paper presented at International Reading Association, New Orleans, Louisiana, May 1974.

Steg, D. and A. D'Annunzio, "Effects of Individualized Learning Procedures on Children with Specific Learning Disabilities," Developmental Medicine and Child Neurology, 1974.

Steg, D. and A. D'Annunzio, "Helping Problem Learners during the Early Childhood Years," paper presented at the American Educational Research Association, Chicago, Illinois, 1972.

Steg, D. and A. D'Annunzio, "Some Theoretical and Experimental Considerations of Cybernetics, Responsive Environments, Learning and Social Development," paper presented to the International Congress of Cybernetics, London, England, September 1969.

Steg, D., M. Mattleman and D. Hammill, "Effects of Individual Programmed Instruction on Initial Reading Skills and Language Behavior in Early Childhood," paper presented at the International Reading Association, 1968.

Steg, D. and R. Schulman, "Remarks on the Possible Economic Significance of 'Pre-School' Education Technology," Drexel University, 1974.

Steg, D., "The Oralographic Learning System," The Language Arts Center of the New Jersey Association for Children with Learning Disabilities, Convent Station, New Jersey, (undated).

Steg, D., "The Limitations of Learning Machines and Some Aspects of Learning," Focus on Learning, A Journal of the School of Education, Indiana University of Pennsylvania, 1, (Spring 1971).

Zaslov, S. and R.I. Frazier, "A Comparison of the Edison Responsive Environment Learning System with an Alternative System for Teaching Reading," a report sponsored by the Division of Research and Development of the Maryland State Department of Education, 1969.

97-08-22 minor repair
glue spine